The Book of Mormon and Other Hidden Books

The Book of Mormon and Other Hidden Books

"Out of Darkness unto Light"

John A. Tvedtnes

The Foundation for Ancient Research and Mormon Studies (FARMS)
at Brigham Young University
Provo, Utah

Cover design by Rebecca Sterrett
Cover photography by John Rees

John A. Tvedtnes earned an M.A. in Linguistics and an M.A. in Middle Eastern Studies—Hebrew, from the University of Utah. He is assistant research director at the Foundation for Ancient Research and Mormon Studies.

The Foundation for Ancient Research and Mormon Studies (FARMS)
at Brigham Young University
P.O. Box 7113
University Station
Provo, Utah 84602

Printed in the United States of America
07 06 05 04 03 02 01 00 6 5 4 3 2 1

Library of Congress Cataloging-in-Publication Data

Tvedtnes, John A.
The Book of Mormon and other hidden books / John A. Tvedtnes.
p. cm.
Includes bibliographical references and index.
ISBN 0-934893-53-5 (pbk. : alk. paper)
1. Book of Mormon--History. I. Title.

BX8627 .T84 2000
289.3'22--dc21

00-056125

Contents

Acknowledgments

Though I must take full responsibility for the contents of this work, the contribution of others cannot be minimized. The pioneering work of Hugh Nibley heads the list. It was he who first demonstrated, in several of his books and articles, that the idea of books hidden to come forth to later generations was not only feasible, but factual. In the latter part of the nineteenth century, Elder Orson Pratt brought to the attention of the Latter-day Saints the existence of inscribed metallic plates. Half a century later, a young missionary named Gordon B. Hinckley, who later became President of the LDS Church, wrote an article for the *Improvement Era,* in which he noted the existence of inscribed metal plates from the ancient Near East in the British Museum. Franklin S. Harris Jr., and Ariel Crowley first compiled lists of inscribed metallic tablets from the ancient Near East and other parts of the world, to which Hugh Nibley, Paul Cheesman, and Elder Mark E. Petersen added their contributions. Franklin S. Harris Sr., and later Thomas Stuart Ferguson noted the ancient Persian practice of burying inscribed metallic plates in stone boxes—a theme developed and examined in depth by H. Curtis Wright, who has explored at length writing on metallic plates and the keeping of records in treasuries. I thank Curtis for writing the introduction to this volume.

I am also indebted to my FARMS colleague Steven W. Booras, who had noted stories of hidden books in several ancient texts. Steve, who has written an article that appears as an appendix to this present volume, has encouraged me to complete this work and we have thrilled together each time new information was uncovered. Others who have provided valuable insights and encouragement are Terrence L. Szink, John Gee, Brian Hauglid, Matthew Roper, and Ron Myatt. I thank FARMS editor Mary Mahan for her helpful suggestions. I am also grateful to other members of the FARMS Publications staff, including Alison Coutts, Wendy Christian, Carmen Cole, Julie Dozier, Paula Hicken, and Linda Sheffield.

Introduction

by H. Curtis Wright

Latter-day Saints cannot know enough about antiquity. But they cannot by searching find it out completely: they cannot know it all by any means available to them, nor can they learn what may be known of it by surfing electromagnetic info-waves or surveying public beaches of mass communication. They also cannot trust "modern" research to supply detailed information about the ancient world because in the end no one—not even the scholarly genius who studies it night and day—knows very much about it. The celebrated and unabashedly commercialized Internet, Web pages and all, which thus far, at least, leads to virtually every destination in the modern world, goes almost nowhere in the ancient world.

A case in point. I've recently learned through FARMS of parents in the Midwest who have been caught in the cross fire between their Mormon daughter and their Baptist daughter over the issue of metallic documents in antiquity. Their Mormon daughter taught them the gospel from the

Book of Mormon in Illinois, and they were receptive to it—until they moved to Missouri, where their Baptist daughter began to unteach everything related to the Book of Mormon ideas her parents were taught by her Mormon sister. A major part of their Baptist daughter's attack on their Mormon daughter, accordingly, was the hypothesis that no one in antiquity has ever written anything at all on metals of any kind.[1] As might be expected, moreover, the father of these disputatious sisters, an eminently fair man concerned for both his daughters, tried to prove this assumption true or false via the Internet—only to find, after countless hours of fruitless searching, insufficient evidence to test it. Shortly after that, his Mormon daughter happened to read an article in the initial twenty-first-century issue of the *Ensign*, where she learned that a few Brigham Young University professors associated with FARMS knew something about ancient writings on metal surfaces. She contacted FARMS immediately, FARMS contacted me, and I sent her a large package of scholarly evidence, which included a fifty-four-page bibliography of learned writings about ancient metallic epigraphy that document the actual existence of literally thousands of metal documents all over the ancient world. And if this book by John Tvedtnes (which deals with ancient inscriptions and much else) had already been published, I would have sent it, too. Happily for all of us, the Latter-day Saints include researchers like Tvedtnes, who are absolutely determined to learn everything they can about antiquity, not in order to prove the gospel—for nothing short of an actual revealed witness communicated by God to an individual person can do that—but in order to prevent rejections of the gospel based on false or uninformed assertions.

Something of the ancient world is known, of course, through written texts and the detritus of obscured and forgotten civilizations. What that world was like, however, can only be discovered; it cannot be anticipated, for it is wildly unpredictable and strangely unlike our world. That is why God, who not only knows the past but knows it perfectly, always startles "modern" thinkers, whatever and whenever their cultural milieus, by revealing things about the past that they don't know and therefore reject out of hand because they find them strange, foreign, absurd, antiquated, ridiculous, and generally repulsive to their "modern" mind-sets. That is where this book comes in.

If it existed in only one ancient copy, says Tvedtnes, the Book of Mormon may have been unique. But in virtually every other way it resembles many ancient books. In this present volume, Tvedtnes shows perhaps fifty things about ancient records that must have been hilarious in 1830 but make perfect sense today: the ubiquity of intentionally hiding books in all kinds of ingenious containers made of many materials, including stone boxes and ceramic jars; books incised on obdurate surfaces, like metals, bones, and ivory; inked papyri and parchments treated with swaddling cloths soaked in cedar and citrus oils to prevent decay; many sealed and open records; waterproofing sealants like bitumen and white lime mortar; caves serving as repositories of treasures buried in many sacred mountains; the ancient perception of permanence and eternalism associated with the preservative functions of writing; and numerous ancient traditions of angels as writers and guardians of written records. Many twentieth-century discoveries of ancient documents have made all of this visible, as has the restoration of lost scriptures by actual revelation from God to Ezra and Jeremiah. Steven Booras's appendix on the *Apocalypse of Paul* (Paul reportedly wrote and sealed up his vision of the third heaven in a stone box and buried it underneath his house) also sheds light on these ancient practices.

I shall say no more, lest I spill all the beans about this book and leave nothing to the imagination of its potential readers. That would be a mistake; but if I can interest them in actually reading it, I will have done my job.

Note

1. See chapter 8, where John Tvedtnes has disclosed, almost casually and perhaps without realizing it, the origin of this spurious assumption in Baptist lectures against Mormonism delivered at Salt Lake City in 1885, reworked as a book published in 1886 and 1887, and republished without change in 1965 and 1980. See Martin Thomas Lamb, *The Golden Bible; or, the Book of Mormon: Is It From God?* (New York: Ward and Drummond, 1886). Critics of Mormonism, it goes without saying, should have better sources than that for their knowledge of antiquity; and perhaps they do. But if they don't, they must realize that Mormon scholars like Tvedtnes will not hesitate to point it out.

chapter 1

Speech from the Dust

> *He said there was a book deposited, written upon gold plates, giving an account of the former inhabitants of this continent, and the source from whence they sprang. . . . Also, that there were two stones in silver bows—and these stones, fastened to a breastplate, constituted what is called the Urim and Thummim—deposited with the plates; and the possession and use of these stones were what constituted "seers" in ancient or former times; and that God had prepared them for the purpose of translating the book. (Joseph Smith—History [JS—H] 1:34–35)*

With these words Joseph Smith introduced to the world the concept of a sacred history, written in ancient times on metallic plates and hidden away to be revealed in the last days. The existence of the records comprising the Book of Mormon was revealed to him by the resurrected Moroni, the last in a line of prophetic Nephite scribes.

"While he was conversing with me about the plates," Joseph later recorded, "the vision was opened to my mind that I could see the place where the plates were deposited, and that so clearly and distinctly that I knew the place again when I visited it" (JS—H 1:42). Joseph's visit was not long in coming; he went the next morning. It was a hill later to be called Cumorah, near Manchester in Ontario County, New York.

> On the west side of this hill, not far from the top, under a stone of considerable size, lay the plates, deposited in a stone box. This stone was thick and rounding in the middle on the upper side, and thinner towards the edges, so that the middle part of it was visible above the ground, but the edge all around was covered with earth. Having removed the earth, I obtained a lever, which I got fixed under the edge of the stone, and with a little exertion raised it up. I looked in, and there indeed did I behold the plates, the urim and thummim, and the breastplate, as stated by the messenger. The box in which they lay was formed by laying stones together in some kind of cement. In the bottom of the box were laid two stones crossways of the box, and on these stones lay the plates and the other things with them. (JS—H 1:51–52)

Joseph attempted to remove the plates from the box but was forbidden by the messenger, who told him to return for instruction at the same time each year for the next four years. During his last visit, on 22 September 1827, Joseph took custody of the plates (see JS—H 1:53–54, 59). Using the translation devices provided by the Lord, he produced the Book of Mormon, which was first published in 1830. It was "the book to be revealed" (D&C 128:20).

We presume that it was Moroni who hid the plates in the New York hill, though this is never explicitly stated in the scriptures or by Joseph Smith. During his time as scribal custodian of the Nephite records, Moroni indicated that he would "hide up" the plates (Mormon 8:4, 14).

Hiding Records in the Book of Mormon

The Book of Mormon practice of hiding records in the earth for safekeeping did not begin with the Nephites. Years before the Nephites hid up their records, the Lord told the brother of Jared to "seal up" the record he was writing with two stones prepared for its future translation (see Ether 3:22–24, 27–28; 4:1–5). When Ether, the last of the Jaredite prophets, "finished his record . . . he hid them in a manner that the people of Limhi did find them" (Ether 15:33). After its discovery by a group of Nephite explorers, the record was translated by a prophet using special stones the Lord prepared for that purpose, in the same manner that Joseph Smith translated the Nephite record (see Mosiah 8: 9–12; 28:11–19).

Just as Ether hid the Jaredite record in the final years before his people's destruction, so, too, did Ammaron conceal the Nephite record in that nation's last years. Nephi$_1$ foresaw this a thousand years before it happened (see 1 Nephi 13:35). In "the three hundred and twentieth year from the coming of Christ," Ammaron, "being constrained by the Holy Ghost, did hide up the records which were sacred—yea, even all the sacred records which had been handed down from generation to generation . . . And he did hide them up unto the Lord, that they might come again unto the remnant of the house of Jacob, according to the prophecies and the promises of the Lord" (4 Nephi 1:48–49).

After hiding up the records, Ammaron went to ten-year-old Mormon, "a sober child, and . . . quick to observe," and charged him that, when he was about twenty-four years of age, he should go to the hill Shim, where Ammaron had "deposited . . . all the sacred engravings concerning this people" (Mormon 1:2–3). At that time he should retrieve the plates of Nephi, leaving the rest, and make a record of the events of his time (see Mormon 1:4). At the appointed time, "seeing that the Lamanites were about to overthrow the land, [Mormon] did go to the hill Shim, and did take up all the records which Ammaron had hid up unto the Lord"(Mormon 4:23). Several decades later, the records were again in danger of being taken by the Lamanites:

> And it came to pass that when we had gathered in all our people in one to the land of Cumorah, behold I, Mormon, began to be old; and knowing it to be the last struggle of my people, and having been commanded of the Lord that I should not suffer the records which had been handed down by our fathers, which were sacred, to fall into the hands of the Lamanites, (for the Lamanites would destroy them) therefore I made this [abridged] record out of the plates of Nephi, and hid up in the hill Cumorah all the records which had been entrusted to me by the hand of the Lord, save it were these few plates which I gave unto my son Moroni. (Mormon 6:6; see also Ether 15:11)

After hiding up the bulk of the Nephite records in the hill Cumorah, Mormon turned his abridgment over to his son, Moroni, to complete. Moroni ultimately hid the abridgment plates as well, though he never mentioned where:[1]

> And I am the same who hideth up this record unto the Lord; the plates thereof are of no worth, because of the commandment of the Lord. For he truly saith that no one shall have them to get gain; but the record thereof is of great worth; and whoso shall *bring it to light*, him will the Lord bless. For none can have power to *bring it to light* save it be given him of God; for God wills that it shall be done with an eye single to his glory, or the welfare of the ancient and long dispersed covenant people of the Lord. And blessed be he that shall *bring this thing to light*; for it shall be *brought out of darkness unto light*,[2] according to the word of God; yea, it shall be

> *brought out of the earth, and it shall shine forth out of darkness*, and come unto the knowledge of the people; and it shall be done by the power of God. (Mormon 8:14–16)[3]

Following his work with the Book of Mormon, Joseph Smith was instrumental in bringing to light other ancient works of scripture, including part of a revelation written by John the apostle (D&C 7), lost writings of Moses and Enoch (Moses 1, 6–7; D&C 107:40–57), and the Book of Abraham. He also restored some missing portions of the Bible, such as Joseph Smith—Matthew in the Pearl of Great Price, D&C 45, and portions of the Joseph Smith Translation.[4] The Lord also encouraged Oliver Cowdery to look into "all those ancient records which have been hid up, that are sacred" (D&C 8:11).

Hiding Records in the Ancient Near East

Joseph Smith's work marked the beginning of an era in which ancient records would be rediscovered in such vast quantities that our knowledge about the ancient Near East would greatly multiply in just a few generations. The discovery of records hidden in the Near East has made headline news in our time. Most notable is the large cache of documents known as the Dead Sea Scrolls, which began coming to light in 1947. Other hidden documents have been found elsewhere in Israel, Egypt, Iraq, and Iran. Moreover, some Near Eastern peoples, such as the Mandaeans and the Yezîdîs, continue to hide their sacred records in boxes placed in the ground and in caves.

The Book of Mormon as a Hidden Book

In this book, we shall demonstrate that various elements of the Book of Mormon story have antecedents in the ancient world that were not known to Joseph Smith or his contemporaries. Among these are the concept of writing and hiding books in such a way that they could be discovered by future generations; the use of special containers, such as stone boxes, in which to hide records; and hiding the books in mountains. We shall also see that ancient and medieval people commonly believed that sacred books were entrusted to the care of angels, who would deliver them to mankind at the appropriate time. Analogously, the angel Moroni delivered the plates of the Book of Mormon to Joseph Smith.

Some critics will see this volume as additional "proof" of their contention that Joseph Smith simply made up the story of the Book of Mormon from information available to him. Consequently, I hasten to add that most of the documents cited herein were not discovered until long after the publication of the Book of Mormon and that the likelihood that any of the traditions were known to Joseph Smith, a New England farmboy, is virtually nil. The research that produced this volume took several years and the expertise of a number of qualified scholars. It is thus inconceivable that Joseph Smith, with his minimal education, could have invented a story with the same elements by the age of twenty-four, when he published his English translation of the Book of Mormon.

Notes

1. Many LDS scholars maintain that the hill we call Cumorah in New York state is not the hill of that name known from the Book of Mormon, which is possibly situated in southern Mexico. This conclusion is based principally on the internal geography of the Nephite record, which suggests that the hill in which Mormon buried the plates was near the narrow neck of land. From the Book of Mormon description, the narrow neck could not have been in the northeastern United States. Still, no one doubts that Moroni hid the abridgment plates in a stone box in the New York hill, where he directed Joseph Smith to find them. Moroni buried the plates sometime after

A.D. 420, some thirty-five years or more after the great battle at the hill Cumorah (compare Mormon 6:5; Moroni 9:1), giving him plenty of time to travel a great distance from his homeland. It is significant that inside that box Joseph found only the abridgment plates and other sacred relics, but not the whole of the Nephite library (see JS—H 1:52–53).

2. The wording reminds us of Job 28:11: "He bindeth the floods from overflowing; and *the thing that is hid bringeth he forth to light*" (emphasis added).

3. The concept of "bringing to light . . . those parts of my scriptures which have been hidden because of iniquity" is also found in D&C 6:27. Records of evil deeds will also be brought to light, for the books—including the Book of Mormon—will be opened at the judgment (see Daniel 7:9–14; Revelation 20:12; 2 Nephi 29:11; 33:10–15; Alma 37:23–25; 3 Nephi 27:25–26; Moroni 10:27–29; D&C 127:7; 128:6–8; *2 Baruch* 24:1; *1 Enoch* 47:3; 90:20–24*; 2 Enoch 36:3* [A]; 52:15; *3 Enoch* 27:1–2; 28:7; 30:2; 32:1; *4 Ezra* 6:20; *Jubilees*10:17; Qur'an 69:14–23; 81:11–14; 83:8–29). Compare Nephi's statement that "there is nothing which is secret save it shall be revealed; there is no work of darkness save it shall be made *manifest in the light;* and there is nothing which is *sealed upon the earth* save it shall be loosed" (2 Nephi 30:17).

4. See D&C 45:15–16, 60. Also, it roughly parallels Matthew 24 but agrees more with the Luke account.

chapter 2

Hidden Records

And I am the same who hideth up this record unto the Lord; the plates thereof are of no worth, because of the commandment of the Lord. For he truly saith that no one shall have them to get gain; but the record thereof is of a great worth; and whoso shall bring it to light, him will the Lord bless. (Mormon 8:14)

Moroni's hiding of his father's abridgment of the Nephite records served at least two purposes. First, it kept the plates out of the hands of those who would destroy them either to eliminate the evidence (see Enos 1:14; Mormon 6:6)[1] or to profit from the precious metal from which the plates were made (see Mormon 8:14; JS—H 1:46). Second, concealing the plates in the earth preserved them from the elements until the time came for them to come forth (see 1 Nephi 13:35; 14:26; 2 Nephi 27:22; Enos 1:13, 15–16; Words of Mormon 1:11; Mosiah 12:8; Alma 37:4, 18–19; Mormon 5:12–13; 8:16; D&C 3:19).

In recent years, some critics have noted that while ancient manuscripts of the books in the Bible exist, there are no such manuscripts for the Book of Mormon. In making such declarations, however, they ignore the unique character of the Book of Mormon as a hidden book, of which there was only one ancient copy. Mormon prepared this book and passed it on to his son, Moroni, who buried it and later revealed its location to the prophet Joseph Smith.

The concept of hiding books for future generations to discover is evident in a large number of early documents from the ancient Near East, whence came the peoples of the Book of Mormon. The practice has also been confirmed by numerous archaeological discoveries, most of which were made in the Near East.

Secret Books

Hidden books are, by their very nature, also secret. The concept of books meant to be kept secret from unbelievers or the uninitiated is as old as writing. Early Christians preserved the secrecy of some of their writings. For example, in the *Epistle of Peter to James* that prefaces the *Clementine Homilies*, the apostle wrote, "I beg and beseech you not to communicate to any one of the Gentiles the books of my preachings which I sent to you, nor to any one of our own tribe before trial; but if any one has been proved and found worthy, then to commit them to him, after the manner in which Moses delivered *his books* to the Seventy who succeeded to his chair."[2] A similar charge is found in the *Book of the Resurrection of Christ by Bartholomew the Disciple*: "Do not let this book come into the hand of any man who is an unbeliever and a heretic. Behold, this is the seventh time that I have commanded thee, O my son Thaddaeus, concerning these mysteries. Reveal not thou them to any impure man, but keep them safely."[3]

The *Book of the Rolls* claims to be one of the hidden books passed from Jesus to his disciples Simon and James, then from Simeon Cepha (Peter) to Clement, who commanded that it be kept secret from the laiety (see *Book of the Rolls* f.89b). In *Book of the Rolls* f.138b, Peter speaks to Clement of the "secret books of the Hebrews" from which the accuracy of the Israelite genealogies was ascertained after the books of the genealogies had been destroyed. This statement is immediately followed by Mary's genealogy.[4]

Some of the fifth-century documents found in a buried jar at Nag Hammadi (Chenoboskion), Egypt, in 1945 tell a similar tale. In the I,*2 Apocryphon of James*, the apostle James said that he was sending to an unknown recipient a secret book that the Lord revealed to him and Peter. He also indicated that ten months earlier he had sent another secret book that the Savior revealed to him, and he mentioned that all twelve apostles recorded both secret and open sayings that Jesus delivered to each of them (see 1.8–18; 1.28–2.16). Another of the documents (II,*2*; IV,*2*) gives its name near the end: "the Gospel of <the> Egyptians. The God-written, holy, secret book."[5] The document II,*1 Apocryphon of John* 31.28–34 informs us that the resurrected Christ told the apostle John to write down what he had told him and to keep it secure.

Some early Ethiopic Christian documents also speak of secret books written by Christ. In the first section of the *Lefafa Sedek* (Bandlet of Righteousness) we read, "And Jesus wrote with a pen of gold. . . . And [Christ] said unto her (Mary), 'Take this [book] which I have given unto thee. And thou shalt not reveal it to the man who is not able to bear it, or to keep guard over this Book, but [only] to the wise who believe on Me, and who walk in My commandments.'"[6] In *The Book of the Mysteries of the Heavens and the Earth* (folios 62a–b) we find these words: "'Now hearken unto me so that I may tell thee about the Books which are hidden in the New Law. Four are in the Holy Gospel, as the Book sayeth. And there are in it others which our Lord Jesus composed, many which are not written in this book. And in Peter he saith Twelve . . . And of Paul Four . . . And of John Seven . . . And of James One. And behold all these Books are Twenty-eight. And this word is given to . . . those who are followers of Me.' And this Book shall not be revealed to every man whom thou shalt meet, but only to those who are learned and to men of understanding."[7] The same text speaks of hidden books from the time of the biblical patriarch Serug (Sîrâk in Ethiopic), great-grandfather of Abraham (see Genesis 11:21–23): "And from Sîrâk [there were] two [books] even as he himself saith, 'Until the reason therefore shall be found, hide my word.'"[8] Abraham noted that "the records of the fathers" had come into his hands (Abraham 1:31).

Another group who believe in keeping some writings secret from nonbelievers are the Mandaeans of Iraq and Iran. The Mandaic *Haran Gawaita* warns them not to reveal the contents of the books in the anonymous writer's library "in the presence of foolish persons."[9] Another Mandean text, *The World of Light*, speaks of *uthras* (angels) reciting "hidden books."[10] The Mandaean *Story of Shum bar Nu* (Shem, son of Noah) contains a declaration from Shum often found in Mandaean literature: "I do not forget my hidden books."[11]

The writing of Nicotheus "the hidden" is mentioned numerous times, for example, by Porphyry, by Zosimos the alchemist in *On the Letter Omega* and in the *Untitled Treatise* in the Bruce Codex, and in Manichaean writings. A Greek magical papyrus, the *Eighth Book of Moses*, orders the reader to "dispose of the book so it will not be found."[12]

In one tradition, the practice of keeping books secret goes back to the time of biblical Ezra, who is said to have written ninety-four books. The Lord told him to make twenty-four of these public but to keep seventy for the wise (see *4 Ezra* 14:44–48). This tradition is recounted in one of the books of the biblical Apocrypha, reminding us that the Greek word *apocrypha* means "hidden" and originally denoted books that were not to be circulated among the general public.

The Egyptian priest Calasiris, during his visit to Delphi, declined to answer all the questions put to him by the Greeks, saying that "prophets alone may read and learn" from the "sacred books."[13]

The Hermetica

Among the traditions common to alchemy and freemasonry is one of ancient texts handed down by the Egyptian scribal god Thoth, who is identified with the Greek messenger god Hermes. The traditions are explained principally in the *Corpus Hermiticum*, in which we read (13.13) that Hermes Trismegistus told his son Tat (a later form of the name Thoth) that he had writings for him that he should not share with the masses. Though the texts are known largely because they were used by medieval European alchemists, the corpus actually originated in Egypt. Clement of Alexandria (circa 160–215) noted that the forty-two sacred books of the Egyptians were all written by Hermes (see *Stromata* 17.1.46). Other early church fathers who cited Hermetic texts are Lactantius (260–330), Cyril of Alexandria (died 444), and Marcellus of Ancyra (died circa 374).[14]

Some Hermetic texts contain elements found in other stories of hidden books. One Arabic tradition, told by al-Qifṭî in his *Taʾrīkh* (History), describes a Babylonian named Hermes who recorded the wisdom of antediluvian mankind. The records were recovered after the flood.[15] A similar story is told in the Arabic *Kitāb d̲aḫīrat Aliskandar* (Book of the Treasures of Alexander): Hermes deposited the books, which were meant to be recovered later, in the sea.[16] In other tales, as noted later in this chapter, it was Noah who hid the texts. Some Hermetic works seem to identify Hermes with Enoch, who, according to the pseudepigraphic literature, left books behind when he was translated. Thus the Greek *Kore Kosmou* 8 indicates that Hermes wrote the mysteries of the heavens in sacred books, which he hid away before being "received into the sanctuary of the everlasting zones." Hermes intended that the books remain "unseen and undiscovered by all men who shall go to and fro on the plains of this land, until the time when Heaven, grown old, shall beget organisms worthy of you."[17]

Of particular interest is the story of Apollonius, who visited Trophonius and found, in an underground passage, a holy book which he removed and placed on display in Antium.[18] The Hermetic text known as the *Book of Apollonios, the Sage, on the Causes*, describes how Apollonius found this holy book: He "entered a chamber, and behold, I met with an old man sitting on a throne of gold, a tablet of green emerald being in his hand." Apollonius stole the tablet, which contained "the *Secret of Creation* and the *Knowledge of the Causes of the Things*."[19] Widengren suggests that this mysterious book is probably identical to the well-known Hermetic text known in Arabic as *Sirr ʾal-ḫaliḳah* (Secret of Creation).[20]

The *Tabula Smaragdina* (Emerald Tablet), an alchemical tract thought to date to the mid-thirteenth century, recounts the legend of the original emerald slab on which the teachings of Hermes were supposedly written in Phoenician. Alexander the Great is said to have discovered the tablet in the tomb of Hermes when he came to Egypt. In a variant story, found in Johann Albert Fabricus's sixteenth-century *Bibliotheca Graeca,* Abraham's wife Sarah removed the tablet from Hermes' tomb in the cave at Hebron, where the patriarchs were later buried.[21] The Arabic version of the *Tabula* notes that a man named

Balinas (from the Greek Apollonius) found the book in "a dark chamber." The book was written in Syriac, "the primordial language," and was in the possession of "an old man sitting on a throne of gold, a tablet of emerald being in his hand."[22]

De Virtutibus Herbarum, a first-century-A.D. Hermetic text attributed to one Thessalos, tells how the author made his way to Egypt to continue his literary studies. During this time, he sought to attain hidden knowledge. At Thebes he met an aged priest who prepared him for a vision by means of a three-day fast, and on the fourth day they entered a special chamber. There Thessalos encountered the god Asclepius (Imhotep), who delivered to him a book from which he could learn.[23]

Widengren notes that "the entering of a dark, subterranean chamber in order to find a book of revelation is a theme often recurring in Egyptian and Hellenistic tales" and that "it has further been rightly emphasized that, in this literature, descent into the nether world and ascent to heaven always correspond."[24] To illustrate the latter point, he cites "the so-called *Krates-Book* [which] relates how Krates is elevated to heaven, where he has an experience of the same kind as Apollonios" in the underworld. Krates saw "an old man, the most beautiful of men, sitting on a throne-stool and wearing white garments, in his hand a shining tablet, containing a writing . . . And I inquired about the old man, and it was said to me: this is Hermes Trismegistos."[25] According to Pastor of Hermas, it is an elderly woman wearing a white robe and seated on a chair who delivers the book. (See the discussion in chapter 5, "Angels as Guardians of Hidden Books.")

Support for the medieval Hermetic tradition is found in other sources as well. The Arabic *Kitāb al-falakīyah al-kubrā* (Book of the Great Astrologers) "is said to have been deposited by Hermes in an underground cave."[26] The Egyptian *Berlin*

Medical Papyrus states that it was discovered rolled up in a case under the feet of an Anubis statue in the days of Tet (or Thoth, who was identified with Hermes), after whose death it was transmitted to King Sent (a second-dynasty monarch) and then restored to the feet of the statue. The same story is told in Papyrus Ebers 856, which contains a recipe "according to what was found in writing under Anubis' feet in Letopolis. It was brought to the majesty of King Smty."[27]

A large stela found at the Egyptian site of Abydos tells how King Neferhotep I wanted to see writings from the earliest times of Atum. He went to the library and searched through the papyri, finding a document that no previous scribe had found. From the long-lost text, he learned of the god Osiris and reinstituted his cult. Another large stela at Abydos indicates that Ramses IV did not neglect any of the sacred books written by Thoth, because he wanted to properly learn of the gods. He particularly wanted to know the mysteries of Osiris.[28] One Egyptian papyrus, *Papyri Graecae Magicae (PGM)* XXIVa, claims to be a copy of a holy book found in the archives of Hermes/Thoth.[29]

Chapter 137 of the Egyptian Book of the Dead reads, "And thou shalt write down these things in accordance with the instructions which are found in the books of Prince Herutātāf, who discovered them in a secret coffer (now they were in the handwriting of the god [Thoth] himself (*i.e.*, they were written in hieroglyphs) and had been deposited in the Temple of the goddess Unnut, the Lady of Unu) during a journey which he was making in order to inspect the temples, and the temple-estates, and the sanctuaries of the gods."[30]

An important Christian Egyptian Hermetic document is the Nag Hammadi text known as the *Discourse on the Eighth and Ninth.* In this fifth-century-A.D. document, found concealed in a large jar buried in the earth, Hermes cautioned his son to "keep silent about what is hidden" and told him that the praise he sings to God should "be written in this imperishable book."[31] Hermes then told him, "My son, write this book for the temple at Diospolis [Thebes] in hieroglyphic characters." After his son promised to do so, he said, "My <son>, write the language of the book on steles of turquoise . . . in hieroglyphic characters." "I command that this teaching be carved on stone, and that you place it in my sanctuary," surrounded by divine guardians. "And put a square milk-stone at the base of the turquoise tablets and write the name on the azure stone tablet in hieroglyphic characters." Again the son said he would do it, whereupon Hermes said, "And write an oath in the book, lest those who read the book bring the language into abuse, and not (use it) to oppose the acts of fate." Of he who is not "begotten at the start by God," "he will not be able to read the things written in this book."[32]

An important cache of documents came out of Thebes, Egypt, in the early nineteenth century. The third- or fourth-century-A.D. papyri, thought to have been concealed in a tomb many centuries ago, comprise a temple archive containing temple rituals, including detailed instructions for making records on metal plates. The collection was acquired by the Alexandrian merchant Giovanni Anastasi in 1828, and the documents, now housed in London, Paris, Berlin, and Leiden, are similar in content (and perhaps even handwriting) to an alchemical papyrus held in Stockholm. The Paris papyrus contains a ritual for rendering a person immortal that is similar to some of the initiatory Hermetica, and it includes the prayer found at the end of the *Asclepius* text from Nag Hammadi. One of the Leiden papyri (Papyrus Leiden I 395) may also contain Hermetic material and is entitled *A Holy Book, called Monas, or the Eighth Book of Moses*. It refers to another work by Moses, *The Key;* to a "holy book" by Hermes, *The Wing;* and to an untitled work by the Egyptian priest Manetho.[33]

Some Hermetic traditions made their way into freemasonry. According to Masonic tradition, Enoch invented writing, and fearing that secrets would be lost in the coming flood, he engraved them on a white oriental porphyry stone, which he hid in the earth.[34] Another Masonic tradition holds that the two pillars of Solomon's temple were hollow and that ancient records were hidden therein.[35]

What is significant about the Hermetica for the present study is their long-standing tradition of documents hidden away for use by the wise. Equally important is the fact that some of the Hermetic documents were themselves concealed in ancient times and discovered relatively recently. Such Hermetic texts confirm the antiquity of the practice followed by some of the Nephite scribes in the Book of Mormon, who also hid up records to come to light at a future time.

The Story of Rabbi Abraham Eleazar

The Hermetic works of ancient Egypt were preserved for the West by European kabbalists and alchemists. One of the later alchemists, Rabbi Abraham Eleazar, in his 1735 *Uraltes Chymisches Werck* (Age-Old Chemical Work), noted that when Jerusalem was destroyed by the emperor Vespasian in A.D. 70, the "Fathers walled in and buried the secrets." Those who went in search of the hidden books were destroyed by a fire. The rabbi indicated that the books were concealed "at the entrance to the Holy of Holies," beneath a stone two cubits in depth that was marked with the Hebrew word for fire. They would remain hidden until the coming of Elijah and the Messiah. Eleazar also wrote of "the book of the secrets of Tubal-Cain," a "secret book" that was passed down to the prophet Moses and described, among other things, "the movement of the stars of heaven" and "the movement and rotation of the earth." The tale is reminiscent of Abraham's gleaning knowledge of the earth and the heavenly bodies from records handed down from "the fathers" (Abraham 1:31).

Eleazar claims that he "found this secret written on copper tablets by Samuel Baruch of our race, in figures, in Chaldaic, Syriac, and Arabic language," difficult to understand, though "the great Jehova soon opened it up for me, by His power, so that I could grasp and understand these secrets." The rabbi copied the material engraved on the copper tablets onto tree bark, known from other sources as material for writing.

The story of Rabbi Abraham Eleazar is retold by the eminent twentieth-century Jewish scholar Raphael Patai.[36] After discussing the rabbi's transcription of the text onto tree bark, Patai notes that this is reminiscent of the alchemist Flamel's assertion that the Book of Abraham the Jew "was made of thin barks . . . its cover was of very thin copper."[37] He includes the following in his footnote to the Flamel reference: "The idea that sacred texts were originally inscribed on metal tablets recurs in the Mormon belief that the *Book of Mormon* came down inscribed on gold tablets. Important documents were in fact inscribed on metal tablets and preserved in stone or marble boxes in Mesopotamia, Egypt, etc."[38] Patai references this idea to an article by LDS scholar H. Curtis Wright and thanks another LDS scholar, John M. Lundquist, for bringing this information to his attention.[39]

Parts of Eleazar's story resemble that of Joseph Smith. In addition to its original text being on plates, the book the rabbi found was said to have been written "in Chaldaic, Syriac, and Arabic" characters. Similarly, when Martin Harris took a transcription made by Joseph Smith from the Book of Mormon plates to Professor Charles Anthon in New York City, Anthon characterized the writing as "Egyptian, Chaldaic, Assyriac, and Arabic" (JS—H 1:64).

The Preservation of Hidden Books

The Book of Mormon records were clearly intended to be kept hidden to preserve them for future generations (see 1 Nephi 13:35–36; 4 Nephi 1:49; title page of the Book of Mormon). Several Nephite prophets asked God to protect the records over time (see Enos 1:13–18; compare 1 Nephi 3:19–20; 5:21; 2 Nephi 27:22; Jacob 1:3; Mosiah 28:20; Alma 37:14, 18, 21; Ether 12:22). This would explain their hiding them up "unto God." After Ether finished his record, he "hid them in a manner that the people of Limhi did find them" (Ether 15:33).[40]

In an early Jewish text, the *Testament of Moses* 1:16–18, Moses instructed Joshua on how to preserve the books (parchments) he was leaving in his charge: anoint them with cedar (oil?) and deposit them in earthen jars until the day of recompense.[41] We can compare this with Hermes' anointing of the holy books with "the drug of imperishability," noted in the earlier discussion of the Hermetic literature.[42] The Third Section of the Ethiopian *Lefafa Sedek,* patterned after the ancient Egyptian Book of the Dead, instructs readers, "Guard ye it (*i.e.* the Book), and make it to endure, and ye shall be saved from the fire."[43]

The Mandaeans of Iraq and Iran, who claim to be descendants of the disciples of John the Baptist, have a number of traditions about the preservation of sacred books. According to *Mandaean Canonical Prayerbook* 73, a letter sent from heaven and sealed by God is hung about the neck of the soul when it is sent to the Gate of Life. Prayer 74 gives instructions about how to seal the letter in a bottle with clay and impress the clay with a ring.

Burying the Books

The Book of Mormon is but one of a number of ancient texts that were buried in the ground and later brought to light. Others, including large caches such as the Dead Sea Scrolls and the Nag Hammadi texts, are discussed in chapter 10, "The Records Come Forth." A number of early traditions also note the practice of burying books in the the ground, some suggesting that the practice began with the first man. Hugh Nibley noted the Jewish tradition recounted by Bin Gorion that Adam received a golden book from the archangel Michael and "hid it in the crevice of a rock."[44] The twelfth-century rabbi Moses Maimonides reported a Sabaean tradition that writings of Adam still existed in the ground (see *Moreh Nebukim* 3.29).

The second recension of the medieval *Book of Noah* tells how Enoch was shown in a dream the location (in a cave) of the heavenly book delivered to Adam. After reading the book, he hid it away. It was later delivered to Noah, who also hid it away.[45] Eusebius, citing Polyhistor, recorded that Noah inscribed a history of everything and buried it at Sippar (*Chronicon* 1.19). The first recension of the *Book of Noah* indicates that the book received by Noah contained cures for the various illnesses afflicting mankind. On a similar note, the Talmud says that King Hezekiah hid away the Book of Cures (see TB *Berakot* 10b; TB *Pesaḥim* 56a).

Jubilees 8:1–4 reports that Cainan, son of Arpachshad (Noah's grandson), was taught by his father to write. This enabled him to transcribe a stone he found that contained writings of his ancestors, but he kept the book's existence from the knowledge of Noah. A similar story is found in *Zohar* Genesis 76a, which, commenting on Genesis 11:2, indicates that "they found remnants of the secret wisdom that had been left there by the generation of the Flood, and with that they made their attempt to provoke the Holy One, blessed be He."[46] *Book of the Rolls* f.121b notes that "when Nimrod was passing through the East, he deposited books making known what Bouniter the son of Noah had taught him."[47]

Similar stories are told of the ark builder by non-Judaeo-Christian writers. Berossus, the third-century-B.C. Babylonian historian, wrote that the god Chronos appeared to Xisuthros (the Babylonian Noah) in a vision to warn him of the flood. Chronos told Xisuthros to bury in Sippar all available writings to preserve them during the deluge, after which the flood survivors were to retrieve and disseminate them to all mankind.[48] As mentioned previously, in Arabic and Masonic traditions it was Hermes who hid the records before the coming of the flood.

Paul Cheesman has pointed out two accounts of sacred texts hidden by Mesoamerican Indians. The first comes from an early Spanish friar, who learned from an Otami Indian man a tradition about a book that spoke of God and Christ but had perished after being buried in the ground by its guardians.[49] The other is the "Golden Book" of the Maya Indians, said to have been hidden away to prevent it from falling into the hands of the invading Spanish. Tradition indicates that the fifty-two gold plates comprising the record contained the history of the Maya.[50]

It should be noted that the practice of burying records was not restricted to those records that were considered sacred. Hugh Nibley noted that when the fabulous Arab king of Hira, Nu'man, built his White Palace around A.D. 400, he ordered that a copy of Arabic poems be buried beneath the palace for future generations.[51] A more extreme example concerns the oaths of the Gadianton robber band, which oaths were buried and later retrieved (see Helaman 11:10, 26). Similarly, in an Armenian document called by one translator *Adam, Eve and the Incarnation*, Satan tricks Adam into making a pact with him by having him place his hand on a stone, leaving an imprint of Adam's hand and fingers. Satan then buries the stone in the Jordan river, but later, at the baptism of Christ, it was destroyed.[52]

Records Buried in Tombs

While some records were buried in the ground, others were buried in tombs. Mentioned earlier was the Hermetic tradition of records buried in the tomb of Hermes, known to the Egyptians as Thoth. Egypt is, in fact, a prime example of using tombs to preserve sacred records. In early Egyptian history, texts designed to assist the dead were carved on the coffin itself. Later, papyri and even metallic plates with such spells were buried with the mummies. Many of these are in the tradition of what has been called the Book of the Dead. Wall inscriptions are typically found in the tombs of Egyptian royalty and government officials. Because they frequently recount the accomplishments of the deceased, these have been a source of important information for historians.

In connection with the Egyptian practice, the story of the Joseph Smith papyri and mummies comes readily to mind. A small booklet found among the Kirtland Egyptian Papers, held by the LDS Church (KEPE6), is labeled "Valuable Discovery of *hid[d]en reccords* that have been obtained from the ancient bur[y]ing place of the Egyptians. Joseph Smith Jr."

Writing about A.D. 1226, the Arab writer Idrîsî noted that a few years before, a group of Arabs had dug for treasure in the pyramid of the pharaoh Mycerinus (Menkaura) at Giza, Egypt. After six months of hard labor, they found the decayed remains of a man with some golden tablets inscribed in a language none of them understood. The tablets were taken for their gold content, suggesting that they were probably melted down.[53]

Examples of metal records buried in tombs is well attested. The early Greek writer Plutarch said that when the tomb of Alcmene, mother of Hercules, was excavated, a bronze tablet with a long inscription resembling Egyptian writing was found (see *Moralia*, "De Genio Socratis," 577E–F).[54] Similarly, Agesilaos of Sparta, opening a tomb at Haliartos, found an inscribed bronze tablet.[55] The nine gold plates of Orphism were interred in coffins as guidebooks for the dead,[56] and the Phoenicians, following an Egyptian practice, wrote letters to the dead on small rolls of thin sheets of lead. These rolls were then dropped into the tomb through openings designed for that purpose.[57]

In 1980 archaeologists opened an ancient tomb adjacent to the Scottish Presbyterian church of St. Andrew in Jerusalem. There they discovered two small rolled-up strips of silver with a Hebrew inscription. Using paleographic evidence, they dated the rolls to the end of the seventh century B.C. or the beginning of the sixth century B.C., the time of Lehi. Both plates include quotations of the priestly blessing from Numbers 6:24–26.[58]

Interment of the dead and of texts in tombs is analogous to the burial of records in the ground. Just as the dead will be resurrected, so too the records will come forth to future generations. Sometimes, as in the case of the Book of Mormon, the concealed documents are placed inside a coffinlike box, as we shall discuss in chapter 3, "Hiding Records in Boxes." Indeed, in Judaism, worn-out synagogue scrolls are buried in a solemn funeral service—a practice that will be discussed in chapter 9, "Books in the Treasury."

Summary

This chapter has used numerous examples to illustrate the long history of concealing documents. While various parts of the world share that tradition, it is most prominent in the ancient Near East, the land from which the Book of Mormon people emigrated to the New World. From this we can suggest that the concealment of the Book of Mormon in the earth is prima facie evidence of the book's ancient origins.

Notes

1. Enos 1:14 notes that the Lamanites wanted to destroy the Nephites, their records, and their traditions. King Benjamin later noted that had it not been for the written records they possessed, the Nephites would have "dwindled in unbelief" like the Lamanites because of the false traditions passed down by their Lamanite ancestors (Mosiah 1:5). Alma believed that the Nephite records would someday convince the Lamanites of the falsity of those traditions (see Alma 9:16–17). His friends, the sons of Mosiah, hoped to convince the Lamanites of this very thing by using the scriptures they possessed (see Alma 17:9; 18:34–40; 21:9, 17; 23:3; 24:7; 25:6; 26:24).

2. Alexander Roberts and James Donaldson, eds., *Ante-Nicene Fathers* (Peabody, Mass.: Hendrickson, 1994), 8:215. Originally published in 1886.

3. Montague Rhodes James, *The Apocryphal New Testament* (Oxford: Clarendon, 1955), 182.

4. See Margaret Dunlop Wilson, ed. and trans., *Apocrypha Arabica* (London: C. J. Clay, 1901), 1.

5. *The Gospel of the Egyptians,* 69, in James M. Robinson, ed.,

The Nag Hammadi Library, 3rd ed. (San Francisco: HarperCollins, 1990), 218.

6. Ernest A. Wallis Budge, *The Bandlet of Righteousness: An Ethiopian Book of the Dead* (London: Luzac, 1929), 63.

7. Ernest A. Wallis Budge, *The Book of the Mysteries of the Heavens and the Earth and Other Works of Bakhayla Mîkâ'êl (Zôsîmâs)* (London: Oxford University Press, 1935), 123–24.

8. Ibid., 107.

9. E. S. Drower, *The Haran Gawaita and the Baptism of Hibil-Ziwa* (Vatican: Biblioteca Apostolica Vaticana, 1953), 17.

10. Werner Foerster, *Gnosis: A Selection of Gnostic Texts,* trans. Robert McLachlan Wilson (Oxford: Clarendon, 1974), 2:154.

11. Geo Widengren, *The Ascension of the Apostle and the Heavenly Book* (Uppsala, Sweden: University of Uppsala, 1950), 73, citing the text published by M. Lidzbarski, *Das Johannesbuch der Mandäer* (Giessen: Alfred Töpelmann, 1915), 2:63.

12. Hans Dieter Betz, ed., *The Greek Magical Papyri in Translation: Including the Demotic Spells* (Chicago: University of Chicago Press, 1986), 179.

13. Garth Fowden, *The Egyptian Hermes: A Historical Approach to the Late Pagan Mind* (Cambridge: Cambridge University Press, 1986), 53, citing Heliodorus.

14. See ibid., 207–9.

15. Cited in Widengren, *Ascension of the Apostle,* 83–84.

16. Cited in ibid., 83–84 n. 4.

17. Ibid., 82. The Greek text is included in a note. The story is also recounted in Fowden, *Egyptian Hermes,* 33.

18. See Philostratus, *Life of Apollonius of Tyana,* 8.19–20.

19. Widengren, *Ascension of the Apostle,* 78–79, citing the Arabic text and the German translation in J. Ruska, *Tabula Smaragdina. Ein Beitrag zur Geschichte der hermetischen Literatur* (Heidelberg: Winter, 1926), 135.

20. See Widengren, *Ascension of the Apostle,* 79.

21. Both texts are noted in Raphael Patai, *The Jewish Alchemists* (Princeton, N.J.: Princeton University Press, 1994), 22–23.

22. Cited in Widengren, *Ascension of the Apostle,* 77–78. Widengren refers to the Arabic text and German translation in Ruska, *Tabula Smaragdina,* 112–14.

23. See Fowden, *Egyptian Hermes,* 162–64. See also the discussion in Robert Kriech Ritner, *The Mechanics of Ancient Egyptian Magical Practice* (Chicago: Oriental Institute of the University of Chicago, 1993), 218–19.

24. Widengren, *Ascension of the Apostle,* 80. The Roman historian Ammianus Marcellinus wrote that in Egypt there were "subterranean passages, and winding retreats, which, it is said, men skillful in the ancient mysteries, by means of which they divined the coming of a flood, constructed in different places lest the memory of all their sacred ceremonies should be lost. On the walls, as they cut them out, they have sculptured several kinds of birds and beasts, and countless other figures of animals, which they call hieroglyphics." *Roman History* 22.15.30, in C. D. Yonge, trans., *The Roman History of Ammianus Marcellinus* (London: George Bell and Sons, 1902), 311–12.

25. Widengren, *Ascension of the Apostle,* 81, citing the Arabic text and the German translation in J. Ruska, *Arabische Alchemisten* (Heidelberg: C. Winter, 1924), 16–24. Widengren compares the old man with the ancient of days or God, in Daniel 7:9. While Joseph Smith identified the "ancient of days" as Adam, or Michael (a fact supported by some pseudepigraphic texts that have Adam seated with the books of judgment), in *1 Enoch* (from which many scholars believe Daniel borrowed the terminology) and other early Jewish texts, the title is used for God.

26. Widengren, *Ascension of the Apostle,* 80 n. 3.

27. Robert K. Ritner, *Egyptian Magical Practice under the Roman Empire: The Demotic Spells and their Religious Context,* vol. 18 of *Aufstieg und Niedergang der römischen Welt* (Berlin: Walter de Gruyter, 1995), 3367 (part 18, section 5).

28. See Georges Posener, *De La Divinité du Pharaon* (Paris: Imprimerie Nationale, 1960), 71–72. The stela has since disappeared, probably a victim of the black market in Egyptian antiquities.

29. See Ritner, *Egyptian Magical Practice,* 3367.

30. Ernest A. Wallis Budge, *The Book of the Dead* (New Hyde Park, N.Y.: University Books, 1967), 660–61. For the use of temples to preserve sacred texts, see the discussion in chapter 9 of this volume, "Books in the Treasury."

31. VI,6 *Discourse on the Eighth and Ninth* 59.13–14; 60.13–16, in Robinson, *Nag Hammadi Library,* 325. Hermes, under his name Trismegistus, is one of the participants in the dialogue found in another Nag Hammadi text, VI,*8 Asclepius 21–29* 66.26; 69.1, 28; 74.18, 33; 78.14, 31, in which his son Tat is also mentioned (72.30). This text may be the *Perfect Discourse* attributed to Aesclepius in some of the Hermetic literature.

32. *Discourse on the Eighth and Ninth* 61.18–20, 25–30; 62.1–15, 22–27; 63.1, 4–5, in Robinson, *Nag Hammadi Library,* 326.

33. See Fowden, *Egyptian Hermes,* 168–73.

34. See Graham Hancock, *The Sign and the Seal* (New York: Crown, 1992), 182, citing Kenneth Mackenzie, *The Royal Masonic Cyclopaedia* (Wellingborough: Aquarian Press, 1987; first published 1877), 200–202.

35. See Hancock, *Sign and the Seal,* 369–70, 573 n. 38.

36. See Patai, *Jewish Alchemists,* 239–53. All quotes used in this section are from Patai.

37. Flamel's story is recounted in chapter 5 of this volume, "Angels as Guardians of Hidden Books."

38. Patai, *Jewish Alchemists,* 573 n. 19.

39. See H. Curtis Wright, "Ancient Burials of Metal Documents in Stone Boxes," in *By Study and Also by Faith,* ed. John M. Lundquist and Stephen D. Ricks (Salt Lake City: Deseret Book and FARMS, 1990), 273–334.

40. The records of the Nephite secret combination, sponsored by the devil, were also concealed in the earth and brought forth later (see Helaman 11:10, 26).

41. See James H. Charlesworth, *The Old Testament Pseudepigrapha* (Garden City, N.Y.: Doubleday, 1983), 1:927. This kind of preparation using oil may be what is meant by one of the Dead Sea Scrolls (4Q536), which speaks of "writ[ing] the words of God in a book which does not wear out." Florentino García Martínez, *The Dead Sea Scrolls Translated,* 2nd ed. (Leiden: E. J. Brill, 1996), 264. Note also the *Cologne Mani Codex,* in which an angel tells Adam "take and write these things which I reveal to you on most pure papyrus, incorruptible and insusceptible to worms." P. Colon. inv. nr. 4780, 49–50, in Ron Cameron and Arthur J. Dewey, *The Cologne Mani Codex* (Missoula, Mont.: Scholars Press, 1979), 39.

42. See the discussion in chapter 8 of this volume, "A Book That Does Not Wear Out."

43. Budge, *Bandlet of Righteousness,* 78.

44. Hugh Nibley, *Enoch the Prophet* (Salt Lake City: Deseret Book and FARMS, 1986), 151, citing M. J. Bin Gorion, *Die Sagen der Juden* (Frankfurt: Kütter and Loening, 1913), 1:263.

45. The Hebrew text was published in Adolph Jellinek, *Bet ha-Midrasch,* 3rd ed. (Jerusalem: Wahrmann, 1967), 3:156–59.

46. Harry Sperling and Maurice Simon, trans., *The Zohar* (New York: Rebecca Bennet Publications, 1958), 1:259. The story is reminiscent of the finding of the concealed records of the Gadianton band (see Helaman 11:10, 26).

47. Wilson, *Apocrypha Arabica,* 37.

48. See Berossus, according to Polyhistor and Abydenus, cited in W. G. Lambert and A. R. Millard, *Atra-Hasis: The Babylonian Story of the Flood* (Oxford: Clarendon, 1969), 135–36. The story is also found in Eusebius (*Chronicon* I.3).

49. See Peter De Roo, *America Before Columbus* (New York: Lippincott, 1900), 224–25, cited in Paul R. Cheesman, *Ancient Writing on Metal Plates: Archaeological Findings Support Mormon Claims* (Bountiful, Utah: Horizon, 1985), 52.

50. See Hyatt Verrill, *America's Ancient Civilizations* (New York: B. P. Putnam's Sons, 1953), 23, 42, cited in Cheesman, *Ancient Writing on Metal Plates,* 53.

51. See Hugh Nibley, *An Approach to the Book of Mormon,* 3rd ed. (Salt Lake City: Deseret Book and FARMS, 1988), 24 n. 19, citing Jawad ʿAli, *Tarikh al-ʿArab qabl al-Islam* (Baghdad: Matbaʿat, 1950), 1:14.

52. See Michael E. Stone, *Armenian Apocrypha relating to Adam and Eve* (Leiden: E. J. Brill, 1996), 53, 65–67. For other translations of the same story, which exists in three different versions, see also W. Lowndes Lipscomb, *The Armenian Apocryphal Adam Literature* (Atlanta: Scholars Press, 1990), 138–41, 268–69.

53. The story is reported in Budge, *Book of the Dead,* xix n. 3.

54. My thanks to William J. Hamblin for this information. See his "Sacred Writings on Bronze Plates in the Ancient Mediterranean" (FARMS, 1994), 13.

55. See Lillian H. Jeffery, *The Local Scripts of Archaic Greece* (Oxford: Clarendon, 1963), 55–56, cited by Wright, "Ancient Burials of Metal Documents," 278.

56. See William K. C. Guthrie, *Orpheus and Greek Religion: A Study of the Orphic Movement* (New York: Norton, 1966), 176, pl. 8–10, cited by Wright, "Ancient Burials of Metal Documents," 279. See also the discussion in C. Wilfred Griggs, "The Book of Mormon as an Ancient Book," *BYU Studies* 22/3 (1982), 259.

57. See Ernest A. Wallis Budge, *Amulets and Superstitions* (London: Oxford University Press, 1930), 253.

58. The finds were reported by Gabriel Barkay, "The Divine Name Found in Jerusalem," *Biblical Archaeology Review* 9/2 (1983): 14–19, and "Priestly Blessings on Silver Plates" (in Hebrew), *Cathedra* 52 (1989): 46–59. The discoveries are discussed by William J. Adams Jr., "Lehi's Jerusalem and Writing on Metal Plates," *Journal of Book of Mormon Studies* 3/1 (1994): 204–6; "More on the Silver Plates from Lehi's Jerusalem," *Journal of Book of Mormon Studies* 4/2 (1995): 136–37. See the discussion in John Gee and John A. Tvedtnes, "Ancient Manuscripts Fit Book of Mormon Pattern," *Insights,* February 1999.

chapter 3

Hiding Records in Boxes

I looked in, and there indeed did I behold the plates, the Urim and Thummim, and the breastplate, as stated by the messenger. The box in which they lay was formed by laying stones together in some kind of cement. In the bottom of the box were laid two stones crossways of the box, and on these stones lay the plates and the other things with them. (JS—H 1:52)

Visitors to the spot where Joseph Smith retrieved the gold plates confirmed his account of the box in which Moroni had hidden them. David Whitmer, in an interview with P. Wilhelm Poulson in 1878, said, "I saw the place where the plates were found, and a great many did so, and it awakened an excitement at the time, because the worst enemies of 'Mormonism' stirred up the confusion by telling about the plates which Joseph found, and the 'gold bible' which he was in possession of, so he was in constant danger of being robbed and killed." Poulson asked, "How did the place look?" Whitmer replied, "It was a stone box, and the stones looked to me as if they were cemented together. That was on the side of the hill, and a little down from the top."[1]

In the early morning hours of 22 September 1827, as Joseph prepared to return to the hill to recover the plates buried by Moroni, he asked his mother if she had a chest with a lock and key. Seeing her anxiety, he told her, "Never mind, I can do very well for the present without it."[2] Later that morning he asked her about having a chest made, whereupon she told him of a cabinetmaker who could perform the task.[3] Still later, Joseph sent his younger brother Don Carlos to ask Hyrum, another brother, to get a chest with lock and key and have it ready for his return with the plates, which he had hidden in a decayed birch log about three miles from the family home.[4] By the time Joseph returned to the house with the plates, which were wrapped in his linen frock, Hyrum had emptied a wooden chest and brought it to his parents' home. Joseph locked the plates inside the chest at that time.[5] Later on, the breastplate containing the interpreters was also kept in the chest.[6]

As he was bringing the plates home, Joseph was attacked by men who sought to take them from him because of the value of the metal, which had "the appearance of gold."[7] While he had custody of the plates, Joseph took precautions to protect the plates by hiding them in various places: in a hollow carved out of a decaying tree, beneath the hearth, in a pile of flax, and in a box hidden inside a cask filled with beans.[8]

Joseph's wish to keep the plates in a box may have been inspired by the stone box in which Moroni had hidden the plates some fourteen centuries earlier. He may also have had in mind a vision in which his father, Joseph Smith Sr., was shown a box, the contents of which he was to eat in order to gain wisdom.[9] The plates from which the Book of Mormon was translated were not the first sacred text known to have been kept in a box. A large number of documents and archaeological discoveries confirm the antiquity of the practice, which predated Moroni by many centuries. Records were kept in arks and foundation stones, as well as in boxes made of stone, metal, and earthenware.

The Ark of the Covenant

The ark of the covenant constructed in Moses' day was the first box used in ancient Israel to house relics and sacred records. According to Hebrews 9:4, it held "the golden pot that had manna, and Aaron's rod that budded, and the tables of the covenant." That the tables of the law were kept in the ark is confirmed in Deuteronomy 10:1–5 and 1 Kings 8:9 (= 2 Chronicles 5:10).

The ark evidently held other records as well, for we read in Deuteronomy 31:26 that the Lord told Moses, "Take this book of the law, and put it in the side of the ark of the covenant of the Lord your God, that it may be there for a witness against thee." In the introduction to his *Mishneh Torah*, the twelfth-century Jewish rabbi Maimonides commented on Deuteronomy 31:26. He noted that Moses had inscribed thirteen copies of the Pentateuch, then delivered one to each of the twelve tribes of Israel and placed the master copy in the ark.[10] *Petirat Mosheh*, recounting the same story, notes that the angel Gabriel took this thirteenth scroll and brought it to the heavenly court. It there became the scroll from which the souls of the pious read.[11]

Commenting on the biblical story of the ark as the cause of the collapse of the Philistine god Dagon (see 1 Samuel 5:1–7), St. Ephraim Syrus, in the third of his *Hymns on the Nativity*, suggested that it was the book hidden in the ark that was the cause of the miracle.[12] A number of early traditions indicate that the ark itself was subsequently hidden away for later recovery—a topic discussed in chapter 6, "Hiding Sacred Relics."[13]

An ancient text known as the *Damascus Document* (CD V, 2–5), copies of which were discovered in both the genizah of the Old Cairo synagogue in Egypt[14] and among the Dead Sea Scrolls, confirms that the written law of Moses was kept in the ark: "However, David had not read the sealed book of the law which was in the ark, for it had not been opened in Israel since the day of the death of Eleazar and of Jehoshua, and Joshua and the elders who worshipped Ashtaroth had hidden the public (copy) until Zadok's entry into office" as high priest in David's day.[15]

Some scholars have suggested that the *Damascus Document* refers not to the ark of the covenant, but to another sealed box (the word "ark" means simply "box"). Ben Zion Wacholder has noted that *Targum Pseudo-Jonathan* on Deuteronomy 31:26 "refers to an additional container" and that an early rabbi, Judah ben Laqish, recorded in Tosefta *Sotah* 7:18 that there were two arks, "one of which contained a *sepher torah* [Pentateuch] and the other of which preserved the broken fragments of the original law-tablets."[16]

Samaritan tradition also reports that records were kept in the ark. One Samaritan document (BM 1732A)[17] says that Moses copied "the holy Torah from the book which was written by the finger of God" and "opened the Ark of Testimony and he placed the Book of the Law, which was written by the finger of God in it, by the side of the two Tablets upon which were engraven the Ten Words,[18] and placed upon the Ark the covering (kaporet) which no one could lift from the Ark up to this very day."[19] The Samaritan *Chronicle Adler* notes that the priest Eli (known from the Bible as the one who raised the prophet Samuel) "made for himself an ark of gold, wherein he placed the books written in the handwriting of his ancestor, our lord Ithamar."[20]

The Samaritan *Tolidah* tells how Abisha, great-grandson of Aaron, wrote a scroll of the law that was, for a long time, kept in a Samaritan synagogue in Elon Moreh. One day, the priest charged with displaying it to the people "carried the Scroll away from the synagogue to Gilgal in Ephraim, where the people quarreled with him about it; and as they were arranging themselves in Gilgal, and the Scroll was opened, there occurred in the world a great earthquake and thunderings of lightning, and a mighty wind lifted the Scroll out of the ark wherein it lay, and it was carried up and whirled into the air by the wind, while the community was watching, trembling and weeping. But they strengthened their hearts and took hold of the end of the Scroll, and it happened that a fragment was torn off."[21]

Related to these stories about the ark as a repository for the law of Moses is a story in *Pseudo-Philo* 26:1–15. As those verses explain, God commanded Kenaz to place books and stones engraved with the names of the twelve tribes into the ark and conceal it on the mountain beside the altar (see also *Chronicles of Jerahmeel* 57:11–21).

To this day, Jews and Samaritans alike keep the scroll of the Torah (law) of Moses in a cabinet known as an ark. It is typically covered with a small curtain representing the veil that separated the holy of holies of the ancient temple or tabernacle (where the original ark of the covenant was kept) from the rest of the sanctuary. While some of this symbolism is not present in Joseph Smith's account of the hiding place of the plates, the stone box in which they were deposited clearly served the same purpose as the ark in Moses' day. The two receptacles are also alike in that in addition to the records, each contained other sacred artifacts. This will be further discussed in chapter 6, "Hiding Sacred Relics."

An Ancient Practice

One early tradition suggests that the earthly practice of keeping sacred documents in boxes is based on the heavenly pattern. In *3 Enoch* 27:1–2, we read that the angel in charge of the heavenly archives keeps a scroll in a sealed box. The box is to be opened and the scroll is to be read in the heavenly court.

Pirqe Rabbi Eliezer 50 notes that the records of the Persian king were placed "in the king's box," whence they could be retrieved and read when necessary.[22]

The tenth-century Arab chronographer al-Kisaʾi wrote that prior to Adam's death, Adam told Seth how in his heavenly vision he had seen what was "written on the Canopy of the Throne and the gates of Paradise, the layers of the heavens and the leaves of the Tuba tree." In addition, "God had given Adam a white cloth from Paradise and placed it in the coffer."[23]

The idea is also found in early Christian and Jewish lore. At the end of the Ethiopic version of the *Apocalypse of Peter,* after telling Clement of the transfiguration, Peter instructed him to hide the revelation in a box. In an early Jewish legend, Rabbi Yohanan noted that as he and others sailed in a ship, they spotted in the water a box studded with precious stones and pearls. A diver went to retrieve the box, but a fish guarding it attacked him. The diver drove the fish away by throwing a hide full of vinegar on it, but when he reached for the box, a heavenly voice told him to leave it because it contained threads that would be used in the future to make garments for the righteous (see TB *Baba Batra* 74a–b).

A text from an ancient Egyptian temple archive that calls itself "the tenth (?) Hidden [Book of] Moses" (*PGM* XIII. 734–1077) describes how to inscribe a text on a gold or silver lamella (plate) and place it "in a clean box."[24] Another ancient Egyptian text tells how Horus, son of Panishi, slept overnight in a temple, where the god Thoth told him in a dream that he would find a box containing a book written by Thoth himself concealed in a naos within the temple. After copying the magical text, Horus returned the original to its place.[25] Another Egyptian document, the *Berlin Medical Papyrus,* expressly states that it is a copy of an earlier book discovered rolled up in a case concealed beneath the feet of a statue of the god Anubis. Chapter 137 of the Egyptian Book of the Dead mentions "the books of Prince Herutataf, who discovered them in a secret coffer."[26]

An Egyptian text from the thirteenth century B.C. (Papyrus Cairo 30646) tells of Setne Khamwas, son of King Ramses II, who learned of a book of magic written by the scribal god Thoth and kept in the tomb of a prince named Naneferkaptah. He went to the tomb and found the book, which radiated a strong light, and tried to take it. His efforts were interrupted by the spirits of Naneferkaptah and his wife, Ahwere, who recounted the book's tale. An old priest had told Nanef that Thoth's book of magic was hidden in a gold box inside a silver box, inside an ebony and ivory box, inside a box of juniper wood, inside a copper box, inside an iron box concealed in the river at Coptos. It was defended by serpents, scorpions, and various reptiles, which Naneferkaptah had to kill in order to obtain the book. Naneferkaptah then took the book and copied it onto a papyrus roll. Various misfortunes befell him and his wife and he was buried with the book. Setne was not dissuaded and removed the book from the tomb, but his father later ordered him to return it.[27]

The idea of hiding sacred records in boxes has continued to more recent times. In the early sixteenth century, a story arose that the judgment of Jesus, written in Latin (Hebrew, according to some versions), had been discovered in a box in Vienne, southern France. Several decades later, in 1580, a new version was published. This was said to have been found at Aquila (also called Aquill, Aguila, or Abruzzi), in the kingdom of Naples (Italy), anciently called Amiternum (or Amitorum) and said to be the birthplace of Pontius Pilate. Though both versions of the story were published and circulated, they were denounced by some sixteenth-century scholars. In the 1580 story, the document in Hebrew was on a copper plate enclosed in three boxes (of marble, iron, and the innermost of stone) in a ruined wall. In 1839 the story resurfaced in France. In this version Napoleon's men, during the French occupation of the kingdom of Naples (1806–1815), found the brass or copper plate in an ebony box kept in the sacristy of the Carthusian charterhouse, near Naples. Dominique Vivant Denon, who had charge of removing art treasures to France, left the copper plate in the chapel of Caserta, probably the royal chapel of the Neopolitan kings, but brought back a translation and a copy of the plate. The original plate was sold to a Lord Howard after Denon's death.[28]

Stone Boxes

The use of stone boxes to house documents is known from the Mediterranean world from which Lehi came.[29] In the early 1900s, archaeologists uncovered a granite box at Alexandria, Egypt, which held the writings of a late Greek author.[30] In 1944 a farmer in the western Peloponnesus of Greece was digging a well when, at a depth of twenty feet, he found a stone box. Smashing the lid, he found a scroll on which he and others saw writing. He informed police, but because of the civil war with the Communists, the local director of antiquities could not come immediately. When at length he arrived, he found that the scroll had been thrown on the dunghill and had disintegrated.[31] More recently, Greek archaeologist Spyridon

Marinatos found at Mesenia a marble chest that he suggested may have been "a library box."[32]

Roman lore holds that the seventh-century king Numa ordered that he not be cremated, but buried instead in a stone coffin alongside another such coffin that was to contain holy books he had written. When he died, his request was obeyed and the two stone sarcophagi were sealed with lead. The body and books were interred at the foot of Janus Hill. Four or five centuries later, the coffins were accidentally discovered and opened. Numa's body had decayed, but his books had all been preserved. Hemina and Pliny both reported that the scrolls had been treated with citrus oil to preserve them.[33]

In 1970, the Jordanian government announced that it had purchased eight parchment scrolls that had reportedly been discovered in a stone chest inside a tomb. Written in a previously unknown script but thought by some to be Philistine documents, their provenance could not be determined because they had not been discovered by archaeologists. A Jordanian entrepreneur living in Jerusalem had acquired them from the unnamed discoverers and had sold them to the Jordanian Department of Antiquities in June 1966. The dealer believed that the documents had come from an ancient site in the region of Hebron, south of Jerusalem.[34]

According to the preface of the *Apocalypse of Paul*, the document was discovered during the fourth century in a stone box buried beneath a house in Tarsus, when a young man followed the instructions of an angel and searched for it. The story, which closely parallels that of the discovery of the Book of Mormon in a number of details, is discussed in chapter 5, "Angels as Guardians of Hidden Books," and in the appendix by Steven Booras, "The Book of Mormon and the *Apocalypse of Paul*."

Metal Boxes

The use of metal boxes to store important writings is also attested. The eleventh-century Arab chronographer al-Thaᶜlabi mentioned a writing that was sealed in an iron box.[35] Similarly, in 1965 a set of nineteen inscribed gold plates was found in a bronze box. The plates, held together by a pin-and-hinge system, were found beneath the Wanggung-ri pagoda in the Chollabuk province of South Korea.[36] The bronze box had been placed inside a stone box in the eighth century A.D. and contained the *Diamond Sutra* from the Buddhist scriptures.

Drower noted that "during times of stress and danger, the Mandaeans of Iraq and Iran 'buried the books', and this has been done, according to them, many times."[37] The sacred texts of the Mandaeans of Iraq and Iran are typically "wrapped in white cloths and kept in a box, often a metal box" and are never written "on parchment," only on "papyrus, metal, and stone."[38]

The Yezîdîs, who inhabit the Kurdistan area of Turkey, keep books that are considered so secret that one man who revealed information concerning them was actually punished with death.[39] Their two most sacred books, *The Black Book* and *The Book of Enlightenment* (or Revelation) are kept hidden away until festival time. Most Yezîdîs do not know where they are kept, and no Christian or Muslim is permitted to see them. "In times of danger the manuscripts are kept locked in a wooden and silver box, measuring thirty-three centimetres long, twenty-two centimetres wide, and seven centimetres high, which is hidden in a cave having a concealed entrance." Three keys to the box are kept, and on the lid is a depiction of the seven angels and other nature symbols.[40] On a related note, another hidden document comes from the Temple of Sheikh 'Adî, the principal Yezîdî shrine, which is said to have originally been a Nestorian monastery deserted by the monks. Pulling down the altar to bury their leader there, the Yezîdîs found therein a Syrian inscription that they dutifully hid away.[41]

Two medieval Jewish texts, *Sepher ha-Razim* (Book of Mysteries) and the *Book of Noah,* indicate that Noah possessed the heavenly book delivered to Adam and "placed (the book) in a golden cabinet and brought it first into the ark to learn from it the times of the day and to investigate from it the times of the night."[42]

Sanctuary/Palace Foundation Boxes

From discoveries made since Joseph Smith's time, we now know that the kings of ancient Mesopotamia hid written documents in boxes, often of carved stone, that were buried in the foundations of their temples and palaces. The most comprehensive discussion of foundation burials is by H. Curtis Wright, from whom we draw much of the information included in this section.[43]

One of the earliest foundation boxes was a stone chest from about 2900 B.C. discovered during excavations at Tel Brak.[44] During excavations at Mari of the Ur III period (circa 2100–2000 B.C.), André Parrot discovered six inscribed bronze plates deposited in the corners of the foundations of the Nin-Ḫur-Sag temple constructed by King Niwar-Mer. The plates were deposited directly on the mud bricks used in the construction.[45] Another of Mari's rulers, Apil-kin, hollowed out bricks in which to hide the records buried in the foundations of his buildings. One such box contained a bronze plate encased in wood.[46]

A number of Sumerian kings are known to have left written records in foundation boxes. One of the earliest, dating to circa 3000 B.C., was found in the temple of Dagan. Now housed at the Louvre in Paris, the stone square box, complete with lid, contained an inscribed bronze plate, a foundation deposit of King Ishtup-Ilum. Also found in the cavity in the brick wall with the box were other written records—a tablet of white limestone and one of schist.[47]

During his excavations at the ancient city of Ur, near Babylon, C. Leonard Woolley found, in a building built in the ninth year of Rim-Sin, king of Larsa (circa 1990 B.C.), a burnt brick box built into the wall. The box contained a copper figure of the king and a dedication tablet.[48]

In 1937, an inscribed gold tablet was found buried beneath the foundation of a building erected by the queen of the ancient Sumerian city of Umma.[49] A metal foundation tablet of King Warad-Sin of Larsa (1843–1823 B.C.) is also known, as is a copper foundation tablet containing an inscription of Simat-Inanna, the wife of the Sumerian king Rim-Sin (1822–1763 B.C.).[50] At Ur, Woolley found, in the ruins of a building of the mid-seventh century B.C., a series of boxes containing statuettes. One of the boxes contained a bronze plaque.[51]

The Assyrians, who later controlled Mesopotamia, also left foundation deposits. Excavation of the Ishtar temple built by king Tukulti-Ninurta I (1244–1208 B.C.) uncovered various buried relics, including inscribed tablets, glass beads, and bits of ivory, all laid out on a stone slab placed atop the mud-brick foundation. The inscribed tablets included thirteen of gold or silver and seven each of lead and alabaster. Other inscribed gold and silver tablets were found throughout the complex.[52]

A foundation box from the ancient city of Apqu (Bumariyah or Tell Abu-Maria), in Iraq, made its way to Philadelphia, where its broken pieces were reassembled. The box bears an inscription commissioned by King Ashurnasirpal

II (883–859 B.C.) on the sides and the lid. A limestone box bearing this king's name was found at Balawat, near the ancient Assyrian capital Nineveh. It contained two inscribed clay tablets. A third inscribed tablet of the same size but made of marble was found lying on a nearby altar. The site archaeologist speculated that ancient priests placed it there to read but did not return it to the box before the temple was destroyed.[53]

A pair of gold and silver plates commissioned by Ashurnasirpal II exists. Their provenance is unknown, though the inscription found on the plates makes it clear that they were foundation burials for a palace.[54] A text of King Ashurbanipal I (circa 668–631 B.C.), written on a clay prism, also describes the founding of the temple of Nergal at Kutha "upon tables of silver and gold."[55]

A stone box from the time of Shalmaneser III (858–824 B.C.) was found in the ruins of the west gate of the outer wall of the ancient city of Assur, but any inscribed tablets that it may have contained were missing.[56]

King Sargon II (722–705 B.C.) repeats throughout his annals that he kept records on plates of gold, silver, bronze, and lead.[57] In 1854, during excavations of his palace at Khorsabad, six small inscribed plates (gold, silver, bronze, tin, and lead, with one alabaster) were found in a stone box buried beneath the palace foundation. The box, along with the lead and alabaster tablets, were lost when the ship carrying them sank into the Tigris River in Iraq on 23 May 1855. The four surviving plates—of gold, silver, bronze, and tin—were taken to Paris and are housed in the Louvre.[58]

Wright hastens to note that the provenance of some of the Assyrian boxes is unknown. Some may have been used in ancient libraries rather than buried in foundations. He points out that a half-dozen statues of Nabu, which were found at

Nimrud and Arslan Tash in northern Syria, show the deity holding a square box in his hands. The association of the box with Nabu, the god of writing, suggests it was meant to contain records.[59]

The neo-Babylonians (Chaldeans), who put an end to the Assyrian hegemony in the seventh century B.C., similarly left records deposited in the foundations of public buildings. Excavation of the temple of Ningal at Ur uncovered a limestone tablet, a steatite tablet, and three copper tablets from two earlier kings (Warad-Sin and Kurigalzu II, between whom there was a considerable gap in time). The tablets had been reburied when the temple was refurbished about 650 B.C. At Sippar, near Babylon, excavators found a lidded stone box containing an inscribed stone from the time of the Babylonian king Nabopolassar (626–605 B.C.).[60] The box was probably originally buried in a foundation.

The Persians continued the practice of depositing metal records in stone foundation boxes after they conquered Babylon in 539 B.C. In 1926 at Hamadan (ancient Ecbatana), Persia (now Iran), archaeologist Ernst E. Herzfeld discovered two small tablets, one silver and the other gold. Hidden inside a stone box laid in the foundation of the palace, the tablets bore inscriptions from Darius I (521–485 B.C.) about the erection of palaces in the city. Suspecting that similar foundation tablets might be found in Darius's palace at Persepolis, archaeologists made a concerted effort to locate such records in 1933. At Persepolis, two pairs of plates (one silver and one gold in each pair) were found in stone boxes placed in the foundation corners of the palace. In all, six plates were found, inscribed in three languages: Old Persian, Elamite, and Babylonian. Darius originally had a box containing a gold and a silver tablet in each corner of his audience hall, but only two of the boxes remained to be discovered. The surviving plates are in the National Archaeological Museum in Tehran, Iran.[61]

In 1930 a gold tablet containing a ten-line inscription from Ariaramnes, great-grandfather of Darius I, was found at Hamadan, the ancient site of Ecbatana. Additional records on gold tablets found at the same site were laid down by Arsames (the son of Ariaramnes), Artaxerxes III, and Darius II.[62] These records were probably originally buried in foundations.

Foundation boxes containing written documents are known outside Mesopotamia as well. Hugh Nibley compared the Mesopotamian foundation burials with the tradition "that the wise Arab King Nu'man of Hira ordered a copy of the poems of the Arabs to be buried in his White Palace."[63] A square depression was found at each corner of the Haldis Temple at Toprakkale, near Lake Van in Turkey, probably from the eighth century B.C. Two of these depressions each contained a square bronze plate and scraps of gold and silver sheets. Nothing was inscribed, and it may thus be that the Arabs adopted the Mesopotamian practice of burying plates in foundation stones but did not write on the plates.[64]

Egypt also has its share of foundation deposits. Dozens of small metallic plates were found in the foundations of the Serapis temple, which housed an ancient library. Ten such foundation plaques, with hieroglyphic and Greek inscriptions from the time of King Ptolemy III (246–221 B.C.) were found in 1943 by Alan Rowe. Three were metal plates (one each of gold, silver, and bronze), five were opaque glass, one was faience, and one was made of mud. A similar set of ten plaques from the same king were found the following year in another foundation trench. A year later, a third set was found in another corner of the foundation. Ultimately, ten more deposit holes were uncovered. Some had been plundered in earlier times, but a total of 43 foundation tablets were recovered from an estimated 130 originally deposited.[65]

The city of Alexandria, Egypt, also has foundation deposits. A plaster box was found in the Harpocrates Shrine, and the Roman Serapeum included rectangular limestone coffers in niches in its long underground passages. In 1847 a granite box was discovered in the garden of the Consulate General of Prussia. Its Greek inscription, "For three volumes by Dioscurides," suggests that it originally contained books, probably written on papyrus rolls, that may have been sold on the antiquities market. The 380-pound box had already been lost in 1848.[66]

Foundation deposits are also known from the Far East. A copy of *The Law or Dharma Preached by the Buddha*, revered in Pali Buddhism, was found concealed in the brick chamber of an old mound at Hmawza, in the Prome district of Burma. It consisted of twenty leaves of gold and two gold covers.[67] Two other inscribed gold plates were found in the same region, in the village of Maunggun in a brick built into an old pagoda.[68]

Earthenware Containers

The preservation of documents in containers other than boxes is also attested. Manuscripts from pharaonic and Roman Egypt have frequently been found in jars.[69] A large cache of Old Kingdom execration texts, written on small ostraca, was found buried in a clay jar near the great pyramids in Giza in 1955.[70]

In 1931 thirty papyrus leaves were discovered buried in jars in a cemetery or church ruins near Aphroditopolis. The texts included both Old and New Testament books, several leaves from the pseudepigraphic *1 Enoch,* and a Christian homily written in the fourth or fifth century A.D. Many of the manuscripts were purchased by A. Chester Beatty, an American living in England, and the University of Michigan at Ann Arbor.

Most now reside in the Chester Beatty Library in Dublin, Ireland.

During the latter half of the nineteenth century, local Egyptians discovered at Thebes (probably in a tomb) an earthen jar containing nineteen papyri. They were purchased in about 1875 by Lord Amherst of Hackney, England, and in 1912 they were purchased from his estate by J. Pierpont Morgan and left privately with a Mr. Lamacraft, a British Museum expert on mounting. In 1945 Charles F. Nims found the papyri at the British Museum and in 1947 arranged to have them transferred to the Pierpont Morgan Library in New York. The underlying language of one of the Amherst papyri is Aramaic, but the papyrus is written in Egyptian demotic script. Although the text is a collection of pagan hymns, it was in part derived from the biblical Psalm 20. The papyrus is thus a religious document containing a quote from the Bible and written in a "reformed Egyptian" script, carefully concealed in a protective container and hidden away—all elements known from the story of the Book of Mormon.[71] Many dozens of other early biblical documents that were purchased from Egyptian antiquities dealers may have come from similar caches.

In December 1982, excavations at the Sri Lanka site of Anuradhpura uncovered fragments of a broken clay pot. Beneath the fragments were seven inscribed gold plates, and archaeologists surmised that Buddhist monks in the ninth-century monastery had hidden the book in the clay pot during an enemy attack but were unable to retrieve it. The text on the plates is a well-known Buddhist sutra. On the basis of the size of the extant text, it was suggested that as many as one hundred such plates may lie hidden in the vicinity.

In 1996 a collection of thirteen birch-bark scrolls from the ancient Buddhist kingdom of Gandhara, on the Pakistani-Afghan border, was found preserved in pottery jars.

The most well-known caches of documents hidden in pottery are the Nag Hammadi texts and the Dead Sea Scrolls. The former, comprising forty-seven separate texts in thirteen codices, were found in a single large clay pot buried near the village of Nag Hammadi in Egypt, where they had been concealed about A.D. 400. Many of the approximately eight hundred Dead Sea Scrolls were preserved in clay pots hidden in caves south of Jericho, near the northwestern shore of the Dead Sea. About half the scrolls were found in Cave 4 and had evidently been hidden away in haste, for no pottery vessels were found in that cave.

One of the Dead Sea Scrolls is made of copper and comprises a list of various treasures hidden away for the future. Known as the *Copper Scroll* (3Q15), it specifically mentions goblets, cups, jars, vases, and jugs. Some of these vessels contained gold and silver, while others held written documents. Lines 4–5 in column VI note the burial place of an amphora containing a book. The beginning of column 8 states that books and ritual vessels had been hidden in an aqueduct. Some of the concealed treasures were hidden "bene[ath the] large [stone]" (V, 2–4), "in the stone . . . under it" (VIII, 5), "under the large slab" (XI, 6–7), "under the black stone" (XII, 2), or near "a stone held in place by two supports" (X, 9). These stones are reminiscent of the large stone laid atop the box in which Moroni concealed the plates of the Book of Mormon. At the end of the *Copper Scroll,* we read that "in the tunnel which is in Sechab, to the North of Kochlit . . . a copy of this text and its explanation and its measurements and the inventory of everything, item by item" (XII, 10–13).[72]

In his *Ecclesiastical History* 6.16, written about A.D. 324, Eusebius reported that the church father Origen (A.D. 184–253) had found an ancient translation of the Book of

Psalms "in a jar near Jericho in the time of Antoninus, the son of Severus."[73] This would have been between A.D. 211 and 217. Notably, it was just a few miles south of Jericho that the Dead Sea Scrolls were discovered in jars hidden in caves.

Some ancient texts also speak of preserving written documents in clay pots. Paul may have alluded to the practice when he told the Corinthians, "If our gospel be hid, it is hid to them that are lost," and noted, "We have this treasure in earthen vessels" (2 Corinthians 4:3, 7). An early Jewish text, the *Testament of Moses*, also mentions the process of preserving documents in clay pots. In this text, Moses instructed Joshua on how to preserve the books, or parchments, he was leaving in his charge: anoint them with cedar (oil?) and deposit them in earthen jars until the day of recompense (see 1:16–18).[74] Similarly, according to the *Book of Jasher* 47:26–29, the patriarch Jacob concealed documents in an earthen vessel. The Bible describes the prophet Jeremiah doing the same (see Jeremiah 32:14).

Two small silver plates and two small gold plates from the reigns of Shalmaneser I (1274–1245 B.C.) and Tukulti-Ninurta I (1244–1208 B.C.) were found inside a container that was formed by lacing together the rims of two bowls. The container was placed in the ground and then covered by a larger bowl and buried. It is thought that these plates were reburied in the time of Shalmaneser III (858–824 B.C.).[75]

During times of plague, or sickness, the Mandaeans place magic exorcism rolls between two bowls (one inverted above the other) and bury the bowls by the threshold of their house or by a grave.[76] Sometimes they inscribe metal dishes or plaques with magical formulas and bury them beneath the threshold to prevent the entry of demons, especially into reed huts.[77]

Other Containers

Ancient documents have been found in containers other than boxes and pots. In 1958 two bronze tablets from the end of the first century B.C. or the early first century A.D. were found hidden beneath two roofing tiles in the Spanish town of Minigua.[78]

In the late 1940s, farmers in the Bertiz valley near the Turkish province of Maras found a buried bronze sphere that contained thin silver-lead plates from the late seventh century B.C. (about the time of Lehi) bearing twenty-two lines of Semitic inscriptions.[79] A similar story is known from antiquity. Pausanius recorded (circa 370 B.C.) a legend in which Epiteles, son of Aeschines, had a dream in which he was told where to dig to rescue the Great Goddess shut up in her brazen chamber. Digging at the spot, he discovered a bronze urn containing a very thin sheet of tin rolled up like a scroll and inscribed with the mysteries of the Great Goddess.[80]

In 1964 three gold plates and one bronze plate from about 500 B.C. were found at the southern Italian site of Pyrgi. Written in Phoenician (a form of Canaanite) and Etruscan, the plates were hidden in a rectangular niche between two temples. The niche was constructed of blocks of tufa and three tiles, and the plates were concealed beneath a heap of pottery fragments.[81]

Summary

This chapter has shown that the practice of concealing records in boxes, particularly stone boxes, is an ancient one. It predates the Book of Mormon by many centuries and was still being practiced when Moroni deposited the plates in the stone box from which Joseph Smith later removed them. With the exception of the biblical account of the ark of the covenant, however, none of this information was available in Joseph Smith's day. This lends authenticity to his account and to the record known as the Book of Mormon.

Notes

1. *Deseret Evening News,* 16 August 1878, 2.
2. Lucy Mack Smith, *History of Joseph Smith by His Mother, Lucy Mack Smith,* ed. Preston Nibley (Salt Lake City: Bookcraft, 1958), 102.
3. See ibid., 104.
4. See ibid., 107.
5. See ibid., 109.
6. See ibid., 111–13.
7. Testimony of Eight Witnesses; compare JS—H 1:34.
8. See Smith, *History of Joseph Smith,* 107–8, 112–13, 118.
9. See ibid., 47. Two biblical prophets, Ezekiel and John the Revelator, were told to eat books (see Ezekiel 2:8–3:3; Revelation 10:8–10; compare Jeremiah 1:9).
10. See Moses Ben Maimon (Maimonides), *Mishneh Torah, Ha-Qadmah.* Support for the idea also comes from the Jerusalem Talmud (see TY *Taʿanit* 4.2), which notes that three master copies of the Pentateuch were kept in the temple at Jerusalem, against which other copies could be checked (see also *Sipre* 2.356, *Soperim* 6.4; *ʾAbot de Rabbi Nathan* 2:46).
11. The story is recounted in Louis Ginzberg, *The Legends of the Jews* (Philadelphia: Jewish Publication Society of America, 1988), 3:439–40. I am indebted to John W. Welch, who refers to the account in his "Doubled, Sealed, Witnessed Documents: From the Ancient World to the Book of Mormon," in *Mormons, Scripture, and the Ancient World: Studies in Honor of John L. Sorenson,* ed. Davis Bitton (Provo, Utah: FARMS, 1998), 419–20.
12. See Philip Schaff and Henry Wace, eds., *Nicene and Post-Nicene Fathers,* Second Series (Peabody, Mass.: Hendrickson, 1994), 13:232. The book was originally published in 1898.

13. See 2 Maccabees 2:1–8; *4 Baruch* 3:7–19; TB *Yoma* 54a; *Conflict of Adam and Eve* IV, 10.16–17.

14. The purpose of the genizah is discussed in chapter 9 of this volume, "Books in the Treasury."

15. Florentino García Martínez, *The Dead Sea Scrolls Translated,* 2nd ed. (Leiden: E. J. Brill, 1996), 36.

16. Ben Zion Wacholder, "The 'Sealed' Torah versus the 'Revealed' Torah: An Exegesis of Damascus Covenant V, 1–6 and Jeremiah 32, 10–14," *Revue de Qumran* 12/47 (December 1986): 357 n. 21.

17. BM denotes documents held in the British Museum, London.

18. In Hebrew, the ten commandments are called "the Ten Words."

19. Moses Gaster, *The Asatir: The Samaritan Book of the "Secrets of Moses"* (London: Royal Asiatic Society, 1927), 303–5.

20. John Bowman, ed. and trans., *Samaritan Documents relating to Their History, Religion and Life* (Pittsburgh: Pickwick Press, 1977), 89.

21. Ibid., 47–48.

22. Gerald Friedlander, trans., *Pirḳê de Rabbi Eliezer* (New York: Hermon Press, 1965), 398 n. 3. The manuscript read "pot" (or "vessel"), but the translator suggested that "box" was meant.

23. W. M. Thackston Jr., trans., *The Tales of the Prophets of al-Kisa'i* (Boston: Twayne, 1978), 81–82. Seth's possession of the coffer passed to him by Adam is also noted on page 85, in connection with the fact that "the guardianship passed to Seth, and the sons of his father obeyed him."

24. Hans Dieter Betz, ed., *The Greek Magical Papyri in Translation, Including the Demotic Spells* (Chicago: University of Chicago Press, 1986), 194.

25. See Serge Sauneron, *The Priests of Ancient Egypt,* trans. Ann Morrisett (New York: Evergreen Profile, 1960), 125.

26. Ernest A. Wallis Budge, *The Book of the Dead* (New Hyde Park, N.Y.: University Books, 1960), 660–61.

27. See Miriam Lichtheim, *Ancient Egyptian Literature: A Book of Readings* (Berkeley: University of California Press, 1980), 3:126–38. A recap of the story is also found in Garth Fowden, *The Egyptian Hermes: A Historical Approach to the Late Pagan Mind* (Cambridge: Cambridge University Press, 1986), 59–60.

28. The story is told in Per Beskow, "The Copperplate from Aquila," in *Strange Tales about Jesus* (Philadelphia: Fortress, 1983), 16–24. In chapter 6 of that book, Beskow tells the story of the coming forth of the Book of Mormon. The story of the Aquila document is also told in Edgar J. Goodspeed, "The Death Warrant of Jesus Christ," in *Famous "Biblical" Hoaxes* (originally *Modern Apocrypha*) (Grand Rapids, Mich.: Baker, 1956), 92–96.

29. Stone boxes are also known from the New World, though their purpose remains unknown. Paul Cheesman, while teaching at Brigham Young University, collected information on and photographs of more than fifty stone boxes found in Central and South America. See Paul R. Cheesman, *Ancient Writing on Metal Plates: Archaeological Findings Support Mormon Claims* (Bountiful, Utah: Horizon, 1985), 77–80.

30. See H. Curtis Wright, "Ancient Burials of Metal Documents in Stone Boxes," in *By Study and Also By Faith*, ed. John M. Lundquist and Stephen D. Ricks (Salt Lake City: Deseret Book and FARMS, 1990), 283. Wright cites Adolph J. Reinach, "Dioskourides g tomoi," *Bulletin de la Société Royale d'Archéologie d'Alexandria* 11 (1909): 350–70.

31. The story was reported by Gilbert Highet, "The Wondrous Survival of Records," *Horizon* 5 (November 1962): 93, and is cited by Wright, "Ancient Burials of Metal Documents," 273–74.

32. Wright, "Ancient Burials of Metal Documents," 293 n.

33. The story is reported in Plutarch, *Numa* 12.2–5; Pliny, *Naturalis historia* 13.27.84–86; Livy, *Ab Urbe Condita* 40.29.3–6; Lactantius, *Divinarum institutionum libri VII* 1.22.5; Valerius

Maximus, *Factorum et Dictorum Memorabilia* 1.1.12; Augustine, *De civitate Dei* 7.34.7–11; *De Viris Illustribus Urbis Romae* 3.3. See the discussion in Wright, "Ancient Burials of Metal Documents," 275–76 and notes. The ancient practice of burying books in tombs is noted in chapter 2 of this volume, "Hidden Records."

34. See the note in *Kadmos* 10 (1971): 102–3.

35. See al-Thaʿlabi, *Qisas al-Anbiya'* (Cairo: Mustafa al-Babi al-Halabi wa-Awladuhu, A. H. 1340), 246. Hugh Nibley was the first to bring this information to the attention of Latter-day Saints. I am grateful to Brian Hauglid for confirming details of the story from the Arabic text.

36. The plates are housed in the Seoul National Museum.

37. E. S. Drower, *The Mandaeans of Iraq and Iran* (Leiden: E. J. Brill, 1962), 22.

38. Ibid., 22–23.

39. See R. H. W. Empson, *The Cult of the Peacock Angel: A Short Account of the Yezîdî Tribes of Kurdistân* (London: H. F. and G. Witherby, 1928), 146.

40. See ibid., 151–52.

41. See ibid., 33.

42. Michael A. Morgan, trans., *Sepher ha-Razim, The Book of the Mysteries* (Chico, Calif.: Scholars Press, 1983), 18–19. For the Hebrew text of the *Book of Noah,* see Adolph Jellinek, *Bet ha-Midrasch* (Jerusalem: Wahrmann, 1967), 3:159. The story is examined in more detail in chapter 5 of this volume, "Angels as Guardians of Hidden Books."

43. See Wright, "Ancient Burials of Metal Documents." The article was based on Wright's earlier study, *Ancient Burials of Metallic Foundation Documents in Stone Boxes,* University of Illinois Graduate School of Library and Information Science Occasional Papers, no. 157 (Champagne, Ill.: University of Chicago, 1982), 1–42. Wright drew on Richard Ellis's Yale University doctoral dissertation on Mesopotamian foundational deposits.

44. See Wright, "Ancient Burials of Metal Documents," 282, and the bibliography in his footnote 61.

45. See ibid., 285.

46. See ibid., 286.

47. See ibid., 285–86. For a photo of the box, see Cheesman, *Ancient Writing on Metal Plates,* 78.

48. See Wright, "Ancient Burials of Metal Documents," 287.

49. See F. Thureau-Dangin, "Une tablette en or provenant d'Umma," *Revue d'Assyriologie et d'archéologie orientale* 34 (1937): 177–82.

50. See C. J. Gadd, "Babylonian Foundation Texts: 1. Limestone and copper tablets of a wife of Rim-Sin," *Journal of the Royal Asiatic Society* (1926): 679–88.

51. See C. Leonard Woolley, "Babylonian Prophylactic Figures," *Journal of the Royal Asiatic Society* (October 1926): 689–713. For the use of foundation boxes to conceal sacred relics (as opposed to written records), see chapter 6 of this volume, "Hiding Sacred Relics."

52. See Wright, "Ancient Burials of Metal Documents," 288–89, and his notes.

53. See ibid., 291. For a photo of the box, see Cheesman, *Ancient Writing on Metal Plates,* 78.

54. See Wright, "Ancient Burials of Metal Documents," 289.

55. Ibid., 290.

56. See ibid., 292.

57. See ibid., 293 and note.

58. See ibid., 293–94 and notes.

59. See ibid., 293.

60. For a photo of the box and its contents, see Cheesman, *Ancient Writing on Metal Plates,* 79.

61. The Darius plates were first brought to the attention of the Latter-day Saints by Franklin S. Harris (Sr.), "Gold Plates in Persia," *Improvement Era* (December 1940): 714–15, 764, and were later noted by Thomas Stuart Ferguson, "Gold Plates and the Book of

Mormon," *Improvement Era,* April 1962, 232–33, 270–71. See the discussion in Wright, "Ancient Burials of Metal Documents," 280 and the bibliography in nn. 51–56.

62. The Ariaramnes and Arsames inscriptions are noted in David Diringer, *The Alphabet: A Key to the History of Mankind,* 3rd ed. (New York: Funk and Wagnalls, 1968), 1:138. See the discussion in Wright, "Ancient Burials of Metal Documents," 282 and the bibliography in nn. 57–58. Of the inscriptions found at Hamadan, one silver tablet and three gold tablets had been cut by looters, from whom they were rescued before being melted down.

63. Hugh Nibley, *An Approach to the Book of Mormon,* 3rd ed. (Salt Lake City: Deseret Book and FARMS, 1988), 24.

64. See Wright, "Ancient Burials of Metal Documents," 294–95.

65. See ibid., 283, 296–98, and notes.

66. See ibid., 299–301.

67. See C. Duroiselle, "Excavations at Hmawza," *Annual Report of the Archaeological Survey of India* (1926–27): 171–79; "The Goldleaf Pali Manuscript of Old Prome," *Report of the Superintendent, Archaeological Survey of Burma* (1938–39): 12. Both are cited by Wright in "Ancient Burials of Metal Documents," 279–80.

68. See Maung Tun Nyein, "Maunggun Gold Plates," *Epigraphica Indica* 5 (1898–99): 101–2, cited by Wright, "Ancient Burials of Metal Documents," 280.

69. See K. Preisendanz, *Papyrusfunde und Papyrusforschung* (Leipzig: Hiersemann, 1934), 113, cited by Wright, "Ancient Burials of Metal Documents," 309 n. 28.

70. See A. M. Abu Bakr and J. Osing, "Ächtungstexte aus dem Alten Reich," *Mitteilungen des Deutschen Archaologischen Instituts Abteilung Kairo* 29/2 (1973): 97–133.

71. For a discussion and bibliography, see John A. Tvedtnes and Stephen D. Ricks, "Jewish and Other Semitic Texts Written in Egyptian Characters," *Journal of Book of Mormon Studies* 5/2 (1996):

156–63; John Gee and John A. Tvedtnes, "Ancient Manuscripts Fit Book of Mormon Pattern," *Insights,* February 1999.

72. The English translation used here is taken from Martínez, *Dead Sea Scrolls Translated,* 461–63.

73. Schaff and Wace, *Nicene and Post-Nicene Fathers,* 1:263.

74. See James H. Charlesworth, *The Old Testament Pseudepigrapha* (Garden City, N.Y.: Doubleday, 1983), 1:927.

75. See Richard S. Ellis, *Foundation Deposits in Ancient Mesopotamia* (New Haven: Yale University Press, 1968), 98; W. Andrae, *Die jüngeren Ischtar-Tempel in Assur* (Leipzig: Hinrich, 1935), 51–54. Both are cited by Wright in "Ancient Burials of Metal Documents," 280, 288.

76. See Drower, *Mandaeans of Iraq and Iran,* 25.

77. See ibid., 50.

78. See H. Nesselhauf, "Zwei Bronzeurkunden aus Minigua," *Mitteilungen des deutschen archäologischen Institute (Madrid)* 1 (1960): 142, cited by Wright, "Ancient Burials of Metal Documents," 279.

79. See Muhibble Anstock-Darga, "Semitische Inscriften auf Silbertäfelchen aus dem 'Bertiz'-Tal (Umgebung von 'Maras')," *Jahrbuch für kleinasiatische Forschung* 1 (1950): 199–200, cited in Nibley, *Approach to the Book of Mormon,* 24, 452 n. 22.

80. See Pausanius, *Description of Greece* 4.26.6–8, in *Pausanias's Description of Greece,* ed. J. G. Frazer (New York: Biblo and Tannen, 1965), 1:218–19. I am grateful to William J. Hamblin for bringing this to my attention in his "Sacred Writings on Bronze Plates in the Ancient Mediterranean" (FARMS, 1994), 12–13.

81. The volume of publications on the Pyrgi inscriptions is too large to give here. They are among the most well studied of ancient inscriptions.

chapter 4

Sealed Books

Wherefore, it is an abridgment of the record of the people of Nephi, and also of the Lamanites—Written to the Lamanites, who are a remnant of the house of Israel; and also to Jew and Gentile—Written by way of commandment, and also by the spirit of prophecy and of revelation—Written and sealed up, and hid up unto the Lord, that they might not be destroyed—To come forth by the gift and power of God unto the interpretation thereof—Sealed by the hand of Moroni, and hid up unto the Lord, to come forth in due time by way of the Gentile—The interpretation thereof by the gift of God. (Title Page of the Book of Mormon)

The scriptures and other ancient texts occasionally speak of "sealed" books. The term is used to denote two different things. Sometimes it refers to a book that has somehow been sealed shut, such as by sewing or by applying an impressed wax or clay seal. In other cases, the word "sealed" means "hidden," referring to a book that is secreted in a hiding place.

Isaiah 29:11–14 speaks of "the words of a book that is sealed." This book cannot be read by the learned but is delivered to the unlearned to read. Though Isaiah seems to have been referring to Jerusalem and its inhabitants,[1] Nephi, in his typical fashion of likening Isaiah's words to his own people (see 1 Nephi 19:23–24; 22:8; 2 Nephi 6:5; 11:2, 8), paraphrased this portion of Isaiah in 2 Nephi 27:6–26 and used it as a prophecy of the coming forth of the Book of Mormon. "The Lord God," he declared, "shall bring forth unto you the words of a book, and they shall be the words of them which have slumbered. And the book shall be sealed" (2 Nephi 27:6–7; see 26:16–17; 27:8–9, 10–11, 13, 15, 17). Nephi detailed the coming forth of the Nephite record, along with the role of the three witnesses and the incident involving Professor Charles Anthon (see 2 Nephi 27:9–26; JS—H 1:64–65).[2]

Nephi noted that "the book shall be hid from the eyes of the world" and "be sealed" by the power of God to come forth in "the own due time of the Lord" (2 Nephi 27:7, 10, 12; see 27:8, 11, 15, 17, 21). In the Lord's name, Nephi further instructed the future translator that after completing his work, he should "seal up the book again, and hide it up unto me, that I may preserve the words which thou hast not read, until I shall see fit in mine own wisdom to reveal all things unto the children of men" (2 Nephi 27:22; compare 30:3). The terms "seal up" and "hide up" seem to mean the same thing. This is clear from other Book of Mormon passages. For example, the Lord instructed the brother of Jared to write an account of his people and "seal them up, that no one can interpret them; for ye shall write them in a language that they cannot be read" (Ether 3:22; see 3:27). Furthermore, Jared was to take the two interpreter stones and "seal them up also with the things which ye shall write" (Ether 3:23). Sealing up the records made it possible for the Lord to "show them in mine own due time unto the children of men" (Ether 3:24, 27–28).

After abridging the account of the Jaredite record, Moroni noted that the Lord "commanded me that I should seal them [the plates of Ether] up; and he also hath commanded that I should seal up the interpretation thereof; wherefore I have sealed up the interpreters, according to the commandment of the Lord," that they might come forth at a later time (Ether 4:5–6). This parallels the passage in which Moroni said, "I am commanded that I should hide them up again in the earth" (Ether 4:3). The fact that the interpreters were likewise sealed suggests that sealing up is the same as hiding (see Ether 3:24, 28; 4:6).

Near the end of his own record, Moroni noted, "And I seal up these records," obviously referring to the abridgment that Joseph Smith translated (Moroni 10:2). Indeed, the title page of the Book of Mormon indicates that the plates containing the record were "written and sealed up, and hid up unto the Lord, that they might not be destroyed—To come forth by the gift and power of God unto the interpretation thereof—Sealed by the hand of Moroni, and hid up unto the Lord, to come forth in due time by way of the Gentile—The interpretation thereof by the gift of God."

Of special interest in this passage is the notation that the record was hidden up "unto the Lord." Ammaron hid up the records "unto the Lord," as did Mormon (Mormon 1:2; see 1:3; 4:23; 5:12; Ether 15:11). Evidently, Nephites commonly hid up their precious things to the Lord (see Helaman 12:18; 13:18–20, 35; Mormon 1:18; compare Job 3:21; Matthew 25:18, 24–25).

The parallel to sealing or hiding records up to the Lord is for an individual to be sealed unto life eternal. Joseph Smith told William Clayton, "Your life is hid with Christ in God, and so are many others. Nothing but the unpardonable sin can prevent you from inheriting eternal life for you are sealed up by the power of the Priesthood unto eternal life, having taken the step necessary for that purpose."[3] This is the sealing by the Holy Spirit of promise that is mentioned in the scriptures (see Ephesians 1:13; 4:30; 2 Corinthians 1:22; Revelation 7:3; D&C 76:53; 124:124; 131:5; 132:7, 18–19, 26). It preserves an individual to come forth in the day of the Lord, on the morning of the first resurrection. In like manner, scriptures sealed or hidden up to the Lord are "to come forth . . . in the own due time of the Lord" (1 Nephi 14:26; see 2 Nephi 26:17; 30:17). And, like the sealing up of individuals to eternal life, the revelation of the sealed records comes through the keys of the priesthood (see D&C 28:7; 35:18).[4]

That sealing refers to hiding is also suggested in *Testament of Adam* 3:6, where Seth declared, "We sealed the testament and we put it in the cave of treasures."[5] Eusebius, in his *Praeparatio evangelica* 9, cited a passage from Artapanus to the effect that Moses "wrote the name [of God] on a tablet and sealed it."[6]

Other Sealed Books

The scriptures speak of other sealed books to come forth in the last days. One of these comes from Daniel. An angel told Daniel, "But thou, O Daniel, shut up the words, and seal the book, even to the time of the end" (Daniel 12:4). "And he said, Go thy way, Daniel: for the words are closed up and sealed till the time of the end" (Daniel 12:9). The angel further spoke of the time "to seal up the vision and the prophecy" (Daniel 9:24).

Nephi was permitted to see the same vision given to the apostle John, as recorded in the book of Revelation, but allowed to write only part of what he saw. The Lord instructed

Nephi, "But the things which thou shalt see hereafter thou shalt not write; for the Lord God hath ordained the apostle of the Lamb of God that he should write them. And also others who have been, to them hath he shown all things, and they have written them; and they are sealed up to come forth in their purity, according to the truth which is in the Lamb, in the own due time of the Lord, unto the house of Israel" (1 Nephi 14:25–26). The sealing of John's record is mentioned in Revelation 10:4: "I was about to write: and I heard a voice from heaven saying unto me, Seal up those things which the seven thunders uttered, and write them not." John was subsequently commanded, "Seal not the sayings of the prophecy of this book: for the time is at hand" (Revelation 22:10). Apparently, the sealed portion of John's revelation consisted of things he saw but did not write, while the things he actually wrote were not sealed.

In his revelation, John saw a heavenly "book written within and on the backside, sealed with seven seals" that only Christ, the Lamb, was worthy to loose (Revelation 5:1; see 5:2, 5–9). Each seal represented a period of time in the earth's history (see D&C 77:6–7), and as the Lamb opened each seal, a different vision was unfolded (see Revelation 6:3, 5, 7, 9, 12; 8:1). Some scholars have identified the sealed book of Revelation with the Mesopotamian tablets of destiny that denoted kingship among both the gods and mortals.[7] It would thus be a symbol of Christ's rule. One of the Dead Sea Scrolls (4Q550), thought by some scholars to be the prototype from which the book of Esther was composed, is similarly described. The fragmentary text speaks of the Persian king whose name is missing and says that "the books of his father were to be read in front of him; and among the books was found a scroll [sealed with] seven seals of the ring of Darius, his father."[8] Like the tablets of destiny, the text then goes on to establish who should rule the Persian empire.

The heavenly book whose seals only Christ could open is reflected in an Ethiopic document called *Lefafa Sedek* (Bandlet of Righteousness), which purports to be the heavenly book in question: "And then all his [i.e., Michael's] angels gathered themselves together that they might have that Book read [to them] by Christ, the Son of God. Now that Book had been sealed with the Seal of the Father, and the Son and the Holy Ghost, and no one had the power [or was authorized] to open that book, except the Four-and-Twenty Priests of heaven, and the Four Evangelists.[9] And the Four Evangelists took that Book, and they opened the seal thereof, and they looked therein, and they read it out aloud so that [the angels] might hear."[10]

The medieval Jewish *Zohar* Genesis 55b says that "when Adam was in the Garden of Eden, God sent down to him a book by the hand of Raziel, the angel in charge of the holy mysteries. . . . In the middle of the book was a secret writing explaining the thousand and five hundred keys which were not revealed even to the holy angels, and all of which were locked up in this book until it came into the hands of Adam."[11] The word rendered "mysteries" in this passage is *raz*, the first element in the name of the angel Raziel, and *Raziel* means "secrets of God."

In Mandaean lore, a letter sealed by God is sent from heaven to the soul of a righteous person, who must wear it around the neck when sent to the Gate of Life at death.[12] Similarly, the ancient Egyptians placed letters of recommendation to various gods in the coffin with their dead. These letters were typically folded and tied around the middle with a fiber thread.[13] In at least one instance (see Papyrus Rhind II), the god

Thoth is depicted holding the letter in his right hand, which is stretched out toward Osiris, the god of the dead, while his left hand grasps the hand of the deceased, whom he is leading toward Osiris.[14] The Christian *Hymn of the Soul* or *Hymn of the Pearl*, a parable of the plan of salvation incorporated into the *Acts of Thomas*, also speaks of a sealed letter sent from the king (meaning God) to one of his sons who had come to the earth, which is symbolized by Egypt.[15] The eleventh-century Arab chronographer al-Thaᶜlabi told of a book sealed with gold that was sent to King David from heaven. The book contained thirteen questions to be put to Solomon.[16] A sealed letter from heaven is also mentioned in *Odes of Solomon* 23:

> And his thought was like a letter, and his will descended from on high. And it was sent from a bow like an arrow that has been forcibly shot. And many hands rushed to the letter, in order to catch (it), then take and read it. But it escaped from their fingers; and they were afraid of it and of the seal which was upon it. Because they were not allowed to loosen its seal; for the power which was over the seal was better than they. But those who saw the letter went after it; that they might know where it would land, and who should read it, and who should hear it. . . . The letter was one of command. . . . And the letter became a large volume, which was entirely written by the finger of God.[17]

Sealed and Open Records

The heavenly book with the seven seals seen by John obviously was not merely hidden away, but actually sealed to be opened at a later time. In the Bible are examples of sealing documents with the king's ring or seal (see 1 Kings 21:8; Esther 3:12; 8:8, 10; Daniel 6:17; compare Job 14:17). The ancient Mesopotamians made two copies of legal documents, such as contracts, one open for public consultation and the other sealed to prevent tampering with the official record. Often, one text, written on a plain clay tablet, was sealed inside the other, written on a hollow clay "envelope," and a seal was rolled over the text on the envelope. A damaged seal was considered to be evidence that the document had been tampered with. Most private archives consisted of these doubled, sealed documents.

The practice of preparing two copies, one sealed and one open, is also known from ancient Israel, as described in the Bible and other early Jewish texts. For example, in *Jasher* 27:12–14 we read that Jacob's purchase of the birthright in exchange for the pottage was formally documented: "And Jacob wrote the whole of this in a book, and he testified the same with witnesses, and he sealed it, and the book remained in the hands of Jacob."[18] Later, after returning from Syria, Jacob wrote a book of purchase for the property agreement he had struck with Esau after Isaac died.[19] He put it with "the command and the statutes and the revealed book, and he placed them in an earthen vessel in order that they should remain for a long time, and he delivered them into the hands of his children" (*Jasher* 47:29).[20] When Esau's family later challenged the right of Jacob's sons to bury their father in the cave, the Israelites produced "all the records; the record of the purchase, the sealed record and the open record, and also all the first records in which all the transactions of the birth-right are written" (*Jasher* 56:57;[21] the story is also found in TB *Soṭah* 13a, *Pirqe Rabbi Eliezer* 39, and Rashi on Genesis 49:21).

The contrast between sealed and open purchase records intended to be preserved is also made in Jeremiah 32, from which the *Jasher* account may have borrowed. Jeremiah's cousin Hanameel asked him to purchase a field,[22] and Jeremiah drew up "the evidence of the purchase" and "sealed it" after having witnesses sign the document. He then instructed his scribe, Baruch, "Take these evidences, this evidence of the purchase, both which is sealed, and this evidence which is open; and put them in an earthen vessel, that they may continue many days." The prophet used this event to prophesy that the people of Judah would, after their captivity in Babylon, return to possess their lands once again (see Jeremiah 32:8–15, 44; compare 13:3–11; 19:1, 10–11).

Another ancient text that mentions both sealed and public, or revealed, documents is the *Damascus Document* (CD V, 2–5), copies of which were discovered in both the genizah of the Old Cairo synagogue in Egypt and among the Dead Sea Scrolls. The *Damascus Document* notes that the "sealed book of the law" was kept in the ark, while the public copy was stored elsewhere.[23] Ben Zion Wacholder, who discusses this aspect of the document at length,[24] notes that "the 'sealing' may refer to the contents of the document, to the document itself, or to its mode of storage." He concludes that the fact that the sealed document was kept in the ark "shows that the primary reference . . . is not to the sealing of the text but to the depositing of the scroll."[25] In partial support of this idea, he notes the similarity in the Hebrew wording of Moses' command to the Levites to place the book of the law in the ark (see Deuteronomy 31:26) and Jeremiah's instructions to Baruch about the hiding of the records he had written (see Jeremiah 32:10).[26]

Wacholder notes that scholars hold differing opinions regarding the meaning of the sealed and public documents. One view is that legal documents were folded and sewn shut (the sealed portion) and that its main points were written on the back of the document. This summary constituted the public document.[27] The other view is that two separate documents were prepared, one hidden away and the other turned over to the individual who needed the document as evidence of, for example, a purchase. The former view has the support of both the Mishnah (where *Baba Batra* 10:1 speaks of the folding of documents) and the fact that documents of this nature were found in the Bar Kochba caves of Wadi Murabbaᶜat and at the nearby site of Masada. The idea of two separate documents is supported by the reference to both sealed and public documents in Jeremiah 32:11, 14.[28]

The existence of sealed and open documents may shed light on passages that refer to a sealed portion of the Book of Mormon. While the entire book was sealed in the sense of being hidden up, a portion was physically sealed shut so that Joseph Smith could not translate it. Nephi's prophecy of the book explains:

> But the words which are sealed he shall not deliver, neither shall he deliver the book. For the book shall be sealed by the power of God, and the revelation which was sealed shall be kept in the book until the own due time of the Lord, that they may come forth; for behold, they reveal all things from the foundation of the world unto the end thereof. And the day cometh that the words of the book which were sealed shall be read upon the house tops; and they shall be read by the power of Christ; and all things shall be revealed unto the children of men which ever have been among the children of men, and which ever will be even unto the end of the earth. But behold, it shall come to pass that the Lord God shall say unto him to whom he shall deliver the book: Take these words which are not sealed and deliver them to another, that he may show them unto the learned, saying: Read this, I pray thee. And the learned shall say: Bring hither the book, and I will read them. Touch not the things which are sealed, for I will bring them forth in mine own due time; for

I will show unto the children of men that I am able to do mine own work. (2 Nephi 27:10–11, 15, 21)

Moroni followed the example of Nephi (see 2 Nephi 27:21–22) and instructed the future translator of the work—Joseph Smith—to not translate "the things which I have sealed up." He may have meant that Joseph should not take the original plates of Ether, which Moroni had hidden; however, the comment has generally been taken to mean that a physical seal had been placed on some of the plates so that Joseph Smith could not use that portion.[29]

That sealed things are hidden is confirmed by Nephi's statement that "there is nothing which is secret save it shall be revealed; there is no work of darkness save it shall be made manifest in the light; and there is nothing which is sealed upon the earth save it shall be loosed" (2 Nephi 30:17). The keys of loosing that which has been sealed were committed to Joseph Smith. As the Lord declared, "I have given him the keys of the mysteries, and the revelations which are sealed, until I shall appoint unto them another in his stead" (D&C 28:7). "And I have given unto him the keys of the mystery of those things which have been sealed, even things which were from the foundation of the world, and the things which shall come from this time until the time of my coming" (D&C 35:18). It was by this power that the prophet Joseph Smith gave us the Book of Mormon and other restored scriptures from ancient times.

Summary

Like other aspects of hidden documents, the practice of sealing records is known not only from the Book of Mormon, but from other ancient Near Eastern texts. Sealed documents are designed to serve as legal testimony, usually for future generations, and it is perhaps in this light that we should understand some of Moroni's comments in the last chapter in the Book of Mormon. Moroni first noted, "I seal up these records" (Moroni 10:2), then informed his future audience how they can know the truth of those records by asking God (see Moroni 10:3–5). After some words of exhortation, he wrote:

> And I exhort you to remember these things; for the time speedily cometh that ye shall know that I lie not, for ye shall see me at the bar of God; and the Lord God will say unto you: Did I not declare my words unto you, which were written by this man, like as one crying from the dead, yea, even as one speaking out of the dust? I declare these things unto the fulfilling of the prophecies. And behold, they shall proceed forth out of the mouth of the everlasting God; and his word shall hiss forth from generation to generation. And God shall show unto you, that that which I have written is true. (Moroni 10:27–29)

Along with the ancient examples cited in this chapter, the Book of Mormon has come forth in our day from the box in which it was sealed and buried. It calls for us to test its authenticity by asking for a divine witness.

Notes

1. For a discussion, see Robert A. Cloward, "Isaiah 29 and the Book of Mormon," in *Isaiah in the Book of Mormon,* ed. Donald W. Parry and John W. Welch (Provo, Utah: FARMS, 1998), 191–248.

2. Mormon, evidently relying on Nephi's prophecy, also refers to "the prophecies of Isaiah" when writing about the book that would be hidden up to come forth at a later time (see Mormon 8:23–26).

3. Joseph Smith, *History of the Church of Jesus Christ of Latter-day Saints* (Salt Lake City: Deseret Book, 1980), 5:391.

4. For other references to sealed records, in heaven and in earth, see Revelation 5:1–9; 6:1, 3, 5, 7, 9, 12; 8:1 and the explanation

in D&C 77:6–7, 10, 13; 88:84; 98:2. Of the wicked acts of men, the Lord said to Moses, "Is not this laid up in store with me, and sealed up among my treasures?" (Deuteronomy 32:34; compare Job 14:17). For the seal on the Lord's treasury for the printing of the scriptures, see D&C 104:61–67. Note also the expression "bind up the law and seal up the testimony" (see Isaiah 8:16 // 2 Nephi 18:16; D&C 88:84; 109:38, 46; 133:72).

5. James H. Charlesworth, *The Old Testament Pseudepigrapha* (Garden City, N.Y.: Doubleday, 1983), 1:994.

6. *The Fragments of Artapanus* 3.26, in ibid., 2:901.

7. See S. H. Hooke, *The Labyrinth* (New York: Macmillan, 1935), 229, cited in Geo Widengren, *The Ascension of the Apostle and the Heavenly Book* (Uppsala, Sweden: University of Uppsala, 1950), 28.

8. Florentino García Martínez, *The Dead Sea Scrolls Translated,* 2nd ed. (Leiden: E. J. Brill, 1996), 291.

9. In Christian tradition, the four evangelists (Matthew, Mark, Luke, and John) are represented by the four beasts that surround the throne of God. According to Revelation 5:8, these beasts, along with the twenty-four elders, were present when Christ broke the seven seals on the book.

10. Third section of the *Lefafa Sedek,* in Ernest A. Wallis Budge, *The Bandlet of Righteousness: An Ethiopian Book of the Dead* (London: Luzac, 1929), 69–70. On page 77 we read, "And straightway God spake unto the Twelve Apostles, and to the Seventy-two Disciples, and commanded them to write copies of this Book. . . . and he who shall lay the Book up in his house, shall never die the death."

11. Harry Sperling and Maurice Simon, trans., *The Zohar* (New York: Rebecca Bennet Publications, 1958), 1:176.

12. See, for example, *The Canonical Prayerbook of the Mandaeans,* 61 (song number 73); *Alma Rišaia Rba* 160, 331.

13. See the discussion and references in Jan Quaegbeur, "P. Brux Dem. E. 8258 une Lettre de Recommandation pour l'au delà," in *Studies in Egyptology,* ed. Sarah Israelit-Groll (Jerusalem: Magnes Press, Hebrew University, 1990), 2:776–95.

14. See the depiction in ibid., 795.

15. See *Hymn of the Soul* 37–55, in Montague Rhodes James, *The Apocryphal New Testament* (Oxford: Clarendon, 1955), 412–13.

16. See al-Thaʿlabi, *Qiṣaṣ ʾal-ʾAnbiyaʾ* (Cairo: Mustafa al-Babi al-Halabi wa-Awladuhu, A. H., 1340), 202. Hugh Nibley was the first to bring this information to the attention of Latter-day Saints. I am grateful to Brian Hauglid for confirming details of the story from the Arabic text.

17. *Odes of Solomon* 23:5–10, 17, 21, in Charlesworth, *Old Testament Pseudepigrapha,* 2:755–56.

18. *The Book of Jasher* (Salt Lake City: J. H. Parry and Co., 1887), 72.

19. Jacob's purchase of the rights to the cave of Machpelah from Esau is mentioned by Rashi on Genesis 46:6, citing *Midrash Tanhuma.* It is also noted in *Pirqe Rabbi Eliezer* 38. According to *Pirqe Rabbi Eliezer* 36, a deed was drawn up for Abraham's purchase of the cave of Machpelah. Gerald Friedlander, trans., *Pirḳê de Rabbi Eliezer* (New York: Hermon Press, 1965), 275–76.

20. *Book of Jasher,* 139.

21. Ibid., 174.

22. Under the law of Moses, real estate could not pass from the family on a permanent basis. Consequently, close relatives were given first choice to purchase land put up for sale (see, for example, Ruth 4:1–9), while land sold to outsiders had to revert to the clan during the jubilee (fiftieth) year (see Leviticus 25:10, 13–16, 25–35; 27:24; Numbers 36:1–12). This ensured that tribal boundaries remained relatively stable.

23. Martínez, *Dead Sea Scrolls Translated,* 36.

24. See Ben Zion Wacholder, "The 'Sealed' Torah versus the 'Revealed' Torah: An Exegesis of Damascus Covenant V, 1–6 and Jeremiah 32, 10–14," *Revue de Qumran* 12/47 (December 1986): 351–68.

25. Ibid., 363.

26. See ibid., 356.

27. For this and other aspects of sealed documents, see the discussion in John W. Welch, "Doubled, Sealed, Witnessed Documents: From the Ancient World to the Book of Mormon," in *Mormons, Scripture, and the Ancient World: Studies in Honor of John L. Sorenson*, ed. Davis Bitton (Provo, Utah: FARMS, 1998), 391–444.

28. See Wacholder, "The 'Sealed' Torah versus the 'Revealed' Torah," 358–59.

29. Elder Orson Pratt said that about two-thirds of the record was "sealed up, and Joseph was commanded not to break the seal; that part of the record was hid up" (*Journal of Discourses,* 3:347).

chapter 5

Angels as Guardians of Hidden Books

An interesting feature of the story of the Book of Mormon is that the book's existence and hiding place were revealed by an angel named Moroni (see JS—H 1:30–35). During his lifetime, this resurrected being was the last guardian of the Nephite records. That responsibility evidently continues to this day, for after completing the English translation, Joseph returned the plates to Moroni (see JS—H 1:60). Yet Moroni's story is not unique.

A number of ancient documents indicate that sacred records are kept by angels.[1] Usually, these documents indicate that the books are kept in the heavenly temple and are intended to be used at the last day to judge the works of men. For example, in *2 Enoch* 52:15 we read that the books written in heaven will be produced on the judgment day. In his vision of the latter-day judgment, Enoch saw the opening of sealed books and an angel keeping a record beside the Lord. In another of Enoch's visions, an angel of the Lord brought the books recording men's deeds from the storehouse to explain them to Enoch, who copied from them 366 books in thirty days (see *2 Enoch* 22:10–23:6). And in still another vision, the archangel Uriel showed Enoch a book of astronomy (see *1 Enoch* 72:1).

The vision of Rabbi Ishmael, recorded in the book of *3 Enoch,* also speaks of heavenly scrolls that were written by angels and that contain the books of the dead and the living (see *3 Enoch* 18:19, 24–25). According to the vision, God will judge the world using information on a scroll kept in a box and guarded by the angel in charge of the archives. Such documents are destined to be opened and read in the heavenly court (see *3 Enoch* 27:1–2; 28:7; 30:2; 32:1). Ishmael saw the heavenly scribes who stood near God in heaven (see *3 Enoch* 33:2). The archangel Metatron, who in his mortal life was known as Enoch, gave Ishmael the books containing the deeds of the wicked, which he was allowed to read (see *3 Enoch* 44:9). Similarly, the Book of Mormon plates were kept in a box and will be used to judge the world.

In a similar story, Abraham is shown a large book on a table at the gates leading to heaven and hell. On either side of the table is an angel with papyrus, pen, and ink. One angel records deeds of righteousness, while the other records the sins of mankind. The souls of the dead are to be judged by these records (see *Testament of Abraham* 12.4–18; 13.9).

Heavenly Visions

During his heavenly vision, the prophet Lehi was given a book to read. From that book he learned of the fate of the city of Jerusalem (see 1 Nephi 1:11–13), and he also learned about the coming of the Messiah (see 1 Nephi 1:19). Lehi's son Nephi experienced the same vision, in which he saw books that are clearly the Bible and the Book of Mormon and other related scriptures (see 1 Nephi 13:20–29, 38–39). He learned that some of what he had seen would later be recorded by the apostle John in what we know as the book of Revelation (see 1 Nephi 14:20–28). He then informed his readers that he had been shown these things by "the angel of the Lord" (1 Nephi 14:29).

In the book of Revelation, the apostle John wrote that he saw heavenly books in his vision. At one point he saw an angel who may have been carrying a book containing the gospel to declare to the inhabitants of the earth (see Revelation 14:6–7). One of the angels "had in his hand a little book open," which the Lord told John to eat (Revelation 10:2; see 10:8–10).[2] Ezekiel, during his vision of the celestial world, was also given a book that he read and was commanded to eat (see Ezekiel 2:8–3:3). This can be compared with Jeremiah 15:16, which describes the prophet eating the Lord's words. Note also Daniel's vision, in which an angel "touched my lips: then I opened my mouth, and spake" and, evidently like Lehi, "retained no strength." Another angel declared that he would show Daniel "that which is noted in the scripture of truth," evidently referring to a heavenly book (Daniel 10:16, 21). These visions are similar to a vision of Joseph Smith Sr. in which he was shown a box whose contents he was to eat in order to gain wisdom.[3] The box parallels the one in which Moroni hid the plates.[4]

Another account that resembles that of Ezekiel and John the Revelator is the record of the prophet Zechariah. Like Moroni when he first appeared to Joseph Smith, the angel awoke Zechariah to deliver his message (see Zechariah 4:1).[5] The angel showed him "a flying roll" or scroll, which represented the curse God would send forth on the land (Zechariah 5:1–3).

The poem "Abou Ben Adhem," written by Leigh Hunt (1784–1859), has a similar theme. An Arab man awakens in the middle of the night and sees in his room "an angel writing in a book of gold . . . the names of those who love the Lord." This modern story shares themes with the account of Joseph Smith and with other more ancient texts, notably the story of V,*2 Apocalypse of Paul*, which will be discussed later in this chapter.

In *Jubilees* 32:21–29, we read that Jacob, during his second vision at Bethel (when returning from Syria), read from seven heavenly tablets brought to him by an angel. The tablets recorded all that would happen to his sons in the future, and Jacob documented this and everything else he saw in the vision. The story is told in first person in a Dead Sea Scrolls fragment, 4Q537 (4QAJa ar), which is sometimes called the *Apocryphon of Jacob*.

The tenth-century Arab chronographer al-Kisaʾi noted that, prior to his death, Adam told Seth that he had seen in a heavenly vision what was "written on the Canopy of the Throne and the gates of Paradise, the layers of the heavens and the leaves of the Tuba tree."[6]

The prophet Isaiah is said to have been taken to the seventh heaven, where, like Abraham before him, he saw Abel, Enoch, and others (see *Martyrdom and Ascension of Isaiah* 9:7–9). An angel brought him heavenly books that named the deeds of the children of Israel (see *Martyrdom and Ascension of Isaiah* 9:19–23). A similar experience is ascribed to the prophet Zephaniah. Following his visit to heaven, Zephaniah was taken to hades, where an angel handed him a rolled manuscript and told him to read it. The manuscript contained all of the prophet's sins and omissions of good works (see *Apocalypse of Zephaniah* [Akhmimic] 7:1–8). He was given another manuscript to read (see *Apocalypse of Zephaniah* [Akhmimic] 7:10–11), but the part of the *Apocalypse* describing its contents, presumably his good deeds, is missing.

The story of the heavenly book is common in the Enoch materials. The angel Uriel showed Enoch the "heavenly tablets" and told him to read their content and note everything they contained (*1 Enoch* 81:1–3). Enoch then recounted to his children that "which I have learned from the words of the holy angels, and have understood the heavenly tablets" (*1 Enoch* 93:2).[7] Later, he spoke about what he had read on the heavenly tablets (see *1 Enoch* 103:2; 106:19).

According to *Zohar* Genesis 217a, Rabbi Judah once "fell asleep and dreamt that he saw four wings outstretched, and R. Simeon ascending on them with a scroll of the Law, and also with all manner of books containing hidden expositions and Agadahs. They all ascended to heaven and were lost to his view. When he woke he said: 'Verily, since the death of R. Simeon wisdom has departed from the earth. Alas for the generation that has lost this precious jewel which used to illumine it and on which higher and lower beings were supported.'"[8]

A second-century A.D. document (Papyrus Oxyrhynchus 1381) from Oxyrhynchus, Egypt, contains the story of the Greek writer Isidor, who put off for some time the translation into Greek of an Egyptian book describing the healing god Imouthes (Asclepius). After a few years Isidor fell gravely ill, and as he lay half asleep one night Asclepius appeared to him in a dream, wearing a shining robe and carrying a book in his left hand. After the apparition disappeared, Isidor understood that he must continue his translation work.[9]

This story is similar to some of the Hermetic literature examined in chapter 2, "Hidden Records." The Hermetic literature describes various individuals who are said to have experienced a vision in which they received a book of arcane lore from an old man who is often said to have been seated on a golden throne. Among those who received the book are Balinas,[10] Apollonius,[11] and Thessalus.[12] The latter, like Isidor, described the giver of the book as the god Asclepius, known to the Egyptians as Imhotep.

As an illustration of how widespread the idea of heavenly records is, note the Maori tradition of Tane, who ascended to the uppermost heaven to retrieve "the three baskets or receptacles of occult knowledge" and "the two sacred stones." There he met with the supreme being, who conducted him to the heavenly sanctuary where the artifacts were kept. He descended to earth, accompanied by some of the heavenly host, but en route the group was attacked by a hostile force who wanted to thwart Tane's mission. These enemies, however, were repulsed, and the receptacles and stones were set up on the earth.[13]

An Angel From On High

A number of stories can be found in which an angel delivers a heavenly book or a long-lost earthly book to a mortal. Perhaps the most well-known is that of Muhammad, who declared that the angel Gabriel presented him a book to read. The book is called the Qur'an, from the Arabic verb meaning "to read." One of the Dead Sea Scrolls (4Q529 I, 6) begins with the claim that it contains the "words of the book which Michael spoke to the angels of God."[14]

Hippolytus noted that the Elchasaites, the earliest Jewish Christian sect, told of a book delivered by a female angel of enormous stature to their founder, one Elchasai, or Alcibiades (see *Refutation of all Heresies* 9.8). According to Eusebius, Origen merely noted that the book had fallen from heaven (see *Ecclesiastical History* 6.38). This would place it in the category of letters from heaven, discussed later in this chapter. In a similar story, another early Christian apostate, Mani (who founded the Manichaean religion) claimed that he received the news contained in the books he wrote from an angel named at-Taûm.[15]

In one of the texts discovered at Nag Hammadi in 1945, an angel instructed a man named Allogenes: "Write down [the things that I] shall [tell] you and of which I shall remind you for the sake of those who will be worthy after you. And you will leave this book upon a mountain and you will adjure the guardian: 'Come Dreadful One.' And after he said these (things), he separated from me. But I was full of joy, and I wrote this book which was appointed for me, my son Messos, in order that I might disclose to you the (things) that were proclaimed before me in my presence."[16]

In another of the Nag Hammadi texts, VI,*1 Acts of Peter and the Twelve Apostles* 2.10–29, Peter described how he encountered "a man . . . wearing a cloth bound around his waist, and a gold belt girded [it]. Also a napkin was tied over [his] chest, extending over his shoulders and covering his head and his hands. I was staring at the man because he was beautiful in his form and stature. There were four parts of his body that I saw: the sole of his feet and a part of his chest and the palms of his hands and his visage. These things I was able to see. A book cover like (those of) my books was in his left hand. A staff of styrax wood was in his right hand."[17] The golden belt is known to have been worn by Jesus in the heavenly temple (see Revelation 1:13), and the shape of the man's clothing allowed him to see the same body parts that Joseph Smith saw when the angel Moroni appeared to tell him about the Book of Mormon (see JS—H 1:31). This man initially told Peter that his name was "Lithargoel . . . the interpretation of which is, the light, gazelle-like stone,"[18] perhaps referring to the interpreters (urim and thummim) by which ancient documents can be translated. Ultimately, the man removed the covering on his head and revealed himself to be Jesus. He then gave the apostles sacred relics, an unguent box, and a pouch or bag containing medicine with which they were to heal the people of the city (see VI,*1 Acts of Peter and the Twelve Apostles* 5.15–18; 9.10–22; 10.31–11.1).

In the Mandaic *Haran Gawaita*, Ruha-Šurbiš, wife of Adonai (a term applied to Jehovah in the Bible), disguised as Hibil-Ziwa (also spelled Hiwil-Ziwa), came to the Nasoraean (Mandaean) Qiqil saying, "I, Hibil-Ziwa, have brought parchment and reed-pen, so write a Root of Life, and a Saying and a Mystery, and disseminate (*them*) send (*them*) forth and act in accordance with them." Qiqil brought parchment and a reed pen and wrote down the text and disseminated it. After her departure, Qiqil recanted, burned the writings, and gave instructions for others to do the same, but the Jews refused to destroy them. The Mandaeans consider these books to be false.[19]

Hugh Nibley noted a Jewish tradition, recounted by Bin Gorion, that Adam received a golden book from the archangel Michael and "hid it in the crevice of a rock."[20] In the *Cologne Mani Codex*, an angel appears to Adam and "he said to him: 'I am Balsamos, the greatest angel of light. Wherefore take and write these things which I reveal to you on most pure papyrus, incorruptible and insusceptible to worms'—and he revealed to him very many other things in the vision as well."[21]

The same text notes that an angel appeared to Sethel, the son of Adam, taking him from world to world.[22] It continues, "Now he spoke with me and said: 'He who is eminently most powerful sent me to you so that I may reveal to you the secrets which you pondered, since you were singled out for the truth. Now all these things that are hidden, write upon bronze tablets and store them up in the desert land.'" Sethel obediently wrote down "all which he heard and saw" and left it for his posterity.[23] The text also points out that angels (with Michael as voice) came down from heaven to Enoch and showed him the places where the righteous and the wicked would live. Enoch then "carefully questioned the angels; and whatever they said to him, he would inscribe in his writings."[24]

The *Cologne Mani Codex* also cites portions of the now-lost *Apocalypse of Enosh* (Enosh was son of Seth and grandson of Adam). The *Apocalypse,* a first-person account, notes that an angel appeared to Enosh (spelled Enos in the King James Bible) and brought him to a mountain, where "He spoke to me and said: 'The Pre-Eminent Almighty One has sent me to you so that I might reveal to you the secret (things) which you contemplated, since indeed you have chosen truth. Write down all these hidden things upon bronze tablets and deposit (them) in the wilderness.'" The abbreviated account then notes that "many things similar to these are in his writings (which) set forth his ascension and revelation, for everything that he heard and saw he recorded (and) left behind for the subsequent generations."[25]

According to *Zohar* Genesis 75b–76a, God gave Adam a book of heavenly wisdom. Adam lost the book by sinning, but after his repentance it was returned to him. The *Sepher ha-Razim* (Book of the Mysteries), sometimes identified with the *Sepher Raziʾel* (Book of the Mysteries of God),[26] is said to have originally been given to Adam in the Garden of Eden by an angel, sometimes called Raphael and sometimes Raziel (meaning "secret of God"). Jealous angels stole the book and threw it into the sea, but God had the angel Rahab retrieve it for Adam. A copy of the *Sepher ha-Razim* was found in the genizah of the Old Cairo synagogue.[27] The story is similar to one told in the Hindu *Bhagavata-Puranu*, where we read that the demon

Hayagriva stole the *Vedas,* or scriptures, from Brahma and placed them in the sea. The god Vishnu, in his incarnation as a fish, recovered the records and gave them to Manu Satyavrata, the Hindu Noah, whom he had rescued from the flood.[28]

Zohar Genesis 37a–b tells a similar tale in regard to the "book of the generations of Adam" mentioned in Genesis 5:1. According to this version,

> God did indeed send down a book to Adam, from which he became acquainted with the supernal wisdom. . . . This book was brought down to Adam by the "master of mysteries," preceded by three messengers. When Adam was expelled from the Garden of Eden, he tried to keep hold of this book, but it flew out of his hands. He thereupon supplicated God with tears for its return, and it was given back to him, in order that wisdom might not be forgotten of men, and that they might strive to obtain knowledge of their Master. Tradition further tells us that Enoch also had a book, which came from the same place as the book of the generations of Adam. . . . This is the source of the book known as "the book of Enoch."[29]

Zohar Genesis 55b tells a similar story:

> When Adam was in the Garden of Eden, God sent down to him a book by the hand of Raziel, the angel in charge of the holy mysteries. In this book were supernal inscriptions containing the sacred wisdom, and seventy-two branches of wisdom expounded so as to show the formation of six hundred and seventy inscriptions of higher mysteries. In the middle of the book was a secret writing explaining the thousand and five hundred keys which were not revealed even to the holy angels, and all of which were locked up[30] in this book until it came into the hands of Adam. When Adam obtained it, all the holy angels gathered round him to hear him read it . . . Thereupon the holy angel Hadarniel was secretly sent to say to him: "Adam, Adam, reveal not the glory of the

Master, for to thee alone and not to the angels is the privilege given to know the glory of thy Master." Therefore he kept it by him secretly until he left the Garden of Eden. While he was there he studied it diligently, and utilised constantly the gift of his Master until he discovered sublime mysteries which were not known even to the celestial ministers. When, however, he transgressed the command of his Master, the book flew away from him. Adam then beat his breast and wept, and entered the river Gihon up to his neck, so that his body became all wrinkled and his face haggard. God thereupon made a sign to Raphael to return to him the book, which he then studied for the rest of his life. Adam left it to his son Seth, who transmitted it in turn to his posterity, and so on until it came to Abraham, who learnt from it how to discern the glory of his Master, as has been said. Similarly Enoch possessed a book through which he learnt to discern the divine glory.[31]

The three recensions of the medieval *Book of Noah* tell the story, though with some variation. According to the second recension, after Adam spent three days in prayer, God sent to him the angel Raziel to deliver the book and read it to him. The angel then ascended in a flame of fire, reminiscent of the conduit of light by which Moroni departed from Joseph Smith (see JS—H 1:43). Adam evidently hid the book away, for four generations later its location (in a cave) was revealed to Enoch in a dream. Enoch read the book and then hid it away. The book was later delivered to Noah by the angel Raphael, and from it he learned how to build the ark. Before entering the ark, Noah hid the book away, but it seems that he later retrieved it, for he passed it to Shem, who transmitted it to succeeding generations.

In the first recension of the *Book of Noah*, the angel Raphael delivered a book of medicinal cures to Noah after the flood.[32] The third recension is closer to the second than it is to the first. In the third version, the angel Raziel delivered the book, written on a sapphire stone, to Adam. Noah eventually gained possession of the book, and from it he learned how to build the ark. This version differs from the second in that Noah brought the book with him in the ark and kept it in a golden box.[33] After the flood, he gave it to Shem, from whom it was transmitted to others until the time of Solomon. This third recension forms most of the introduction of another medieval work known today by the title *Sepher ha-Razim*.[34]

One of the Nag Hammadi texts, V,5 *Apocalypse of Adam* 85.3–24, declares: "The words they have kept, of the God of the aeons, were not committed to the book, nor were they written. But angelic (beings) will bring them, whom all the generations of men will not know. For they will be on a high mountain, upon a rock of truth. Therefore they will be named 'The Words of Imperishability [and] Truth,' for those who know the eternal God in wisdom of knowledge and teaching of angels forever, for he knows all things. These are the revelations which Adam made known to Seth his son. And his son taught his seed about them. This is the hidden knowledge of Adam, which he gave to Seth."[35]

According to *Life of Adam and Eve* 51:3–9, Seth, under the guidance of an angel, chronicled the life of his parents, Adam and Eve, on tablets of stone and clay and deposited them in the oratory of his father's house. After the flood many people saw the tablets but did not read them. When Solomon saw them he prayed to the Lord, who sent the angel who had been with Seth when he prepared them and commanded Solomon to build a temple on the site. Solomon built the temple and found on its stones the prophecy of Enoch recorded in *1 Enoch* 1:9 and cited in Jude 1:14–16. In *1 Enoch* 68:1, we read that an angel taught Noah from the book of his ancestor Enoch and that Noah kept the book.

In Jewish and Samaritan tradition, when Moses ascended the mountain to converse with God, he actually went to heaven.[36] One Samaritan text says that "he ascended to heaven, and the Torah [law] was put on his hand."[37] According to *Jubilees* 1:27–2:1, an angel of the presence[38] brought to Moses tablets containing the history of the world, from the first creation until the sanctuary of God would be built forever in the midst of Israel. Moses was instructed to copy part of the account, and this portion formed the basis of the Pentateuch and of *Jubilees* itself. The commentary on the law of Moses written by the Samaritan Marqa *(Memar Marqa)* also says that Moses, enthroned in the presence of God and angels, wrote down the words of the heavenly book as dictated to him by God.[39] The story is confirmed in Moses 1:40–41; 2:1, where we read that God dictated to Moses and told him to write his words in a book (compare with *Jubilees* 1:4–5, 26). In *Pirqe Rabbi Eliezer* 46, we read that when God gave Moses the law, the ministering angels, seeing his actions, gave to the prophets tablets to be used in healing.

In Mandaean belief, the first several secret books were revealed to Adam, including the one known as the *Ginza Rba* (Great Treasure), while others were given to various of his descendants. The Mandaean document known as the *Alma Rišaia Rba* (Great First World) is said to have been originally given, with an oath, by Mara-d̲-Rabuta (a name for God) to the great priest Šišlam-Rba. Šišlam-Rba passed the document down to another, also with an oath, and this new guardian "brought it down to the earth and set guardians in charge of it until world's end."[40] *Alma Rišaia Rba* 115–124 speaks of a heavenly being who brought a sealed letter to Adam.[41] According to the Mandaean text known as *The Thousand and Twelve Questions* 1.1.3, this document was "hidden and guarded" and passed on only under oath.[42]

Drower recorded the traditional Mandaean story *How Dana Nuk Visited the Seventh Heaven*, which resembles some of the other hidden book stories. Dana Nuk, also called Noh (Noah) is said to have possessed "all the sacred books which Hiwel Ziwa gave to Adam," which he kept in a locked room. "One day, when he entered this room, he found a book placed above the others." He burnt the book, then went out to think about what had happened, whereupon the book suddenly appeared before him. This time, he tore it up and cast the pieces into the river. Returning home and unlocking the book storeroom, he found the book once again where it had been. This time he left it and went to sleep. On awaking, he found the book beneath his head and concluded that the book "must be from God [and] must be read." He read the book and taught from it. Three weeks later, another book appeared in the room, and still later five more books appeared. "At last, a book appeared above the others which radiated light as it lay there." This latest book "contained the perfection of the knowledge of God. When he read it, his spirit was glad." Soon afterward, "he was in his garden, praying, when he saw a being of light descending from Awathur [heaven]." This being of light spoke to him of the importance of the eighth book, then took his soul to visit the seven heavens and learn about them.[43]

In some of these accounts, it is God, rather than an angel, who delivers a book to the prophet. Similarly, when Moses went atop the mountain in Sinai, it was God who delivered to him the tablets containing the law (see Exodus 24:12). Likewise, King David told his son Solomon that he had received the pattern for the Jerusalem temple by means of a "writing" from the Lord (1 Chronicles 28:19).

Heavenly Letters

Similar in nature to books brought from heaven by angels are heavenly letters. In Mandaean lore, a letter sealed by God is sent from heaven to the soul of a righteous person, who must wear it around the neck when sent to the Gate of Life at death.[44] During the Mandaean rite of proxy baptism, performed at the annual rededication of the Mandi, a ritual text inscribed on lead sheets using a stylus is brought in. The text, which is wrapped in white cloth, is dipped three times in the water. It contains the *masiqta* (service for the ascension of the souls of the dead) and the *zidqa brikha* (a ritual meal for the dead).[45]

Isaac H. Hall drew attention to two different versions of a letter said to have fallen from heaven in the days of the Nestorian patriarch Athanasius in the year 779.[46] A "letter from heaven" that has been widely published in English over the years first appeared in Latin in the latter part of the sixth century A.D. in Ebusa, a small Balearic island, where the local bishop, Vincentius, accepted it as genuine. The preface notes that "the Letter was written by Jesus Christ, and found under a great stone, round and large, at the foot of the Cross. . . . Under this stone was found the following, written by Jesus Christ. It was carried to the city of Iconium, and published by a person belong to the Lady Cuba. On the Letter was written, 'The Commandments of Jesus Christ Signed by the Angel Gabriel, seventy four [*or* ninety nine] years after our Saviour's birth.'" A modern Greek version of the letter indicates that it was "Found on the Grave of the Mother of God" and was revealed when Joannicius, patriarch of Jerusalem, smote a stone that had fallen from heaven.[47]

According to the Qur'an, Moses, John the Baptist, Jesus, and David received heavenly books (see Surah 2:50; 3:48;

17:57; 19:13, 31). Accordingly, the eleventh-century Arab chronographer al-Thaʿlabi wrote of a book sealed with gold that was sent from heaven to David. The book contained thirteen questions that David was to ask his son Solomon.[48] Indeed, a sealed letter from heaven is mentioned in a work traditionally attributed to Solomon (see *Odes of Solomon* 23:5–10, 17, 21).[49]

An Angel Guards the Record

After Joseph Smith received the plates from the angel Moroni, it became necessary for him to return them from time to time to the angel's keeping. After Joseph "wearied" the Lord with his requests to allow Martin Harris to take the first 116 pages of translation to show to a few others, the angel returned to take possession of both the plates and the interpreters. He returned them to Joseph when he was ready to continue the work.[50] The plates were also taken away for safety considerations. When Joseph and his scribe, Oliver Cowdery, moved from Harmony, Pennsylvania, to Fayette, New York, to continue the translation work at the home of Peter Whitmer Sr., the Lord told Joseph "that he should commit them into the hands of an angel, for safety, and after arriving at Mr. Whitmer's the angel would meet him in the garden and deliver them up again into his hands."[51]

Upon completion of the translation, Joseph evidently returned the plates to the angel, who subsequently showed them to the three witnesses—Oliver Cowdery, David Whitmer, and Martin Harris.[52] Eight more witnesses saw them not long afterward.[53] In an 1878 interview with P. Wilhelm Poulson, David Whitmer said that "the angel, the guardian of the plates, gave the plates up to Joseph for a time, that those eight witnesses could see and handle them."[54] After finishing his work with the plates, Joseph returned them to the angel (see JS—H 1:60).

There were other witnesses as well, two of them women whose families were involved with the translation. Lucy Harris, wife of Martin Harris, had a dream in which a personage (presumably the angel Moroni) appeared to her and showed her the plates.[55] Mary Musselman Whitmer, wife of Peter Whitmer Sr., also received a visit from a messenger who showed her the plates and turned the leaves so that she could see them.[56] Harrison Burgess, a member the church, reported that in 1832, while praying in the woods, he was visited by "a glorious personage clothed in white," who showed him "the plates from which the Book of Mormon was taken."[57]

Some early Jewish and Christian accounts parallel the Book of Mormon story in that an angel is appointed to guard sacred records. For example, *2 Enoch* 33:10–12 notes that the writings of Adam, Seth, Enos, Cainan, Mahalaleel, Jared, and Enoch were to survive until the final age and were to be preserved through the flood by angels. The preservation of the writings of Enoch until the last days is indicated in *1 Enoch* 104:10–13. Accordingly, in *Pistis Sophia* 134, God commanded Enoch to write *1 Jeu* and *2 Jeu* and deposit them in the rock of Ararad (Ararat). God then set a watcher (a member of an angelic class) to protect the books from the coming flood and the rulers who, through envy, might seek to destroy them.[58]

The Ethiopic *Book of the Mysteries of the Heavens and the Earth* also indicates that angels guarded sacred records. It declares, "Now the sons of Moses the prophet preserved a little book (*or*, a few works) which their father had left to them and to their children's children. And when they revealed that book to all men, an angel came, and seized it, and carried it up into heaven. Now, I have related unto thee these many words of mystery: keep them carefully and reveal not [to any man] how thou hast acquired them. And when the angel had said all these things the Apostle went up [into heaven], and the angel who remained taught me all these mysteries."[59]

The second-century Christian writer Hermas, brother of Pius, the bishop of Rome, wrote an account of a series of visions in which he was visited by several angels. One of the celestial beings who appeared during his first vision was an elderly woman "arrayed in a splendid robe, and with a book in her hand."[60] She read to him from a book, naming the calamities that would befall the wicked and the blessings that would come to the righteous in the last days (see Pastor of Hermas, *Vision* 1.3). She later reappeared with the book and allowed Hermas to take it and transcribe its contents, insisting that, when he had finished, he must return the book to her. He wrote, "Thereupon I took it, and going away into a certain part of the country, I transcribed the whole of it letter by letter; but the syllables of it I did not catch. No sooner, however, had I finished the writing of the book, than all of a sudden it was snatched from my hands; but who the person was that snatched it, I saw not" (Pastor of Hermas, *Vision* 2.1).[61] The story bears similarities to Joseph Smith's dealings with the angel Moroni, including the description of the angel's white robe. Another element that ties to the Book of Mormon, which the prophet Joseph translated by the gift and power of God, lies in Hermas's explanation of how he came to understood the meaning of what he had copied from the book: "Fifteen days after, when I had fasted and prayed much to the Lord, the knowledge of the writing was revealed to me" (Pastor of Hermas, *Vision* 2.1).[62] In a subsequent vision, a young man appeared to Hermas and told him that the woman who had delivered the book was the church. She subsequently reappeared to provide additional words for the book, instructing Hermas that he should make two copies and send them to two of the elders to be recopied and sent out to the churches (Pastor of Hermas, *Vision* 2.4).

Another story of a snatched book, told in the Samaritan chronicle known as the *Tolidah,* relates to the Torah scroll held in the high priest's house in Nablus. Said to have been written by Abishaᶜ, son of Phinehas, the grandson of Aaron, it was formerly kept at Elon Moreh. Once, the priest charged to carry the scroll took it to Gilgal, in Ephraim, where the people quarreled with him about it. When the scroll was opened, there was an earthquake, accompanied by lightning and thunder, "and a mighty wind lifted the Scroll out of the ark wherein it lay, and it was carried up and whirled into the air by the wind, while the community was watching, trembling and weeping. But they strengthened their hearts and took hold of the end of the Scroll, and it happened that a fragment was torn off."[63]

In an ancient Egyptian tale examined in detail in chapter 3, "Hiding Records in Boxes," a man named Setne Khamwas is said to have removed a sacred book from the tomb of Naneferkaptah. The dead man appeared to persuade him to return the book, in much the same way as angels are elsewhere said to come to recover sacred records from the hands of mortals.

Two Medieval Stories

From the twelfth and thirteenth centuries come two stories of angels delivering metallic plates. The first of these stories was recapped in 1876 by John William Draper:

> About the close of the twelfth century appeared among the mendicant friars that ominous work, which under the title of "The Everlasting Gospel," struck terror into the Latin hierarchy. It was affirmed that an angel had brought it from heaven, engraven on copper plates, and had given it to a priest called Cyril, who delivered it to the Abbot Joachim. The abbot had been dead about fifty years, when there was put forth, A.D. 1250, a true exposition of the tendency of his book, under the form of an introduction, by John of Parma, the general of the Franciscans, as was universally suspected or alleged. Notwithstanding its heresy, the work displayed an enlarged and masterly conception of the historical process of humanity. In this introduction, John of Parma pointed out that the Abbot Joachim, who had not only performed a pilgrimage to the Holy Land, but had been reverenced as a prophet, received as of unimpeachable orthodoxy, and canonized, had accepted as his fundamental position that Roman Christianity had done its work, and had now come to its inevitable termination. He proceeded to show that there are epochs or ages in the Divine government of the world.[64]

This account parallels that of Joseph Smith in two respects. The first is that an angel delivers metallic plates that are said to contain the "everlasting gospel." Doctrine and Covenants 27:5 speaks of "Moroni, whom I have sent unto you to reveal the Book of Mormon, containing the fulness of my everlasting gospel" (see also D&C 109:65; 135:3). One need not read into this that the Lord really called Cyril and Joachim as he later called Joseph Smith; still, Joachim's declaration, like Doctrine and Covenants 27:5, draws on the imagery of the angel bringing the "everlasting gospel" in Revelation 14:6.

The second parallel element in this story is that Joachim of Floris announced the beginning of a new dispensation of the gospel. But his concept was different from that of Joseph

Smith, for he taught that there were only three dispensations, represented by the Old and New Testaments and the new book brought by the angel. The first dispensation was governed by God the Father, the second by God the Son, and the third would be governed by God the Holy Ghost.

The other medieval tale that draws our attention is that of Nicholas Flamel, a thirteenth-century French alchemist. His story has been translated and published in various places.[65] Flamel lived before the invention of printing and was a copyist, and his account has been summarized by Arthur Waite:

> Now tradition informs us that, whether his application was great, his desire intense, or whether he was super-eminently fitted to be included by divine election among the illuminated Sons of the Doctrine, or for whatever other reason, the mystical Bath-Kôl appeared to him under the figure of an angel, bearing a remarkable book bound in well-wrought copper, the leaves of thin bark, graven right carefully with a pen of iron. An inscription in characters of gold contained a dedication addressed to the Jewish nation by Abraham the Jew, prince, priest, astrologer, and philosopher.
>
> "Flamel," cried the radiant apparition, "behold this book of which thou understandest nothing; to many others but thyself it would remain for ever unintelligible, but one day thou shalt discern in its pages what none but thyself will see!"
>
> At these words Flamel eagerly stretched out his hands to take possession of the priceless gift, but book and angel disappeared in an auriferous tide of light. The scrivener awoke to be ravished henceforth by the divine dream of alchemy; but so long a time passed without any fulfilment of the angelic promise, that the ardour of his imagination cooled . . . in the year 1357, an event occurred which bore evidence of the veracity of his visionary promise-maker, and exalted his ambition and aspirations to a furnace heat.[66]

Flamel's story contains a number of parallels to the story of how the Book of Mormon came into Joseph Smith's hands. The use of metal is common to both records, as is the fact that both sets of plates were engraved. Additionally, the fact that the book could not be readily comprehended but would ultimately be intelligible to the recipient is found in both accounts (see JS—H 1:63–65; compare 2 Nephi 27:15–20). Just as Flamel was told that no others would see the original record, so, too, was Joseph Smith commanded not to show the plates to others except when directed by God. In both cases, the record is delivered by an angel of light, who takes the record away again.

Though Flamel was originally shown the book by an angel, he later recovered it by rather ordinary means—he found it for sale:

> There fell by chance into my hands a gilded book, very old and large, which cost me only two *florins*.
>
> It was not made of paper or parchment, as other books are, but of admirable rinds (as it seemed to me) of young trees. The cover of it was of *brass*; it was well bound, and graven all over with a strange kind of letters, which I take to be Greek characters, or some such like.
>
> This I know that I could not read them, nor were they either Latin or French letters, of which I understand something.
>
> But as to the matter which was written within, it was engraven (as I suppose) with an iron pencil or graver upon the said bark leaves, done admirably well, and in fair and neat Latin letters, and curiously coloured.[67]

Again, some of the parallels with the Book of Mormon are evident, including the "strange kind of letters" in which the record was written. For example, the Testimony of Eight Witnesses at the beginning of the Book of Mormon mentions "the engravings thereon, all of which has the appearance of ancient work; and of curious workmanship."

Flamel set about trying to understand the book. He copied "as much to the life or original as I could, all the images and figures of the said fourth and fifth leaves. These I showed to the greatest scholars and most learned men in Paris, who understood thereof no more than myself: I told them they were found in a book which taught the philosophers' stone. But the great part of them made a mock both of me and that most excellent secret, except one whose name was Anselm, a practiser of psychic and a deep student in this art. He much desired to see my book, which he valued more than anything else in the world, but I always refused him, only making him a large demonstration of the method."[68] This is reminiscent of when Martin Harris took the transcript from the plates to scholars in New York.

At length Flamel went to Leon, Spain, carrying "the extract or copy of the figures or pictures." There he consulted with Canches, a Jewish physician who had converted to Christianity. Upon examining Flamel's copies, Canches became excited at the prospect of a translation, which he began to provide. Anxious to see the original, which Canches declared to be "a thing which was believed to be utterly lost," the two set out for France. Unfortunately, Canches died before reaching Paris, and Flamel was obliged to provide his own translation, which he published as divinely inspired.

The Story of John Dee

John Dee (1527–1608) was an English mathematician and astrologer who made many contributions to the scientific knowledge of his time but also dabbled in the occult and alchemy, as did many other sages of his time and before. He spent much of his life in royal service both in England and abroad (notably Poland and Bohemia).

Dee was fascinated by Bible stories of the patriarchs and prophets, especially by the fact that they had been visited by angels. He also pondered on the "Shewstone," by which the Israelite high priests were able to receive revelation from God. In the 1580s Dee teamed with one Edward Kelly, a scryer well versed in Hermetic literature who claimed to see angelic apparitions in Dee's crystal ball. In 1582 Kelly claimed to have seen successive sets of seven angels, each carrying a tablet with his name written on it. During a subsequent apparition, an angel told the two men that they should not look to the Catholics or the Protestants for truth, but to God and Christ.

Over the years, both God and the angelic visitors dictated to the men a number of books, including a long-lost record made by the antediluvian patriarch Enoch entitled *The Angelic Keys* and another called the *Mystery of Mysteries and the Holy of Holies*. In 1586, however, the voice of God came to Kelly, instructing them to burn the manuscripts. Reluctantly they complied and consigned the books to the fire. As the flames rose, Kelly declared that he saw the form of a man gathering up the ashes and reforming them into books. He then heard the divine voice proclaiming that they would receive the books again and warning that the information contained therein was not to be revealed to the world at large.

In the fall of the same year, as Dee and Kelly were praying in the garden, an angel appeared in the form of a gardener. They knew he was an angel because he stood a full foot off the ground. Kelly followed the angel, who delivered to him most of the books that had been burned and promised that the others would ultimately be restored to them. Kelly brought the books to Dee, who had remained seated beneath the almond tree where they had prayed, and the two rejoiced together.

The Apocalypse of Paul

One of the more fascinating stories of hidden books revealed by angels is about the *Apocalypse of Paul*, whose authorship is attributed to the apostle Paul.[69] Where the Greek and Latin texts end, the Syriac version adds these words:

> And I, Paul, returned unto myself, and I knew all that I had seen: and in life I had not rest that I might reveal this mystery, but I wrote it and deposited it under the ground and the foundations of the house of a certain faithful man with whom I used to be in Tarsus a city of Cilicia. And when I was released from this life of time, and stood before my Lord, thus said he unto me: Paul, have we shown all these things unto thee that thou shouldst deposit them under the foundations of a house? Then send and disclose concerning this revelation, that men may read it and turn to the way of truth, that they also may not come to these bitter torments. And thus was this revelation discovered.[70]

This is immediately followed by an explanation of how the text was discovered, which is also found in the Greek and Coptic versions. In the Latin version, this explanation (which reads same as the Greek) prefaces the text. The explanation relates how, in the fourth century A.D., the time of Theodosius Augustus the younger and Cynegius, a man of Tarsus who was living in Paul's old house was visited by an angel during the night. The angel told the man to tear up the house's foundation and publish what he found. The man thought the words of the angel were untrue, but on the third visit the angel compelled him to break up the foundation. As he dug he found a marble box sealed with lead. The box bore an inscription on the sides, indicating that it contained a revelation of Paul and the shoes he wore on his missionary journeys. The man turned the box over to a judge, who sent it to the emperor Theodosius.

The emperor opened it and found the revelation, then sent a copy to Jerusalem (or, according to the Greek, kept a copy and sent the original).

This story was also told by the early Christian writer Sozomen (see *Ecclesiastical History* 7.19), who rejected the apocalypse as a forgery. It was generally rejected by early writers. In his preface to his English translation of the *Apocalypse of Paul,* Willis Barnstone wrote, "The details of the discovered scriptures calls to mind the detailed evidence associated with the discovery of Mormon scriptures in New York state."[71]

Other Dream Records

Other stories also mention books whose location was revealed by dreams. Chapter 3 noted how Epiteles, a Greek man who lived before the fourth century B.C., learned from a dream the location of a sacred book hidden in the ground. Serge Sauneron cited an Egyptian text in which Horus, son of Panishi (Pawenesh), slept overnight in the temple of Hermopolis, where the god Thoth came to him in a dream. Thoth told Horus to go the next morning into the rooms of the temple in which books were kept, and there he would find a sealed naos. In the naos would be a box containing a magical text written by Thoth himself, which Panishi was to copy and then return to its place. He followed the instructions and, by use of the magic in the book, the Egyptians were able to defeat an invading Ethiopian army.[72] Aspects of the story resemble some of the Hermetic tales discussed in chapter 2, "Hidden Records."

Summary

The story of the angel Moroni delivering a sacred record to the young prophet Joseph Smith has close parallels with some of the ancient and medieval accounts discussed in this chapter. In most of these instances, a heavenly being was appointed as guardian of the record, which he retrieved from the mortal to whom the record had been revealed. We need not assume that all of these tales are true, but the antiquity of some of them suggests that the concept was known anciently.

Notes

1. The stories of angels keeping heavenly records are too numerous to mention here but will be discussed in the chapter on "Writings of the Fathers" in my forthcoming FARMS book, tentatively titled *Testaments of the Twelve Patriarchs: Notes and Reflections.*
2. According to D&C 77:14, the book represented a mission given to the apostle John.
3. See Lucy Mack Smith, *History of Joseph Smith by His Mother, Lucy Mack Smith,* ed. Preston Nibley (Salt Lake City: Bookcraft, 1958), 47.
4. For a discussion of the role boxes play in the hiding of records, see chapter 3 of this volume, "Hiding Records in Boxes."
5. Zechariah's angel, like the angels seen by Ezekiel and John the Revelator, measured the temple in Jerusalem.
6. W. M. Thackston Jr., trans., *The Tales of the Prophets of al-Kisa'i* (Boston: Twayne, 1978), 81–82.
7. James H. Charlesworth, *The Old Testament Pseudepigrapha* (Garden City, N.Y.: Doubleday, 1983), 1:74.
8. Harry Sperling and Maurice Simon, trans., *The Zohar* (New York: Rebecca Bennet Publications, 1958), 2:304.
9. See Garth Fowden, *The Egyptian Hermes: A Historical Approach to the Late Pagan Mind* (Cambridge: Cambridge University Press, 1986), 50–51.
10. Cited in Geo Widengren, *The Ascension of the Apostle and the Heavenly Book* (Uppsala, Sweden: University of Uppsala, 1946), 77–78. Widengren refers to the Arabic text and German translation

in J. Ruska, *Tabula Smaragdina. Ein Beitrag zur Geschichte der hermetischen Literatur* (Heidelberg: C. Winter, 1926), 112–14.

11. See Philostratus, *Vita Apollonii* 8.19.

12. See Fowden, *Egyptian Hermes,* 162–64; Widengren, *Ascension of the Apostle,* 78–79, 81, citing the Arabic text and the German translation in Ruska, *Tabula Smaragdina,* 16–24, 132.

13. See Elsdon Best, *Maori Religion and Mythology* (Wellington, New Zealand: W. A. G. Skinner, 1924), 60–64, 67–68. I am grateful to Matthew Roper for bringing this to my attention.

14. Florentino García Martínez, *The Dead Sea Scrolls Translated,* 2nd ed. (Leiden: E. J. Brill, 1996), 125.

15. See Jean Doresse, *The Secret Books of the Egyptian Gnostics* (New York: Viking, 1960), 227. For a Parthian Manichaean hymn that says the book revealed was by an assembly of angels, see Hans-Joachim Klimkeit, *Gnosis on the Silk Road: Gnostic Texts From Central Asia* (San Francisco: HarperSanFrancisco, 1993), 58.

16. XI,3 *Allogenes* 68.16–31, in James M. Robinson, ed. *The Nag Hammadi Library,* 3rd ed., (San Francisco: HarperCollins, 1990), 500. For a discussion of records hidden on mountaintops, see chapter 7 of this volume, "Mountain Repositories."

17. Robinson, *Nag Hammadi Library,* 290.

18. Ibid., 291.

19. See E. S. Drower, *The Haran Gawaita and the Baptism of Hibil-Ziwa* (Vatican: Biblioteca Apostolica Vaticana, 1953), 13–14. According to their tradition, the Mandaeans are descendants of the disciples of John the Baptist.

20. Hugh Nibley, *Enoch the Prophet* (Salt Lake City: Deseret Book and FARMS, 1986), 151, citing M. J. Bin Gorion, *Die Sagen der Juden* (Frankfurt: Kütter and Loening, 1913), 1:263.

21. P. Colon. inv. nr. 4780, 49–50, in Ron Cameron and Arthur J. Dewey, *The Cologne Mani Codex* (Missoula, Mont.: Scholars Press, 1979), 39.

22. See P. Colon. inv. nr. 4780, 50–52, in ibid.

23. P. Colon. inv. nr. 4780, 54, in ibid., 39–43.

24. P. Colon. inv. nr. 4780, 57, in ibid., 47, see 45–57.

25. John C. Reeves, *Heralds of That Good Realm: Syro-Mesopotamian Gnosis and Jewish Traditions* (Leiden: E. J. Brill, 1996), 142. Reeves's translation and commentary on the *Apocalypse of Enosh* comprises chapter 5 of his book. For a discussion of records hidden on mountaintops, see chapter 7 of this volume, "Mountain Repositories."

26. The story of the book is told in *Pirqe Rabbi Eliezer* and in two medieval kabbalistic works, the *Zohar* and the *Book of Noah*, with variants in the different recensions of the latter. The story in the *Zohar* is based on the one given in the second recension of the *Book of Noah* (see *Zohar* I, 37b, 55b, 58b, 72b, 118a). For a discussion of the subject, with source information, see Louis Ginzberg, *The Legends of the Jews* (Philadelphia: Jewish Publication Society of America, 1911), 1:156–57, 5:117 n. 110, 177 n. 23.

27. For a discussion of the genizah, see chapter 9 of this volume, "Books in the Treasury."

28. See Shakti M. Gupta, *Vishnu and His Incarnations* (Bombay: Somaiya, 1974), 13.

29. Sperling and Simon, *The Zohar*, 1:138–39.

30. Compare the sealed portion of the Book of Mormon.

31. Sperling and Simon, *The Zohar*, 1:176–77.

32. Significantly, the name Raphael means "God heals." Traditionally, this angel has charge over healing powers.

33. Traditionally, the sapphire (often a pearl or some other precious stone) provided light in the ark during the flood and is comparable to the urim and thummim. (See the appendix "Glowing Stones in Ancient and Medieval Lore.")

34. For an English translation, see Michael A. Morgan, trans., *Sepher ha-Razim: The Book of the Mysteries* (Chico, Calif.: Scholars Press, 1983), 17.

35. Robinson, *Nag Hammadi Library*, 286. For a discussion of records hidden on mountaintops, see chapter 7 of this volume, "Mountain Repositories."

36. For a discussion of records hidden on mountaintops, see chapter 7 of this volume, "Mountain Repositories."

37. Widengren, *Ascension of the Apostle,* 46, citing the text published in Wilhelm Gesenius, *Carmina Samaritana e codicibus Londinensibus et Gothanis* (Leipzig: Imensis Typisque Fr. Chr. Guil. Vogelli, 1824), 40.

38. The term "angel of the presence," used in the Bible and other early documents, denotes an angel of superior rank (an archangel) who is allowed to stand in God's presence.

39. See Widengren, *Ascension of the Apostle,* 48–49, citing the text published in A. E. Cowley, *The Samaritan Liturgy* (Oxford: Clarendon Press, 1909), 1:31.

40. *Alma Rišaia Rba* 4–8, in E.S. Drower, *A Pair of Naṣoraean Commentaries (Two Priestly Documents)* (Leiden: E. J. Brill, 1963), 1.

41. In Mandaean lore, other letters from heaven are sent to the souls of the righteous, as noted later in this chapter.

42. E. S. Drower, *The Thousand and Twelve Questions* (Berlin: Akademie-Verlag, 1960), 110.

43. E. S. Drower, *The Mandaeans of Iraq and Iran* (Leiden: E. J. Brill, 1962), 300–305. For the name Noh, see ibid., 307 n. 6.

44. See, for example, E. S. Drower, *The Canonical Prayerbook of the Mandaeans* (Leiden: E. J. Brill, 1959), 61 (song number 73); *Alma Rišaia Rba* 160, 331. Drower notes that the letter is placed in "a small phial . . . in the small pocket over the right breast of the dying person's tunic" (Drower, *Thousand and Twelve Questions,* 14). She also notes that "the dying man himself is also spoken of as 'a letter'" (ibid., 115 n. 9).

45. See Drower, *Mandaeans of Iraq and Iran,* 132.

46. See Isaac H. Hall, note in *Journal of the American Oriental Society* 13 (1889): clv, and "The Story of Arsânîs," *Hebraica* 6 (October 1889–July 1890), 81.

47. For an account, see Edgar J. Goodspeed, "The Letter From Heaven," in *Famous "Biblical" Hoaxes,* (original title *Modern*

Apocrypha) (Grand Rapids, Mich.: Baker, 1956), 70–75, from which I have drawn the quotes. For records hidden in tombs, see chapter 2 of this volume, "Hidden Records."

48. See al-Thaʿlabi, *Qiṣaṣ ʾal-ʾAnbiyaʾ* (Cairo: Mustafa al-Babi al-Halabi wa-Awladuhu, A. H., 1340), 202. Hugh Nibley was the first to bring this information to the attention of Latter-day Saints. I am grateful to Brian Hauglid for confirming details of the story from the Arabic text.

49. The text is described in detail in chapter 4 of this volume, "Sealed Books."

50. See Joseph Smith, *History of the Church of Jesus Christ of Latter-day Saints* (Salt Lake City: Deseret Book, 1980), 1:21. Joseph's mother, recollecting the events years later, indicated that the angel took possession of the translators and the plates after the loss of the 116 pages. See Smith, *History of Joseph Smith,* 133–34.

51. Smith, *History of Joseph Smith,* 149–50.

52. See Smith, *History of the Church,* 1:54–56. See also Testimony of Three Witnesses, published at the front of the Book of Mormon.

53. See *History of the Church,* 1:57. See also Testimony of Eight Witnesses, published at the front of the Book of Mormon.

54. *Deseret Evening News,* 16 August 1878, 2.

55. See Smith, *History of Joseph Smith,* 117.

56. See Andrew Jenson, *The Historical Record* (October 1888): 621, cited in Richard Lloyd Anderson, *Investigating the Book of Mormon Witnesses* (Salt Lake City: Deseret Book, 1981), 30–33.

57. Harrison Burgess, "Sketch of a Life Well Spent," in *Labors in the Vineyard* (Salt Lake City: Juvenile Instructor Office, 1884), 65–66. Although two of these accounts had already come to my attention, all three are noted by Matthew Roper in his "Comments on the Book of Mormon Witnesses: A Response to Jerald and Sandra Tanner," *Journal of Book of Mormon Studies* 2/2 (1993): 169–70.

58. See Carl Schmidt, ed., *Pistis Sophia,* trans. Violet Macdermot (Leiden: E. J. Brill, 1978).

59. Ernest A. Wallis Budge, *The Book of the Mysteries of the Heavens and the Earth and Other Works of Bakhayla Mika'el (Zosimas)* (London: Oxford, 1935), 124, citing folio 62b, column 2.

60. The aged woman in the white robe, who is said to be seated on a chair, is reminiscent of the aged man in a white robe seated on a throne and identified with Hermes Trismegistos, who hands over records in the Hermetic traditions. See the discussion in chapter 2 of this volume, "Hidden Records."

61. Alexander Roberts and James Donaldson, *Ante-Nicene Fathers* (Peabody, Mass.: Hendrickson, 1994), 2:10. Originally published in 1886. Many writers prefer to call the work Shepherd of Hermas. Its title draws upon the fact that one of the angels appeared in the form of a shepherd.

62. Ibid., 2:11. In a subsequent vision, a young man appeared to Hermas and told him that the woman who had delivered the book was the church. She subsequently reappeared to provide additional words for the book, instructing Hermas to make two copies and send them to two of the elders to be recopied for the churches (see Pastor of Hermas, *Vision* 2.4).

63. John Bowman, ed. and trans., *Samaritan Documents Relating to Their History, Religion and Life* (Pittsburgh: Pickwick Press, 1977), 47–48.

64. John William Draper, *History of the Intellectual Development of Europe* (New York: Harper, 1876), 77–78. I am indebted to Ron Myatt for bringing this text to my attention.

65. See, for example, Laurinda Dixon, *Nicolas Flamel: His Exposition of the Hieroglyphicall Figures (1624)* (New York: Garland, 1994).

66. Arthur Edward Waite, *Lives of Alchemystical Philosophers* (London: George Redway, 1888), 96–97.

67. Ibid., 99.

68. Ibid., 102–3.

69. See the appendix by Steven Booras in this volume.

70. *Apocalypse of Paul* 51, in Montague Rhodes James, *The Apocryphal New Testament* (Oxford: Clarendon, 1955), 553–54.

71. Willis Barnstone, ed., *The Other Bible* (San Francisco: Harper and Row, 1984), 537.

72. See Serge Sauneron, *The Priests of Ancient Egypt* (New York: Evergreen Profile, 1960), 125.

chapter 6

Hiding Sacred Relics

> *And ye shall prepare for yourselves a place for a treasury, and consecrate it unto my name. . . . And there shall be a seal upon the treasury, and all the sacred things shall be delivered into the treasury . . . And the avails of the sacred things shall be had in the treasury, and a seal shall be upon it; and it shall not be used or taken out of the treasury by any one, neither shall the seal be loosed which shall be placed upon it, only by the voice of the order, or by commandment. And thus shall ye preserve the avails of the sacred things in the treasury, for sacred and holy purposes. And this shall be called the sacred treasury of the Lord; and a seal shall be kept upon it that it may be holy and consecrated unto the Lord. (D&C 104:60, 62, 64–66)*

One of the striking things about the Book of Mormon record is that Moroni hid the plates in a stone box along with other sacred Nephite relics, including the breastplate and the interpreters, or urim and thummim (see JS—H 1:34–35, 52, 59). The fact that the resurrected Moroni showed all these, along with the sword of Laban, to the three witnesses implies that the sword was also part of the sacred cache (see D&C 17:1).

Indeed, the sword of Laban and the large plates of Nephi were passed down in the line of Nephite kings and may have been emblems of royal and priestly power.[1] King Benjamin turned over the records, the sword of Laban, and the liahona to his son Mosiah when he became king (see Mosiah 1:10, 15–16), and when Nephite kingship was abolished in favor of a system of judges, Mosiah gave the records and the interpreters (and presumably the other artifacts) to Alma, the high priest and first chief judge. Before his death, Alma committed the plates, the interpreters, and the liahona to his son Helaman (see Alma 37).

Like other aspects of the Book of Mormon story, the hiding of sacred relics is an ancient practice, attested in early documents as well as by archaeological discoveries.

Hidden Treasures

The hiding of treasures in the ground seems to have been a common practice among the Nephites (see Helaman 12:18; 13:18–20). The burying of weapons of war by converted Lamanites, to preserve them as a testimony of their repentance, may come from the same tradition (see Alma 24:12–17; 25:14; 26:32; Helaman 15:9). Burying treasures is also known from the Bible. For example, Jacob hid the teraphim beneath a tree, perhaps to make it easier to identify the burial spot for future recovery (see Genesis 35:4). Similarly, in the parable of the talents, one of the servants dug a hole and hid the money in the ground (see Matthew 25:18, 25). Jesus said that "the kingdom of heaven is like unto treasure hid in a field; the which when a man hath found, he hideth, and for joy thereof goeth and selleth all that he hath, and buyeth that field" (Matthew 13:44). Other hidden treasures—perhaps also concealed in the ground—are mentioned in various Bible passages (see 2 Kings

7:8; Job 3:21; Psalm 17:14; Proverbs 2:4; Isaiah 45:3; compare Colossians 2:3).

A Jewish tradition recounts that the Babylonian king Nebuchadnezzar ordered the construction of large copper ships that were then filled with money and hidden beneath the mud of the Euphrates River. On the day that Cyrus, king of Persia, decreed that the Jews could rebuild the temple in Jerusalem, God revealed this hidden treasure to reward him.[2] According to *Targum Rishon* on Esther 1:4, Cyrus dug in the bank of the river and found 680 copper vessels filled with gold and jewels.[3]

A hoard of variously sized silver ingots from the eighth to seventh centuries B.C. was found in a clay pot at En-Gedi. During excavations at es-Samuᶜ (biblical Eshtemoa), archaeologists uncovered five clay jugs from the ninth to eight centuries B.C., filled with twenty-six kilos of silver in various forms (crescents, rings, circlets, bracelets, silver leaves, silver thread, and jewelry in filigree, and molten silver). Some have related the cache to David's sending some of the plunder of the Amalekites to Esthemoa (see 1 Samuel 30:28).

Caches of coins have been found at several archaeological sites in Israel. One of the largest, a trove of 2,920 coins, was found beneath the floor of the fifth-century synagogue at Capernaum. Another 67 coins were found beneath the foundation of the synagogue's benches. In October 1998 a cache of up to 400 coins was uncovered at Beth-Shean in Israel. They had been hidden in the sixth or seventh century A.D. in a large ceramic jug buried beneath the floor of a house. Archaeologist Ofer Sion suggested that the owner had secreted the coins, hoping to return for them at a later time.

Also in 1998, archaeologists working at Tiberias, on the western shore of the Sea of Galilee, uncovered a treasure concealed in three large clay jars in an eleventh-century shop. Each jar had been sealed with a stone and two of them had been hidden beneath the floor. The third jar, the largest, was evidently used as a safe: it was hidden from view but accessible through a hole in the wall. Altogether, these jars contained five to six hundred bronze and brass objects, including various medallions, a glass jar, a large candelabrum, and numerous figurines. Of the eighty-two coins found in the jars, fifty-eight bore the likeness of Jesus with inscriptions identifying him as the Messiah. Yizhar Hirschfield, who conducted the excavation, suggested that the hoard may have been hidden before the Crusaders invaded the city in 1099. The owner, who may have been a dealer or a collector, likely intended to return for his property but was unable to do so.[4]

Among the Dead Sea Scrolls was a record written on a piece of copper eight feet in length. This record is known as the *Copper Scroll* (3Q15). It lists the burial site of treasures, thought by some to have come from the Jerusalem temple, hidden up for future discovery and use. Most of the treasures were buried beneath walls or hidden in tunnels, cisterns, water channels, and even in tombs and burial mounds. The list includes various pots, jugs, and vases, along with "sacred vestments" (I, 9; see also III, 9). The document also mentions caches of gold and silver, including "a chest of money" (I, 3), "containers with seventy talents of silver" (II, 6), "two jugs filled with silver" (IV, 8), "a chest and all its contents and sixty talents of silver" (XII, 5), and a cache of silver hidden "bene[ath the] large [stone]" (V, 2–4). The first six lines in column VI note the burial place of an amphora containing a book or scroll and, beneath the amphora, forty-two silver talents. The beginning of column VIII states that books and ritual vessels were hidden in an aqueduct.[5]

The *Copper Scroll* describes events that took place about the time of the Roman siege of Jerusalem in A.D. 70, but it seems to have a precedent. The medieval Jewish text *Massekhet Kelim* (Tractate of the Vessels) describes how the vessels of the Jerusalem temple were hidden away when the Babylonians conquered Jerusalem in 587 B.C. In connection with this action, "Shimmur the Levite and his associates listed *on a copper tablet* the sacred vessels and the vessels of the Temple which were in Jerusalem and in every place." The vessels were to remain hidden "until the advent of a legitimate king for Israel."[6] Similarly, in the *Apocalypse of Enosh*, cited in the *Cologne Mani Codex*, an angel instructed Enosh (Enos in the King James Bible), son of Adam, to write "hidden things upon bronze tablets and deposit (them) in the wilderness." Enosh "left [the records] behind for the subsequent generations."[7]

It is particularly noteworthy that the *Copper Scroll* indicates that books and other relics were hidden in jars and under stones and were sometimes accompanied by other treasures. This parallels Moroni's hiding the plates with other sacred relics beneath a stone and lends authenticity to Joseph Smith's story of the Book of Mormon.[8]

Sacred Stones

Among the relics concealed with the Book of Mormon plates were "two stones in silver bows . . . that God had prepared them for the purpose of translating the book" (JS—H 1:35). Concealing sacred stones, sometimes with records, is known from several ancient texts.

An early Jewish account tells how Kenaz, father of the Israelite judge Othniel,[9] placed books and sacred glowing stones engraved with the names of the twelve tribes on the mountain beside the altar, as God commanded him (see *Pseudo-Philo* 26:5–15; *Chronicles of Jerahmeel* 57:11–21).[10]

Some stones are said to have writing on them. Chapter 2, "Hidden Records," noted the Hermetic tradition of the emerald tablets on which Hermes is said to have written arcane lore, which he hid up. In Jewish tradition, the tablets on which the Ten Commandments were engraved were large sapphires (see *Pirqe Rabbi Eliezer* 46; *Zohar* Exodus 84a–b). Similarly, according to the third recension of the *Book of Noah*, the heavenly book given to Adam by the angel Raziel was written on a sapphire stone.[11]

In the Samaritan *Asatir* (Secrets) of Moses (2.7), we read that Enoch "learned the Book of Signs which was given to Adam. And these are the twenty-four precious stones, twelve for the time of Divine Favour and twelve for the chosen heads of the sons of Jacob and to the descendants of the servants of the high God."[12] According to the *Pitaron* (Explanation) to the *Asatir*, Adam was given a Book of Signs that was copied on twenty-four precious stones, twelve of which were "hidden away as a secret for the last generation." The other twelve were for "the families of the children of Jacob," and the text suggests they may have been the twelve stones of the high priest's breastplate and hence the stones buried on the mountain by Kenaz.[13]

Other Hidden Relics

The discovery of hidden relics is known from both tradition and archaeology. In a story attributed to Lucian, Rabbi Gamaliel appeared in vision to Lucian about A.D. 415 to reveal the location of the body of Stephen, the first Christian martyr, which became a sacred relic to early Christians. The story is known from Augustine (see *On the Gospel According to St. John* 120.4), from a Slavonic version of Lucian,[14] and from the tenth-century Syriac *Book of the Bee* 47. According to the *Book of the*

Bee, Gamaliel, his two sons, and his brother Nicodemus all became Christians and were buried alongside Stephen.

The Mandaeans placed amulets in the form of terra-cotta bowls, which they inscribed with magical texts, by or under the foundations of their houses.[15] One of the earliest caches of objects, from about 3000 B.C., consisted of some 429 metal objects (including 240 copper mace heads) found in a cave in Nahal Mishmar, Israel.[16]

Iraq, where a number of ancient documents were found in stone boxes (see chapter 3, "Hiding Records in Boxes"), is also known for the discovery of other relics hidden in boxes. George Smith wrote about finding a brick box below a pavement. The box, whose contents are housed in the British Museum, contained six terra-cotta figures with human bodies, heads of lions, and large wings, as well as five small terra-cotta dogs.[17] Dr. Robert Koldewey found similar statuettes in small brick boxes beneath pavements of buildings in Babylon.[18]

Excavators at the Ishtar temple of the Assyrian king Tukulti-Ninurta I (1244–1208 B.C.) uncovered various buried relics, including inscribed tablets, glass beads, and bits of ivory, all laid out on a stone slab placed atop the mud-brick foundation.[19]

From 1924 to 1926, in his excavations of the ruins of a building from the mid-seventh century B.C. at Ur, C. Leonard Wooley found a series of boxes, each box made with three plano-convex bricks. One side of each square was open, and the cover of each box was a pavement brick. Inside each box was usually a single figure or statuette. These boxes were lined up all around rooms against the walls, with the open end toward the center of the room.[20]

Europe is also known for hidden relics. A sixteenth-century writer indicated that in 1530 a "demon" used a crystal to show a priest in the city of Nuremberg a vision of buried treasure. The priest went to the place and found an excavated cavern in which he saw a chest and a black dog lying alongside it. When he entered the cavern, the roof collapsed and crushed him to death.[21]

Near the end of the sixteenth century, the canons of San Giovanni in Laterano, Rome, wanted to repair a house they owned. They sent workmen to remove two large superimposed stones that were in the way. When the workmen broke the upper stone, they found embedded inside it a covered alabaster funerary urn hidden in a space hollowed out between the upper and lower stones. Inside the urn they found ashes, twenty crystal balls, and other small artifacts.[22]

George Kunz noted that small crystal balls have been found in medieval French and English tombs.[23] He further noted that a crystal ball was found in a funerary urn at Hinsbury Hill, Northamptonshire,[24] and that Cardinal Farnese once possessed an urn that included various gems, carved stones, a crystal ball, and six "nuts of crystal."[25]

The Cave of Treasures

A number of ancient texts speak of a cave in which Adam and Eve lived after they were expelled from the Garden of Eden. According to these accounts, the first couple were later interred in the same cave, alongside sacred relics that God had given them. This "Cave of Treasures" was highly revered by Adam's descendants, who came there to pray.

The sacred artifacts are mentioned by tenth-century Arab chronographer al-Kisa'i. He wrote that "God had given Adam a white cloth from Paradise and placed it in the coffer, which He now commanded Adam to open. Adam took out the cloth and spread it out." It contained the forms of all Adam's posterity, which he showed to Seth. "Having seen all this, he was commanded to fold the cloth and put it back into the coffer. Then he took a handful of hair from his beard, placed it in the coffer," and turned over to Seth both the coffer and his ring.[26]

A Christian tradition recorded in *Book of the Rolls* f.96b and f.101b indicates that after God expelled Adam and Eve from the garden, he made them dwell in a cave in the holy mountain that was the foundation of paradise. There Adam found gold, myrrh, and incense—symbols of the Son of God. Adam kept these treasures in the cave, which he had dedicated as a house of prayer. A variant story found in the *Conflict of Adam and Eve* I, 31:9–10 indicates that angels delivered to Adam the gold, incense, and myrrh, which he kept in the Cave of Treasures, also called a place "of concealment."[27]

According to *Testament of Adam* 3:6, Seth wrote the testament, including the history of Adam. He hid it with the body of his father, along with the sacred artifacts later retrieved by the Magi and taken to Bethlehem. According to *Book of the Rolls* f.102b, the *Testament of Adam* was on a scroll possessed by the Magi that "was put by for safe keeping."[28] The tenth-century Syriac *Book of the Bee* 39 mentions this story but gives it no credence.

Cave of Treasures 20b.1 notes that each of the patriarchs from Adam to Noah knew of the coming flood and instructed that after the flood the body of Adam was to be buried in a secret location. Jared, one of Seth's descendants, is said to have told Noah to take the body of Adam, the gold, the incense, and the myrrh on the ark and bury them in a place to be shown him (see *Conflict of Adam and Eve* II, 21:7–11). Methuselah repeated these instructions, according to *Cave of Treasures* 15b.1, *Book of the Rolls* f.109b, and *Conflict of Adam and Eve* III, 5:9–10, 14–18. Accordingly, Noah took the body of Adam, along with the gold, myrrh, and frankincense, with him on the ark (see *Cave of Treasures* 16b.2–17a.1; *Book of the Rolls* f.106a–b, f.110b; *Conflict of Adam and Eve* III, 6.3–5; 7.14–17). According to one account, after the flood Noah and his son Shem took the books of the testaments, along with the gifts of gold, myrrh, and frankincense later used by the magi, and Shem buried them with the body of Adam. They were sealed inside the ark with the seal of Noah (see *Book of the Rolls* f.106b, 109b, 110b, 115a–b). A variant story indicates that Shem and Melchizedek hid these sacred artifacts in what later became Jerusalem (see *Conflict of Adam and Eve* III, 17–19) and were commanded by God to keep the information secret and reveal it to no one (see *Conflict of Adam and Eve* III, 16.10; 18:2). The place where they deposited Adam's body was Golgotha, where Christ later died on the cross (see *Cave of Treasures* 21a.1–2).[29]

A related document, *Book of the Bee* 30, says that the rod of Adam, passed down through the patriarchal line, came to Judah, who gave it in pledge to Tamar (see Genesis 38:18, 25). Because of the wars in which Judah became involved, "an angel took the rod, and laid it in the Cave of Treasures in the mount of Moab, until Midian was built. There was in Midian a man upright and righteous before God, whose name was Yathrô (Jethro). When he was feeding his flock on the mountain, he found the cave and took the rod by divine agency; and with it he fed his sheep until his old age. When he gave his daughter to Moses, he said to him, 'Go in, my son, take the rod, and go forth to thy flock.' When Moses had set his foot upon the threshold of the door, an angel moved the rod, and it came out of its own free will towards Moses."[30] After Moses, Phineas brought the rod into the land of Canaan and "hid the rod in the desert, in the dust at the gate of Jerusalem, where it remained until our Lord Christ was born. And He, by the will of

His divinity, shewed the rod to Joseph the husband of Mary, and it was in his hand when he fled to Egypt with our Lord and Mary, until he returned to Nazareth."[31]

This Christian tale probably derives from the Jewish tradition about the rod. According to *Pirqe Rabbi Eliezer* 40 and *Jasher* 77:38–51, Adam passed his staff to Enoch, from whom it descended to Noah, Shem, Abraham, Isaac, Jacob, and Joseph, eventually coming into the possession of Jethro, who planted it in his garden. When Moses discovered it there, it was covered with written characters.

Sacred Relics and Writings from the Temple

According to Jewish tradition, five things were hidden away when the first temple was destroyed, to be restored when the Lord would rebuild the temple: the sacred fire, the ark, the menorah, the Spirit, and the cherubim (*Midrash Rabbah* Numbers 15.10).[32] The idea of the temple implements, including the two tables of the law, being hidden in the earth before the destruction of Jerusalem—later to be restored—is also found in *2 Baruch* 6:7–9. Where the Midrash and *2 Baruch* differ is in who hid them.

In one account, King Josiah, in preparation for the exile prophesied in Deuteronomy 28:36, hid away the ark, the anointing oil, the jar of manna, Aaron's rod, and the coffer sent as a gift by the Philistines when returning the ark (see TB *Horayot* 12a; TB *Kerithot* 5b). *Midrash Rabbah* Numbers 18:23 indicates that the rod of Aaron was "held in the hand of every king until the Temple was destroyed, and then it was [divinely] hidden away. That same staff also is destined to be held in the hand of the King Messiah."[33]

According to *4 Baruch* 3:7–19, it was Jeremiah who hid the temple vessels in the earth. A similar story in *Lives of the Prophets* 2:11–19 indicates that Jeremiah caused the ark of the covenant and its contents to be swallowed up in a rock. The tablets of the law will remain there, inaccessible until the day of resurrection, when they will be placed on Mount Sinai.

In 2 Maccabees 2:1–8, we read that Jeremiah took the tabernacle, the ark, and the incense altar and hid them in a cave in Nebo, the mountain Moses ascended, to be brought forth after the gathering of Israel from its captivity. According to *ʾAbot de Rabbi Nathan* 41, eight things were made during the creation and later hidden away: the tent of meeting and its furnishings, the ark and the broken tables of the commandments in it, the jar of manna, the cruse of anointing oil, the rod (of Moses), Aaron's staff (with its almond blossoms and flowers), the priestly vestments, and the vestments of the anointed priest.

According to Rabbi Nahman, the ark was hidden away in the chamber of the temple's wood shed: "It happened to a certain priest who was whiling away his time that he saw a block of pavement that was different from the others. He came and informed his fellow, but before he could complete his account his soul departed. Thus they knew definitely that the ark was hidden there" (TB *Yoma* 54a).

In another account, Nabuzaradan, captain of Nebuchadnezzar's army, granted the high priest Simeon's request to give him the ark containing the records. Simeon gathered the ashes of the books, laid them in a pot in a vault, put fire in a censer of brass, threw incense on it, and hung it in the vault over the place where the ashes of the books lay (see *Conflict of Adam and Eve* IV, 10.16–17). A similar story is found in *Book of the Rolls* f.137a, where we read that at the time Nebuchadnezzar took Jerusalem, Simeon asked permission to take "the old writings," which he carried into captivity with him. En route "he saw a well in his way among the borders of the West; and he laid the writings in it, and put with them a bronze vase, filled with glowing coals, and in it sweet smelling incense; he covered up this well, and went to Babylon."[34] Later, according to *Book of the Rolls* f.138a, Ezra recovered the vase full of fire, incense, and writings but found the writings faded and had to restore them by revelation.

Other accounts also credit Ezra with recovery of the temple treasures. According to *Chronicles of Jerahmeel* 77:4–9, an old man led Ezra, Nehemiah, and the elders to a large stone sunk into the Mount of Olives. They rolled the stone away, and some young priests descended into the pit. The priests found something like the lees of oil, like mud and honey, which they placed on the altar, whereupon fire burst out. But the ark was not there; it had been hidden by Jeremiah in a cave on Mount Nebo, along with other items, including tables of stone.

In Jewish tradition, the prophet Elijah will in the last days reveal to Israel the hiding place of the ark of the covenant, the vial of manna, the seven-branched menorah, and the vial of anointing oil.[35]

The Samaritans also have traditions about the hiding of the temple relics. When the Taheb (Messiah) comes, he will rediscover the tabernacle and its furnishings, including the staff of Moses, the pot of manna, and the ark, which were hidden up anciently.[36] In the time of Christ, a man led a Samaritan group up Mount Gerizim, promising to discover the tabernacle vessels. Pilate, recognizing this as a messianic claim (with political implications), intervened (see Josephus, *Antiquities of the Jews* 18.4.1). Interestingly, the Taheb, according to the poem attributed to the fourteenth-century-A.D. Samaritan scholar Abisha ben Pinhas, will be given new scripture.[37]

A Samaritan document in the British Museum concerning the death of Moses declares "that the Favour will become hidden, and the sanctuary of the Lord will be hidden away, and Mount Garizim will be defiled."[38]

The hiding of sacred implements is reflected in the Jewish story of Jacob hiding the garments of Adam and Eve in a hole in the ground to keep them from the unworthy Esau (see *Pirqe Rabbi Eliezer* 24). Similarly, the Bible indicates that the sword David took from Goliath was evidently hidden behind the ephod in the tabernacle, whence David later retrieved it when fleeing from Saul (see 1 Samuel 21:9).

Among the sacred relics that have been concealed are disused portions of temples. The earliest textual reference is from the Apocrypha, where we read of the events that followed the Seleucids' desecration of the altar in the Jerusalem temple: "And when as they consulted what to do with the altar of burnt offerings, which was profaned; They thought it best to pull it down, lest it should be a reproach to them, because the heathen had defiled it: wherefore they pulled it down, And laid up the stones in the mountain of the temple in a convenient place, until there should come a prophet to shew what should be done with them. Then they took whole stones according to the law, and built a new altar according to the former" (1 Maccabees 4:44–47 KJV).

There is also archaeological evidence for the practice of pulling down altars. During excavations at ancient Beer-Sheba, Yohanan Aharoni's team found neatly carved stones from a dismantled altar built into the wall of a storeroom. All the stones were recovered and the altar was reconstructed on the site. Of the four horned altars in the corner, only one was damaged—its horned projection had been broken off.

Aharoni also uncovered a similar situation at the site of Arad, where two worn-out *maṣṣebot*, or covenant altars, that once stood in the holy of holies of the Israelite temple built on the site had been built into the back wall of the room and concealed with plaster. A third *massebah*, obviously newer and in virtually pristine condition, was found in situ in the holy of holies itself.

Summary

This chapter has shown that the ancients commonly concealed sacred relics. Of particular significance for the story of the Book of Mormon is that these relics were sometimes deposited with books and that, like the interpreters Moroni placed with the plates, these relics are sometimes said to have been stones.

Notes

1. That the sword of Laban was a symbol of royalty among the Nephites has been discussed by several scholars. See Todd R. Kerr, "Ancient Aspects of Nephite Kingship in the Book of Mormon," *Journal of Book of Mormon Studies* 1/1 (1992): 85–118; Brett L. Holbrook, "The Sword of Laban as a Symbol of Divine Authority and Kingship," *Journal of Book of Mormon Studies* 2/1 (1993): 39–72; Daniel N. Rolph, "Prophets, Kings, and Swords: The Sword of Laban and Its Possible Pre-Laban Origin," *Journal of Book of Mormon Studies* 2/1 (1993): 73–79.

2. See Esther Rabbai 2:1, in Raphael Patai, *The Children of Noah: Jewish Seafaring in Ancient Times* (Princeton, N. J.: Princeton University Press, 1998), 117.

3. See Bernard Grossfeld, *The Two Targums of Esther,* vol. 18 of *The Aramaic Bible* (Collegeville, Minn.: Liturgical Press, 1991), 30–31. The Aramaic *targumim* (translations) are translations of the books of the Bible with additional material added as an explanation.

4. See "Heavy Metal: Tiberias Yields Islamic Treasure," *Biblical Archaeology Review* (January/February 1999): 18.

5. The English translation used here is taken from Florentino García Martínez, *The Dead Sea Scrolls Translated,* 2nd ed. (Leiden: Brill, 1996), 461–63.

6. John C. Reeves, *Heralds of That Good Realm: Syro-Mesopotamian Gnosis and Jewish Traditions* (Leiden: E. J. Brill, 1996), 152–53.

7. Ibid., 142.

8. See the discussion in chapter 3 of this volume, "Hiding Records in Boxes."

9. He is mentioned in Joshua 15:17; Judges 1:13; 3:9, 11; 1 Chronicles 4:13.

10. For more on glowing stones, see the appendix to this volume, "Glowing Stones in Ancient and Medieval Lore."

11. Sapphires and emeralds are both forms of corundum.

12. Moses Gaster, *The Asatir: The Samaritan Book of the "Secrets of Moses"* (London: Royal Asiatic Society, 1927), 198.

13. Ibid., 193–94.

14. See Montague Rhodes James, *The Apocryphal New Testament* (Oxford: Clarendon, 1955), 565.

15. See Ernest A. Wallis Budge, *Amulets and Superstitions* (London: Oxford University Press, 1930), 247.

16. See Yigael Yadin, *Bar Kochba* (London: Widenfeld, 1971), 217–21.

17. See Budge, *Amulets and Superstitions,* 98, citing George Smith, *Assyrian Discoveries: An Account of Explorations and Discoveries on the Site of Nineveh, during 1873 and 1874* (New York: Scribner, Armstrong, 1875), 78.

18. See ibid., 99.

19. See H. Curtis Wright, "Metal Documents in Stone Boxes," in *By Study and Also By Faith,* ed. John M. Lundquist and Stephen D. Ricks (Salt Lake City: Deseret Book and FARMS, 1990), 288–89, and his notes.

20. See C. Leonard Woolley, "Babylonian Prophylactic Figures," *Journal of the Royal Asiatic Society* (October 1926): 689f.

21. See George Frederick Kunz, *The Curious Lore of Precious Stones* (New York: Halcyon House, 1913), 189, citing Wieri, *De Prestigiis Demonum* (Basileae, 1563), 121.

22. See ibid., 220, citing Bernard de Montfaucon, *Les monumens de la monarchie Françoise qui Comprennent L'histoire de France* (Paris, J. M. Gandouin: 1729), 15.

23. See Kunz, *Curious Lore of Precious Stones,* 221–22.

24. See ibid., 222, citing Akerman, 10.

25. Ibid., citing Sir Thomas Browne, *Hydrotaphia, or Urn Burial,* ed. F. L. Huntley (New York: Meredith, 1966). Originally published in 1658. The Browne piece was an addition to John Aubrey, *Miscellanies upon Various Subjects* (London: Reeves and Turner, 1890), 244.

26. W. M. Thackston Jr., trans., *The Tales of the Prophets of al-Kisa'i* (Boston: Twayne, 1978), 81–82. Seth's possession of the coffer passed to him by Adam is also noted on page 85, in connection with the fact that "the guardianship passed to Seth, and the sons of his father obeyed him."

27. S. C. Malan, *The Book of Adam and Eve, also called The Conflict of Adam and Eve with Satan* (London: Williams and Norgate, 1882), 33.

28. Margaret Dunlop Wilson, *Apocrypha Arabica* (London: C. J. Clay, 1901), 18.

29. In a variant tradition, found in the Armenian Christian *Penitence of Adam,* God himself sealed Adam's tomb with a threefold seal at the time of the patriarch's death. See Michael E. Stone, *The Penitence of Adam* (Louvain: Peeters, 1981), 20.

30. Ernest A. Wallis Budge, *The Book of the Bee* (Oxford: Clarendon, 1886), 50.

31. Ibid., 51. The text further notes that the rod subsequently served as one of the pieces of wood used in the construction of the cross on which Christ was crucified.

32. This tradition is the basis of Revelation 11:15–19.

33. H. Freedman and Maurice Simon, eds., *Midrash Rabbah* (London: Soncino Press, 1961), 6:743. Originally published in 1939.

34. Wilson, *Apocrypha Arabica,* 53.

35. See Pereq Rabbi Yoshiyahu, in Adolph Jellinek, *Bet ha Midrasch,* 3rd ed. (Jerusalem: Wahrmann, 1967), 6:115; Meir Friedmann, *Mekhilta deRabbi Yishma*ᶜ*el* (Vinah: Meir Ish Shalom, 1870), 80.

36. See John Bowman, "Early Samaritan Eschatology," *The Journal of Jewish Studies* 6/2 (1955): 63, 70; John Bowman, *Samaritan Documents Relating to Their History, Religion and Life* (Pittsburgh:

Pickwick Press, 1977), 42, 89–90, 264, 267, 271 n. 10; Alan D. Crown, *The Samaritans* (Tübingen: Mohr, 1989), 272, 273–74; James Alan Montgomery, *The Samaritans: The Earliest Jewish Sect* (New York: Ktav Publishing House, 1968), 248 (originally published in 1907).

37. See Matthew Black, *The Scrolls and Christian Origins* (New York: Charles Scribner's Sons, 1961), 159.

38. From BM 1732A. See Gaster, *The Asatir*, 309.

chapter 7

Mountain Repositories

Convenient to the village of Manchester, Ontario county, New York, stands a hill of considerable size, and the most elevated of any in the neighborhood. On the west side of this hill, not far from the top, under a stone of considerable size, lay the plates, deposited in a stone box. This stone was thick and rounding in the middle on the upper side, and thinner towards the edges, so that the middle part of it was visible above the ground, but the edge all around was covered with earth. (JS—H 1:51)

The Nephites consistently hid their sacred records in hills. Ammaron hid the records in the hill Shim (see Mormon 1:2–3; compare 4 Nephi 1:48–49), whence Mormon retrieved them (see Mormon 4:23). Mormon subsequently hid all but his abridgment of the records in the hill Cumorah and passed the abridgment on to his son Moroni (see Mormon 6:6). Moroni then hid the abridgment in the New York hill that came to be known as Cumorah.[1]

Chapter 6, "Hiding Sacred Relics," noted some stories in which sacred writings and other relics were hidden in mountains. Kenaz, for example, is said to have placed books and stones engraved with the names of the twelve tribes on a mountain beside an altar, as God commanded him (see *Pseudo-Philo* 26:1–15; *Chronicles of Jerahmeel* 57:11–21). Jeremiah is said to have hidden the sacred implements of the temple in a cave on mount Nebo (see 2 Maccabees 2:1–8), though according to other stories he hid them in a cave on the Mount of Olives (see *Chronicles of Jerahmeel* 77:4–9) or, in Samaritan tradition, on Mount Gerizim.

In one of the texts discovered at Nag Hammadi in 1945 (See XI,*3 Allogenes* 68.16–31), an angel instructed Allogenes to write in a book what the angel dictated and to place it "upon a mountain."[2] Two of the Christian Gnostic books found in Egypt, the *Pistis Sophia* and the books of *Jeu*, are said to have been dictated to Enoch in paradise and then hidden on Mount Ararat, where Noah found them after the flood.[3] The *Book of the Invisible Great Spirit* was similarly concealed on Mount Charax.[4] The *Cologne Mani Codex* cites portions of the now lost *Apocalypse of Enosh*, in which an angel brought Enosh to a mountain and instructed him to write on bronze tablets and hide his record.[5]

Masonic tradition holds that the Lord revealed secrets to Enoch atop a mountain and that Enoch, knowing of the forthcoming flood, sought a way to preserve this knowledge. On the top of a high mountain, he erected one pillar of marble and another of brass, and on these pillars he engraved the sciences for the benefit of future generations. He also inscribed his revelation on a gold plate that he concealed in a temple he constructed inside a mountain.[6]

The eleventh-century Arab chronographer al-Thaʿlabi wrote of a group of Jews fleeing persecution who buried a copy of the Torah (law of Moses) in a mountain.[7] Their choice for a burial spot may have been influenced by the fact that Moses had received the law on a mountain.

It is reported that in 1898 in the southern Russian German-speaking settlement of Franzfeld, the sons of Jacob Schaub found twelve small gold plates in a hill, each inscribed with a different animal representing each of the twelve months of the year.[8]

The Tables of the Law

When the Israelites were assembled at Sinai, "the Lord said unto Moses, Come up to me into the mount, and be there: and I will give thee tables of stone, and a law, and commandments which I have written; that thou mayest teach them. And Moses rose up, and his minister Joshua: and Moses went up into the mount of God" (Exodus 24:12–13).

Terrence L. Szink, of the Department of Ancient Scripture at Brigham Young University, suggests that the tables of stone given to Moses on the mountain may not have been prepared by God at that time but may have been hidden there earlier, under the Lord's direction, by a prophet charged with protecting the ancient records.[9] The fact that the two tables had been "written with the finger of God" (see Exodus 31:18; 32:15–16; compare Deuteronomy 4:13; 5:22; 9:9–11) does not mean that he wrote them at the time that he spoke with Moses on the mount. After Moses broke the two tables (see Exodus 32:19; Deuteronomy 9:15–17), the Lord did not simply write up another set but had Moses prepare the new tables (see Exodus 34:1, 4). Moses then spent forty days with the Lord, during which time the prophet, not the Lord, wrote on the tables (see Exodus 34:28–29).

Exodus 34:1 JST informs us that the Lord wrote on the second set of tablets (as in Deuteronomy 10:1–5) but left out the covenant of priesthood contained on the first tablets. Szink notes that Abraham spoke of the covenant of priesthood (see Abraham 1:1–4), suggesting that this was the same record Moses originally received on the mountain. In one passage, Abraham noted that "the records of the fathers, even the patriarchs, concerning the right of Priesthood, the Lord my God preserved in mine own hands; therefore a knowledge of the beginning of the creation, and also of the planets, and of the stars, as they were made known unto the fathers, have I kept even unto this day, and I shall endeavor to write some of these things" (Abraham 1:31). But when Abraham introduced the information about the heavenly bodies and the creation (see Abraham 3:1–5:21), he noted that he had the urim and thummim, by which the Lord told him about these other worlds (see Abraham 3:4). Szink sees this as evidence that Abraham, like Joseph Smith, had to use the urim and thummim to translate the records of his ancestors, because they were written in a language that was unknown to him. It remains possible, however, that the instrument simply gave him additional information, as it did to Joseph Smith when he sought divine revelation.

Noting that the interpreters, or urim and thummim, were associated with—and even sealed up with—records in the cases of Joseph Smith (see JS—H 1:34–35, 52, 59) and the brother of Jared (see Ether 3:21–24, 27–28; 4:5–6; see also Mosiah 8:12–14; 21:27–28; 28:11–17), Szink suggests that Moses also received the urim and thummim with the records on Mount Sinai. The sacred oracle, first mentioned in Exodus 28:30, appears in such a way as to hint that it already existed before the high priestly clothing with which it became associated was made.

Szink's views are partially supported by several early Jewish sources. According to *Pirqe Rabbi Eliezer* 46, the tablets of the law given to Moses atop the mountain were heavenly in origin. When Moses was told to prepare a second set of tablets, God created a quarry of sapphires from which he cut the new stones.[10] Significantly, the revelation is said to have taken place at a cave, which may have been the hiding place of the tablets. According to *ʾAbot de Rabbi Nathan* 2, the tables containing the commandments were inscribed and put away atop the mountain during the six days of creation.

Midrash Rabbah Exodus 40:2 notes that as Moses was about to descend from the mountain, God "brought him the book of Adam and showed him all generations that would arise from Creation to Resurrection, each generation and its kings, its leaders, and prophets."[11] According to *Midrash Rabbah* Genesis 24:3–4, the book in Psalm 69:28 from which one is blotted out is the Book of the Generations of Adam mentioned in Genesis 5, which contains the names of all the souls God made. The text notes that the royal Messiah would not come until all these had been born. This story is partially confirmed by one of the Nag Hammadi texts, V,5 *Apocalypse of Adam* 85.3–24, which notes that the words of God as revealed to Adam and passed on to his son Seth are to be found "on a high mountain, upon a rock of truth."[12]

A Falasha text, the *Death of Moses,* also suggests that the tablets already existed when Moses met God on the mount: "Moses ascended Mt. Sinai to pray to God and opened the Torah to read therefrom. He found five sayings which he was unable to understand. God called unto Moses and said to him: 'I wrote them with mine own hand, and I understand their meaning. Hearken and understand as I tell thee the first word.'"[13]

Additional support for Szink's theory comes from a study by Geo Widengren in *The Ascension of the Apostle and the*

Heavenly Book, wherein he demonstrates that Moses' receipt of the tables of the law on the mountain (see Exodus 24:12) parallels Mesopotamian stories in which kings ascend to heaven to receive the "tablets of destiny" or "tablets of wisdom." In the Babylonian creation epic (Enuma Elish IV, 121–22), these tablets, "sealed" and fastened to the chest like the biblical urim and thummim, grant kingly power to the god Kingu and his successor, Marduk.[14] Reminding us that some scholars believe that the urim and thummim were kept in a bag on the high priest's breast,[15] Widengren cites a text in which Enmeduranki, king of Sippar, is called into the assembly of the gods, placed "on a great golden throne," and given "the tablets of the gods, the bag with the mystery of heaven [and earth]."[16] He further notes the Samaritan tradition that Moses was seated on a great throne in the presence of angels while writing the law.[17] The Arabic version of the *Tabula Smaragdina* declares that the sacred book, written in Syriac, the "primordial language," was found with "an old man sitting on a throne of gold."[18] Wiedengren also suggests that the "testimony" given to the Israelite king by the high priest at the time of his anointing (see 2 Kings 11:12) consists of the tablets of the law.[19]

Records Hidden in Caves

In modern times, several caches of documents have been found hidden in caves. The most famous, of course, are the Dead Sea Scrolls, which were found in eleven caves in cliffs overlooking the northern end of the Dead Sea, not far from the city of Jericho. Only a few large scrolls were recovered, but fragments of more than eight hundred documents were found. The earliest date to the second century B.C. and the latest to the first century A.D. They include books of the Bible, Pseudepigrapha, and other writings.

During 1951 and 1952, another cache of documents was found in two of four large adjacent caves in a canyon known as Wadi Murabbaʿat, south of where the Dead Sea Scrolls were discovered. Among the finds was the earliest Hebrew papyrus found in the Holy Land, containing a list of names and numbers from the seventh or eighth century B.C., written atop a letter of a slightly earlier date. Parts of several books of the Bible were also found, along with documents from the time of the Bar Kokhba revolt (A.D. 132–35). In 1955, in another cave about a kilometer away, a scroll of the minor prophets was found. This scroll contained biblical books from the middle of Joel to the beginning of Zechariah, in the traditional order.

At the same time (1952), several caves in Naḥal Ḥever and Naḥal Ṣeʾēlîm, to the south, were found to have caches of leather and papyrus documents, including fragments of biblical texts, dating from the first century B.C. to the second century A.D. In 1958 a number of Old and New Testament books and other documents were found at Khirbet Mird, the ruins of ancient Hyrcania, on a peak west of where the Dead Sea Scrolls were found. The texts were probably from the Christian monastery that formerly stood on the site. Four years later a cache of fourth-century-B.C. papyri, many with their seals intact, was found in the ʾAbu Shinjah Cave in Wadi Daliyah, about fourteen miles north of Jericho and twelve miles west of the Jordan River. Written in Samaritan, the earliest documents were written circa 375 B.C., while the latest was dated 18 March 335 B.C. They had evidently been brought to the cave by Samaritans fleeing the invading Greek army of Alexander the Great in 331 B.C. Skeletons of about two hundred people were found in the cave, and archaeologists surmised that the people were suffocated by the smoke of a fire set at the entrance to the cave.

In about 1900 at Tuen Huang, in Chinese Turkestan, some fifteen to twenty thousand manuscripts dating between the sixth and seventh centuries A.D. were found after having been walled up in a cave since about A.D. 1035. The documents were written in Chinese, Tibetan, Sanskrit, and other languages.[20] To this day, a religious group known as the Yezîdîs, who live in the Kurdistan area of Turkey, keep their most sacred texts in a box hidden in a cave.[21]

Ancient traditions also indicate that caves were used as repositories for records. Chapter 5, "Angels as Guardians of Hidden Books," noted the Jewish belief that Adam hid the *Sepher ha-Razim* (Book of Mysteries) in a cave, the location of which was revealed to Enoch in a dream, and that Enoch read the book and hid it up again. The eleventh-century Arab chronographer al-Thaᶜlabi noted that an individual had found, in a cave in the Hadramaut region of southern Arabia, ancient gold tablets containing the history of a vanished empire. No one could decipher the text until a traveling artisan was consulted.[22]

In the pseudepigraphic *Narrative of Zosimos*, also known as the *History of the Rechabites*, we read that Zosimos, during his visit to the Rechabites, saw them write their history on stone tablets, which they then gave him (see Greek 7:1; 15:8; Syriac 8:1; 16:8). Chapters 18 through 20 of the Greek version indicate that when he returned to the cave in which he dwelt, Zosimos deposited the tablets beside the altar. When the devil came seeking to destroy him and the book, Zosimos warded him off with prayer. This is a remarkable parallel to the story of Joseph Smith, who was attacked by the devil during his prayer in the sacred grove (see JS—H 1:15–16) and later by men seeking to steal the Book of Mormon plates.

The Cave of Treasures

Chapter 6, "Hiding Sacred Relics," noted a number of early Christian stories in which Adam kept relics from the Garden of Eden in a mountaintop cavern called the Cave of Treasures. In *Conflict of Adam and Eve* I, 31.9–10, the cave is said to be a place "of concealment." After his death, Adam was buried in this cave, along with the treasures.[23] Some accounts indicate that sacred records were concealed in the cave.

In *Testament of Adam* 3:6, Seth declared that he had written the testament, adding, "And we sealed the testament and we put it in the cave of treasures with the offerings Adam had taken out of Paradise, gold and myrrh and frankincense. And the sons of kings, the magi, will come and get them, and they will take them to the son of God, to Bethlehem of Judea, to the cave."[24]

One of the Nag Hammadi texts, the *Gospel of the Egyptians* 68.1–20, known from two copies (III,2 and IV,2), declares: "This is the book which the great Seth wrote, and placed in high mountains on which the sun has not risen . . . The great Seth wrote this book . . . He placed it in the mountain that is called Charaxio, in order that, at the end of the times and the eras . . . it may come forth."[25] A companion text, V,5 *Apocalypse of Adam* 85.3–24, notes that the words of God revealed to Adam and passed on to his son Seth are to be found "on a high mountain, upon a rock of truth."[26]

According to *In Matthaeum Homiliae* II, a fifth-century document falsely attributed to St. Chrysostom, Seth, the son of Adam, wrote a book that was kept in a cave on a mountain named Victorialis.[27] A similar story is told in *Pseudo-Dionysius*, which mentions a book containing revelations from Adam to Seth that was kept on Mount Triumphalis,[28] where it was studied until the time of the Magi, who learned of Christ from its contents.[29]

Jewish tradition also suggests that Adam's book was hidden in a cave. In *Zohar* Genesis 117b–118a, Rabbi Jose walked with Rabbi Judah and discussed points of the law of Moses. When they arrived at a certain place,

> Suddenly R. Jose said: "It comes to my memory that in this place I was once sitting with my father and he said to me: 'When you will reach the age of sixty years you are destined to find in this place a treasure of sublime wisdom.' I have lived to reach that age, and I have not found the treasure, but I wonder if the words spoken by us just now are not the wisdom that he meant. He further said to me: 'When the celestial flame reaches the spaces between your fingers, it will escape from you.' I asked him: 'How do you know this?' He replied: 'I know it by the two birds that passed over your head.'" At this point R. Jose left him and entered a cavern, at the farther end of which he found a book hidden in the cleft of a rock. He brought it out and caught sight of seventy-two tracings of letters which had been given to Adam the first man, and by means of which he knew all the wisdom of the supernal holy beings, and all those beings that abide behind the mill with turns behind the veil among the supernal ethereal essences, as well as all that is destined to happen in the world until the day when a cloud will arise on the side of the West and darken the world. R. Jose then called R. Judah and the two began to examine the book. No sooner had they studied two or three of the letters than they found themselves contemplating that supernal wisdom. But as soon as they began to go into the book more deeply and to discuss it, a fiery flame driven by a tempestuous wind struck their hands, and the book vanished from them. R. Jose wept, saying, "Can it be, Heaven forefend, that we are tainted with some sin? Or are we unworthy to possess the knowledge contained therein?" When they came to R. Simeon they told

> him what had occurred. He said to them: "Were you, perhaps, scrutinising those letters which deal with the coming of the Messiah?" They answered: "We cannot tell, as we have forgotten everything." R. Simeon continued: "The Holy One, blessed be He, does not desire that so much should be revealed to the world, but when the days of the Messiah will be near at hand, even children will discover the secrets of wisdom and thereby be able to calculate the millennium; at that time it will be revealed to all, as it is written, 'For then will I turn to the people a pure language, etc.,' the term *az* (then) referring to the time when the community of Israel will be raised from the dust and the Holy One will make her stand upright; then 'will I turn to the peoples a pure language, that they may all call upon the Lord, to serve him with one consent.'"[30]

Dead Sea Caves

Even before the 1947 discovery of the Dead Sea Scrolls a few miles south of Jericho, there were reports of ancient records hidden in the caves of that region. The fourth-century Christian historian Eusebius reported that the church father Origen (A.D. 184–253) had found an ancient translation of the Book of Psalms "in a jar near Jericho."[31]

In A.D. 805 the Nestorian Syriac patriarch of Seleucia, Timotheus I, wrote to Sergius, metropolitan of Elam, that he had heard from converted Jews that an Arab hunter had found Hebrew scrolls ten years earlier in a cave near Jericho. The Arab hunter told some Jews from Jerusalem, who went to the cave and removed a large number of biblical and other Jewish texts. One of the converted Jews told Timotheus that they had found more than two hundred psalms of David and that some of the texts included the passages cited in Matthew 2:23; 1 Corinthians 2:9; and Galatians 3:13 that were missing from the New

Testament. The patriarch, knowing of the tradition that Jeremiah had buried sacred temple implements prior to the Babylonian attack on Jerusalem in 587 B.C., assumed that the newly discovered books had been placed in the cave by Jeremiah or by his scribe, Baruch.[32]

In 1878 a Jerusalem merchant, Moses Wilhelm Shapira, learned of some Arabs who, fleeing authorities, hid out in a cave in Wadi Mujib, to the east of the Dead Sea. These Arabs reported finding a number of old bundles of rags containing dark leather strips cut from scrolls with very faint writing on them. Shapira purchased fifteen strips. The inked text on the strips, written in paleo-Hebrew script, contained portions of the book of Deuteronomy, mingled with extracts from other books of the Pentateuch, though with some differences from the Masoretic Hebrew text. Shapira took the scrolls to Europe, where they were pronounced fraudulent, mostly on the grounds that the writing disagreed in some particulars with the standard text. Shapira was humiliated in the press and even accused of being the forger. (A few years earlier, he had been duped by some Arabs into purchasing some fraudulent pottery with Moabite inscriptions.) Thinking that he could sell the parchment strips, he and his family had gone into debt in anicipation of the sale. Faced with the humiliation and the possibility of losing all, he committed suicide in March 1884.

The discovery of the Dead Sea Scrolls six decades later prompted a reexamination of the Shapira story. Like the Shapira parchments, the Dead Sea Scrolls were found near the Dead Sea, some wrapped in cloth and some written in paleo-Hebrew script. In both cases, some of the biblical texts differed from what is found in later Hebrew Bibles. Unfortunately, it is no longer possible to examine the original Shapira documents (some were sold at auction), for their whereabouts is unknown.[33]

Companions of the Cave

Medieval (tenth to twelfth centuries) Karaite[34] and Muslim writers wrote of the Magarians (*Maghariya,* from the Arabic word for cave), whose writings were discovered in a cave. Significantly, one of the Dead Sea Scrolls, the *Damascus Document,* copies of which were found in caves, was first discovered in two medieval manuscripts, one from the tenth century and one from the twelfth century, in the genizah of the Old Cairo Karaite synagogue.[35] The Karaite scholar Jacob al-Qirqisani, writing of the founding of the Jewish Sadducean party, noted: "About that time there appeared also the teaching of a sect called Magarians, who were so called because their religious books were discovered in a cave *(maġār).* One of them was the Alexandrian [Philo], whose well-known book is the principal religious book of the Magarians. Next to it in rank is a small booklet called the Book of Yadduᶜa, also a fine work. Of their remaining books none is significant; most of them merely resemble idle tales."[36]

Some of the best studies of the Arabic traditions of the companions of the cave are from Professor Hugh Nibley.[37] He suggests that the companions, often identified with the Sleepers of Nejran, may have been the people of the Qumran community near the caves where the Dead Sea Scrolls were discovered. He further points out that the companions sealed up in a cave something called in Arabic *al-Raqim*, which some scholars have interpreted as engraved metal plates.[38] Nibley notes that one scholar suggested that the plates were sealed in a copper box. Of particular interest is the tradition Nibley cites from the Arab writer Baidawi, who wrote that the apostle Peter had discovered the *al-Raqim* documents and hidden them near Jerusalem.[39]

Summary

This chapter has shown that a number of ancient texts speak of books hidden on mountains or in caves, while some actual document finds have been made in caves or on mountain slopes. It is not surprising, therefore, to find such Book of Mormon personalities as Ammaron, Mormon, and Moroni hiding the sacred records of the Nephites on mountains. It was indeed an ancient practice.

Notes

1. Internal geographical evidence from the Book of Mormon suggests that the hill Cumorah in which Mormon hid the Nephite records was near the narrow neck of land. Scholars tend to place it in southern Mexico. The Book of Mormon does not tell us where Moroni buried the abridgment plates, but it is known that he sent Joseph Smith to the nearby New York hill to retrieve them, so we presume that this was the spot where Moroni deposited them.

2. James M. Robinson, *The Nag Hammadi Library,* 3rd ed. (San Francisco: HarperCollins, 1990), 500.

3. See Jean Doresse, *The Secret Books of the Egyptian Gnostics* (New York: Viking, 1960), 254.

4. See ibid.

5. See John C. Reeves, *Heralds of That Good Realm: Syro-Mesopotamian Gnosis and Jewish Traditions* (Leiden: E. J. Brill, 1996), 142. Reeves's translation and commentary on the *Apocalypse of Enosh* comprise chapter 5 of his book.

6. See George Oliver, *The Antiquities of Free-Masonry* (Lodgeton, Ky.: Morris, 1856), 58–59.

7. See al-Thaʿlabi, *Qiṣaṣ ʾal-ʾAnbiyaʾ* (Cairo: Mustafa al-Babi al-Halabi wa-Awladuhu, A. H., 1340), 242. Hugh Nibley was the first to bring this information to the attention of Latter-day Saints. I am grateful to Brian Hauglid for providing additional details from the Arabic text.

8. See P. Conrad Keller, *The German Colonies in South Russia, 1804–1904* (Saskatoon, Canada: Western Producer, 1968), 248, cited in Paul R. Cheesman, *Ancient Writing on Metal Plates: Archaeological Findings Support Mormon Claims* (Bountiful, Utah: Horizon, 1985), 52.

9. Szink's views, as expressed here, are from private communications. I am grateful for his permission to use his insights, which I suspect he will provide in greater detail at some future time.

10. *Zohar* Exodus 84a–b also indicates that the tablets were made of sapphire.

11. H. Freedman and Maurice Simon, eds., *Midrash Rabbah* (London: Soncino Press, 1961), 3:461. Originally published in 1939.

12. Robinson, *Nag Hammadi Library,* 286.

13. Wolf Leslau, *Falasha Anthology* (New Haven: Yale University Press, 1951), 107.

14. See Geo Widengren, *The Ascension of the Apostle and the Heavenly Book* (Uppsala, Sweden: University of Uppsala, 1950), 10, 12.

15. See ibid., 25–26.

16. Ibid., 7–8, 11.

17. See ibid., 46, citing the Samaritan text in M. Heidenheim, *Bibliotheca Samaritana* (Leipzig: Otto Schulze, 1896), 3:72.

18. Ibid., 77–79. Widengren refers to the Arabic text and German translation of two documents in J. Ruska, *Tabula Smaragdina. Ein Beitrag zur Geschichte der hermetischen Literatur* (Heidelberg: C. Winter, 1926), 112–14, 135. The *Tabula* and other Hermetic texts are discussed in chapter 2 of this volume, "Hidden Records."

19. See ibid., 25. Widengren further suggests that Ezekiel 28:12 be read, "Thou wast a sealer of the preserved (thing)," where the Hebrew word "would thus refer to the 'well-preserved' heavenly tablets" (ibid., 26).

20. See A. Dupont-Sommer, *The Dead Sea Scrolls: A Preliminary*

Survey (New York: Macmillan, 1952), 17; Doresse, *Secret Books of the Egyptian Gnostics*, 120–21.

21. See ibid., 151–52. The Yezîdî practice is described in chapter 3 of this volume, "Hiding Records in Boxes."

22. See al-Thaʿlabi, *Qiṣaṣ ʾal-ʾAnbiyaʾ*, 102. Hugh Nibley was the first to bring this information to the attention of Latter-day Saints. I am grateful to Brian Hauglid for confirming details of the story from the Arabic text.

23. See *Conflict of Adam and Eve* II, 8.8; 9.4, in S. C. Malan, *The Book of Adam and Eve, also called The Conflict of Adam and Eve With Satan* (London: Williams and Norgate, 1882), 114–17; Ernest A. Wallis Budge, *The Book of the Cave of Treasures* (London: Religious Tract Society, 1927), 73.

24. James H. Charlesworth, *The Old Testament Pseudepigrapha* (Garden City, N. Y.: Doubleday, 1983), 1:994.

25. Robinson, *Nag Hammadi Library*, 218.

26. Ibid., 286.

27. The text is noted by A. F. J. Klijn, *Seth in Jewish, Christian and Gnostic Literature* (Leiden: E. J. Brill, 1977), 57–58.

28. According to the *Cave of Treasures*, while the rest of the world fell into sin, Methuselah, Lamech, and Noah "remained in the 'Mountain of the Triumphant Ones'" (Budge, *Book of the Cave of Treasures*, 96).

29. See ibid., 59.

30. Harry Sperling and Maurice Simon, trans., *The Zohar* (New York: Rebecca Bennet Publications, 1958), 2:366–67. The biblical quotes are taken from Zephaniah 3:9.

31. Eusebius, *Ecclesiastical History* 6.16; see Philip Schaff and Henry Wace, *Nicene and Post-Nicene Fathers*, Second Series (Peabody, Mass.: Hendrickson, 1994), 1:263.

32. See Otto Eissfeldt, "Der gegenwärtige Stand der Erforschung der in Palästina new gefundenen hebräischen Handscriften," *Theologische Literaturzeitung* 74 (1949): 597–600; O. Braun in *Oriens Christianus* 1 (1901): 138–52, especially 304–5; G. R. Driver, *The*

Hebrew Scrolls from the Neighborhood of Jericho and the Dead Sea (London: Oxford University Press, 1951), 25–26; J. Hering, "Qumran à l'époque de Charlemagne," *Revue d'Histoire et de Philosophie Religieuse* 41 (1961): 159–60; Michael Baigent and Richard Leigh, *The Dead Sea Scrolls Deception* (New York: Summit Books, 1991), 229. For Eusebius's report of the discovery of a copy of the book of Psalms in a jar near Jericho in the early third century A.D., see chapter 3 of this volume, "Hiding Records in Boxes."

33. See John M. Allegro, *The Shapira Affair* (Garden City, N. Y.: Doubleday, 1965); "The Shapira Affair," *Biblical Archaeological Review* 4/5 (July/August 1979), 12–27.

34. The Karaites are a Jewish sect that rejected the writings of the pharisaic rabbis that characterize orthodox Judaism. Though clearly a minority, the Karaites have communities in various parts of the world even today. The Karaites were particularly prominent in the Middle Ages. Moses Taku, a thirteenth-century rabbinic scholar from Europe, said he learned from his teachers that the early Karaites hid texts in the ground and then claimed to have found ancient books. Perhaps they really did find such books, but the rabbis rejected their claims.

35. For a discussion of the genizah, see chapter 9 of this volume, "Books in the Treasury."

36. Jacob al-Qirqisani Abū Yūsuf Yaʿqūb ibn Isḥāk ibn Samʿawayh al-Qirqisānī, "History of Jewish sects," cited in Leon Nemoy, *Karaite Anthology: Excerpts from the Early Literature* (New Haven: Yale University Press, 1952), 50.

37. See Hugh W. Nibley, "Qumran and 'The Companions of the Cave,'" *Revue de Qumran* 5/18 (April 1965): 177–98; reprinted as "Qumran and the Companions of the Cave: The Haunted Wilderness," in *The Old Testament and Related Studies* (Salt Lake City: Deseret Book and FARMS, 1986), 253–84.

38. The Arabic term *raqq*, deriving from *raqîm* (thin), usually refers to paper or parchment on which one writes and is sometimes used for the writings of Moses or the Qur'an.

39. See Nibley, *Old Testament and Related Studies*, 255–56.

chapter 8

A Book That Does Not Wear Out

Now behold, it came to pass that I, Jacob, having ministered much unto my people in word, (and I cannot write but a little of my words, because of the difficulty of engraving our words upon plates) and we know that the things which we write upon plates must remain; But whatsoever things we write upon anything save it be upon plates must perish and vanish away; but we can write a few words upon plates, which will give our children, and also our beloved brethren, a small degree of knowledge concerning us, or concerning their fathers—Now in this thing we do rejoice; and we labor diligently to engraven these words upon plates, hoping that our beloved brethren and our children will receive them with thankful hearts, and look upon them that they may learn with joy and not with sorrow, neither with contempt, concerning their first parents. (Jacob 4:1–3)

The men whose writings came to be included in the Book of Mormon were very concerned that their records be preserved. Nephi recorded that "the Lord God promised unto me that these things which I write shall be kept and preserved, and handed down unto my seed, from generation to generation"

(2 Nephi 25:21), and Jacob wrote that Nephi told him to "preserve these plates and hand them down unto my seed, from generation to generation" (Jacob 1:3). Enos prayed "that the Lord God would preserve a record of my people, the Nephites; even if it so be by the power of his holy arm, that it might be brought forth at some future day unto the Lamanites. . . . I cried unto him continually . . . that he would preserve the records; and he covenanted with me that he would bring them forth unto the Lamanites in his own due time" (Enos 1:13, 15–16).

King Benjamin also spoke of preserving the plates (see Mosiah 1:4–5), and King Mosiah "took the plates of brass, and all the things which he had kept, and conferred them upon Alma [the younger] . . . and commanded him that he should keep and preserve them, and also keep a record of the people, handing them down from one generation to another" (Mosiah 28:20; see 28:11). Alma, in turn, handed the plates over to his son Helaman, commanding him to "keep them . . . and that ye preserve these interpreters" (Alma 37:21; see 37:8–12, 18–19).

Mormon wrote of the plates, "And they were handed down from king Benjamin, from generation to generation until they have fallen into my hands. And I, Mormon, pray to God that they may be preserved from this time henceforth. And I know that they will be preserved; for there are great things written upon them" (Words of Mormon 1:11). When Moroni delivered his father's abridgment to Joseph Smith in 1827, he told him "that if [he] would use all [his] endeavors to preserve them, until he, the messenger, should call for them, they should be protected" (JS—H 1:59).

Earlier chapters noted that the Nephites preserved their records by keeping them from the hands of the wicked, often by hiding them. Another method of preservation was the writing medium itself—metal plates that were less likely to deteriorate over time.

Alma, describing the plates containing the sacred Nephite records, told his son Helaman, "Behold, it has been prophesied by our fathers, that they should be kept and handed down from one generation to another, and be kept and preserved by the hand of the Lord until they should go forth unto every nation, kindred, tongue, and people. . . . And now behold, if they are kept they must retain their brightness; yea, and they will retain their brightness; yea, and also shall all the plates which do contain that which is holy writ" (Alma 37:4–5).

One of the Dead Sea Scrolls (4Q536) speaks of "writ[ing] the words of God in a book which does not wear out."[1] In the *Cologne Mani Codex*, an angel told Adam to "take and write these things which I reveal to you on most pure papyrus, incorruptible and insusceptible to worms."[2] In the fifth-century-A.D. Gnostic Christian Nag Hammadi text known as VI,6 *Discourse on the Eighth and Ninth,* Hermes told his son that the praise he sang to God should "be written in this imperishable book" (60.13–16).[3]

The indestructible nature of sacred records is reflected in the story of Brik-Yawar, an early copyist of the Mandaean book *Alma Rišaia Rba.* When Brik-Yawar received the scroll, he was afraid: "I took it and cast it into the water but the water did not accept it. Twice I threw it into the fire but the fire did not accept it."[4] When Shaq-Ziwa-Rba later received the document, he wrapped it until he arrived at his sanctuary. Opening the document (called "the treasure"), he discovered that it was "in the handwriting of the Lord-of-Greatness."[5]

One way of preserving texts written on perishable materials was to treat them with oil. Thus in an early Jewish text, the *Testament of Moses* 1:16–18, Moses instructed Joshua to preserve the books (parchments) he was leaving in his charge by anointing them with cedar (oil?) and depositing them in earthen jars until the day of recompense.[6] Similarly, the Roman writers Hemina and Pliny (see *Naturalis historia* 13.27.84–86) noted that the books of King Numa had been preserved by being treated with citrus oil and then buried in a stone coffin. A few centuries later, when the coffins containing the books and Numa's body were discovered, the corpse had decayed but the books were still in good condition.[7]

In the Greek *Kore Kosmou* 8, Hermes hid his books and addressed them, "Ye holy books, which have been written by my imperishable hands, and have been anointed with the drug of imperishability by me who am master over you, remain ye undecaying through all ages, and be ye unseen and undiscovered by all men who shall go to and fro on the plains of this land, until the time when Heaven, grown old, shall beget organisms worthy of you."[8]

Writing on Metallic Plates

In the Book of Mormon, records were frequently kept on metallic plates. This was done not only with Mormon's abridgment,[9] but also with the small and large plates of Nephi,[10] the brass plates obtained from Laban,[11] the records kept by the people of Limhi (see Mosiah 8:5), and Ether's twenty-four gold plates comprising the Jaredite history.[12]

One of the authors of the Book of Mormon, Jacob (son of Lehi), explained why the Nephites kept their secret records on metallic plates: "I cannot write but a little of my words, because of the difficulty of engraving our words upon plates," he declared, but "we know that the things which we write upon plates must remain" (Jacob 4:1). The durability of metal plates was also known in ancient Turkey. At the dedication or renovation of a house or temple, the Hittites deposited a piece of copper in the foundations and recited, "As this copper is firm and sound, so may the house (temple) be firm and sound."[13] The durability of metal records is also noted in the Falasha version of *5 Baruch*,[14] in which an angel accompanied Baruch on a tour of the heavenly Jerusalem:

> Then the angel took me to the east and showed me a golden column on which was engraved an inscription in a thin writing (brighter) than the sun, the moon, and the stars of the sky. I asked him: "What is this golden column and what is this writing on it (that has) the likeness of the sun, the moon, and the shining stars?" He answered me: "The names of the just are written for eternal life on this golden column, where they wax not old or corrupt." I said to him: "Are the names alone engraved upon it; are not the features of the face engraved upon it, too?" He answered and said: "All the features of the faces of the just are engraved for [eternal] life on this golden column, where they neither wax old nor become corrupt. They are engraved with a golden pen; the deeds of the sinners (are engraved) with an iron pen."[15]

A prominent late-nineteenth-century critic of the Book of Mormon wrote, "No such records were ever engraved upon golden plates, or any other plates, in the early ages."[16] Had he known Hebrew, he would have known that Isaiah 8:1 speaks of writing on a polished metal plate with an engraving tool; the terms are mistranslated "roll" and "pen" in the King James Bible. The critic also seems to have been unaware of the fact that the Apocrypha, which was included in about half the King James Bibles in the early nineteenth century, notes that a treaty between the Jews and the Romans in the second century B.C. was inscribed on bronze plates (see 1 Maccabees 8:22).

Other early texts speak of documents written on metallic plates. The *Cologne Mani Codex* says that an angel had appeared to Sethel (biblical Seth), son of Adam and told him secrets that he was to "write upon bronze tablets and store them up in the desert land.'"[17] A similar story is told in the *Apocalypse of Enosh*, cited in the *Cologne Mani Codex*. The angel instructed Seth's son Enosh (Enos in the King James Bible) to write "hidden things upon bronze tablets and deposit (them) in the wilderness." Enosh left these tablets "behind for the subsequent generations."[18]

Arab traditions also speak of documents written on metallic plates. The eleventh-century historian al-Thaᶜlabi wrote of a book sent to David from heaven. The book was sealed with gold and contained thirteen questions to be asked Solomon.[19] Al-Thaᶜlabi also mentioned gold tablets containing the history of a vanished empire. These tablets were found in a cave in the Hadramaut region of southern Arabia.[20] Writing about A.D. 1226, the Arab writer Idrîsî noted a treasure-hunting expedition of a few years before in which a group of Arabs dug into the pyramid of Mycerinus at Giza, Egypt. After six months of hard labor, they found the decayed remains of a man with some golden tablets inscribed in a language none of them understood. The tablets were taken for their gold content, suggesting that they were probably melted down.[21]

Ancient inscribed plates of gold, silver, copper, and lead have been found in such diverse places as China, Java (an Indonesian island), Thailand, India, Pakistan, Portugal, Spain, Italy, Greece, Morocco, Turkey, Iran, Lebanon, Crete, and Korea. A list of sixty-two such discoveries was compiled by Franklin S. Harris Jr. and published in 1957.[22]

The *Elder Edda*, an Old Norse text, contains a prophetic utterance known as the Völuspâ. In this text, the *Aesir* (gods) met "on Ida's plain, and of the mighty earth-encircler speak, and there to memory call their mighty deeds, and the supreme god's ancient lore. There shall again the wondrous golden tablets in the grass be found, which in days of old had possessed the ruler of the gods, and Fiölnir's race."[23]

Summary

The concept of preparing records that will last through many centuries, making them available to later generations, is ancient. Records written on clay (a common practice in what today constitutes the nations of Iraq, Syria, and Turkey) were sometimes baked to make them last longer and were occasionally kept in containers. Documents written on papyrus and parchment, which are considerably more perishable than clay, were often preserved in pottery jars or in tombs. Another method the ancients used to preserve documents was calling on divine guardians to keep the records safe.

Writing on metallic plates was yet another way to ensure the durability of records. Many of the metallic records discovered to date have been found in foundation deposits, often in stone boxes, as was the Book of Mormon. These include records left behind by Sumerian, Hittite, Assyrian, Babylonian, and Persian kings, as well as foundation deposits from other parts of the Near East and from Asia. Some of these are discussed in chapter 3, "Hiding Records in Boxes."[24]

Of all the metals, gold is the one least likely to decay over time. It does not oxidize like iron, silver, copper, or its alloys (bronze and brass), and it does not wear down like lead. Because it is a softer metal, it is easier to engrave, yet unlike lead, which is softer still, it does not readily lose its shape. Consequently, the most durable records would have been written on gold or gold alloy plates and hidden away in stone boxes, which are less likely to degrade than pottery.

Notes

1. Florentino García Martínez, *The Dead Sea Scrolls Translated,* 2nd ed. (Leiden: E. J. Brill, 1996), 264.

2. P. Colon. inv. nr. 4780, 49–50, in Ron Cameron and Arthur J. Dewey, *The Cologne Mani Codex* (Missoula, Mont.: Scholars Press, 1979), 39.

3. James M. Robinson, ed., *The Nag Hammadi Library,* 3rd ed. (San Francisco: HarperCollins, 1990), 325.

4. *Alma Rišaia Rba* 651–54, in E. S. Drower, *A Pair of Naṣoraean Commentaries (Two Priestly Documents)* (Leiden: E. J. Brill, 1963), 52.

5. *Alma Rišaia Rba* 251–57, in ibid., 72. The first-century-A.D. Jewish philosopher Philo, referring to "the Book of the Generation of the Real Man" in Genesis 5:1, notes that good men are not remembered by records in papers that can be destroyed by bookworms, but by the immortal book in which his virtuous actions are recorded (see *De Abrahamo* 11).

6. See James H. Charlesworth, *The Old Testament Pseudepigrapha* (Garden City, N.Y.: Doubleday, 1983), 1:927.

7. For further details, see chapter 3 of this volume, "Hiding Records in Boxes."

8. Geo Widengren, *The Ascension of the Apostle and the Heavenly Book* (Uppsala, Sweden: University of Uppsala, 1950), 82, where he includes the Greek text in a note.

9. See 3 Nephi 5:11; Mormon 2:18; 6:6; 8:5, 14; 9:33; Ether 4:4; 5:2.

10. See 1 Nephi 1:17; 6:1, 3, 6; 9:1–5; 10:1; 19:1–6; 2 Nephi 4:14; 5:4, 29–33; Jacob 1:1–4; 3:13–14; 4:1–3; 7:26–27; Jarom 1:2, 14–15; Omni 1:1, 3, 8, 11, 14, 18, 25, 30; Words of Mormon 1:3–6, 9–10; Mosiah 1:6, 16; 28:11; Alma 37:2; 44:24; 3 Nephi 5:10; 26:7, 11; 4 Nephi 1:19, 21; Mormon 1:4; 2:17–18; 6:6.

11. See 1 Nephi 3:3, 12, 24; 4:16, 24, 38; 5:10, 14, 18–19; 13:23; 19:21–22; 22:1, 30; 2 Nephi 4:2, 15; 5:12; Mosiah 1:3–4, 16; 10:16; 28:11, 20; Alma 37:3; 3 Nephi 1:2; 10:17.

12. See Mosiah 8:9, 11, 19; 21:27; 28:11; Alma 37:21; Ether 1:2, 4, and the preface to Ether.

13. Theodor H. Gaster, in his revision of James Frazer, *The New Golden Bough* (New York: Macmillan, 1963), 171. The concept of the burial of metallic records in palace and temple foundations is discussed in chapter 3 of this volume, "Hiding Records in Boxes."

14. The Falasha, the so-called "black Jews" of Ethiopia, borrowed the sacred book from their Christian neighbors, who have also preserved it.

15. Wolf Leslau, *Falasha Anthology* (New Haven: Yale University Press, 1951), 68.

16. Martin Thomas Lamb, *The Golden Bible: Or, the Book of Mormon. Is It From God?* (New York: Ward and Drummond, 1887), 11.

17. P. Colon. inv. nr. 4780, 50–52, in Cameron and Dewey, *Cologne Mani Codex*, 39–43.

18. John C. Reeves, *Heralds of That Good Realm: Syro-Mesopotamian Gnosis and Jewish Traditions* (Leiden: E. J. Brill, 1996), 142.

19. See al-Thaᶜlabi, *Qiṣaṣ ʾal-ʾAnbiyaʾ* (Cairo: Mustafa al-Babi al-Halabi wa-Awladuhu, A. H., 1340), 202.

20. See ibid., 102. Hugh Nibley was the first to bring this information to the attention of Latter-day Saints. I am grateful to Brian Hauglid for confirming details of the story from the Arabic text.

21. The story is reported in Ernest A. Wallis Budge, *The Book of the Dead* (New Hyde Park, N.Y.: University Books, 1960), 15 n. 5.

22. See Franklin S. Harris Jr., "Others Kept Records on Metal Plates, Too," *Instructor,* October 1957, 318–21. The list was later reprinted in a pamphlet entitled "Gold Plates Used Anciently" (Salt Lake City: The Church of Jesus Christ of Latter-day Saints, 1963); and in Mark E. Petersen, *Those Gold Plates!* (Salt Lake City: Bookcraft, 1979), 4–5. See also Paul R. Cheesman, *Ancient Writing on Metal Plates* (Bountiful, Utah: Horizon, 1985); and his "Ancient Writing on Metal Plates," *Ensign,* October 1979, 42–47. For a survey

of ancient writings on metallic plates with extensive bibliography, see H. Curtis Wright, "Metallic Documents of Antiquity," *BYU Studies* 10/4 (1970): 457–77.

23. Benjamin Thorpe, trans., *The Elder Edda of Saemund Sigfusson,* published with I. A. Blackwell, trans., *The Younger Edda of Snorre Sturleson* (London: Norroena Society, 1907), 8.

24. To date, the definitive article on the subject is H. Curtis Wright, "Ancient Burials of Metal Documents in Stone Boxes," in *By Study and Also By Faith,* ed. John M. Lundquist and Stephen D. Ricks (Salt Lake City: Deseret Book and FARMS, 1990). Wright is currently preparing an exhaustive bibliography of writings on metal plates.

chapter 9

Books in the Treasury

I went forth unto the treasury of Laban. And as I went forth towards the treasury of Laban, behold, I saw the servant of Laban who had the keys of the treasury. And I commanded him in the voice of Laban, that he should go with me into the treasury. And he supposed me to be his master, Laban, for he beheld the garments and also the sword girded about my loins. And he spake unto me concerning the elders of the Jews, he knowing that his master, Laban, had been out by night among them. And I spake unto him as if it had been Laban. And I also spake unto him that I should carry the engravings, which were upon the plates of brass, to my elder brethren, who were without the walls. (1 Nephi 4:20–24)

The earliest records possessed by the Nephites were the brass plates brought from Jerusalem. These plates had been kept in "the treasury of Laban," whence Nephi retrieved them. The concept of keeping books in a treasury, while strange to the modern mind, was a common practice anciently, and the term often denoted what we would today call a library.

Ezra 5:17–6:2 speaks of a "treasure house" containing written records. The Aramaic word rendered "treasure" in this passage is *ginzayyâ*, from the root meaning "to keep, hide" in both Hebrew and Aramaic. In Esther 3:9 and 4:7, the Hebrew word of the same origin is used to denote a treasury where money is kept. Also from this root is the Mishnaic Hebrew word *g^e^nîzāh*, denoting a repository for worn synagogue scrolls, and *gannāz*, meaning "archivist," or one in charge of records. The related Mandaean[1] word *ginza* has several meanings, one of which is "library." For example, in the *Thousand and Twelve Questions* 1.1.203 and 2.7.436 it refers to holy books.

The practice of placing worn-out scrolls in a synagogue treasury, which continues in Judaism today, is noted in Mishnah *Šhabbat* 9:6, where the verb meaning "hide" is from the same root as *genizah*. Sometimes the scrolls are buried in a cemetery. In Israel, it is the practice to actually hold a funeral service at the grave site for the scrolls. Hugh Nibley suggests that the Dead Sea Scrolls, hidden in caves, were actually a genizah.[2] Significantly, the Christian documents found at Nag Hammadi in Egypt were buried near a cemetery.

Several old *genizot* (the plural form of *genizah*) have been discovered. The most well-known was the sealed room uncovered in the ninth-century-A.D. Old Cairo synagogue in Egypt during renovations in 1890. In 1896, two Scottish ladies, Mrs. Agnes Smith Klewish and her sister, Mrs. Margaret Dunlop Wilson of Cambridge University, brought back from the genizah a page from an ancient Palestinian Talmud and a portion of a second-century-B.C. Hebrew text of Ecclesiasticus, or Ben-Sirach, previously known only from the Greek. They turned the materials over to Solomon Schechter, who read talmudic studies at Cambridge. Schechter thereafter went to Cairo, where he was taken to the genizah by the city's chief rabbi, Raphael ben Simon. He recovered many more manuscripts, most of them biblical documents, and sent back 164 boxes containing about 100,000 manuscript fragments for the Cambridge University Library. Cataloging the find took a full decade.

Meanwhile, an equal volume of manuscripts from the same source ended up at various other libraries, including the Bodleian at Oxford and the Jewish Theological Seminary in New York. In all, the Cairo collection included biblical, apocryphal, and Hebrew pseudepigraphic books, as well as Aramaic Targumim, biblical trilinguals (Hebrew/Aramaic/Greek), and other documents, including copies of a text (the *Zadokite Work,* or *Damascus Document*) of which copies were found among the Dead Sea Scrolls half a century later.

Another such synagogue genizah was recently discovered in Jerusalem. During the early 1960s, fourteen scrolls (biblical, sectarian, and apocryphal) were found at the site of Masada, overlooking the Dead Sea from the west. Two of the biblical scrolls were found in pits dug into the floor of a synagogue and covered with earth and stones.

Some documents have been kept securely in Middle Eastern monasteries. For example, a number of early copies of the Bible were discovered in the Greek Orthodox Saint Catherine's Monastery in the Sinai peninsula. The monastery is noted for its library, a portion of which was for a long time sealed off by plaster over the door.

Epiphanius (died A.D. 403) reported that Jewish converts to Christianity told him that the Gospel of John, as translated from Greek into Hebrew, was found in the Jewish "treasuries" at Tiberias, where it was secretly kept along with a copy of the Acts of the Apostles as translated from Greek into Hebrew (see *Panarion* 1.2.3, 6, 7–9; 4,1). One of his informants was a Josephus of Tiberias. This Josephus went to the "'gazophylacium' there which was sealed—'gaza' means 'treasure' in

Hebrew. As many had different notions about this treasury because of its seal, Josephus plucked up the courage to open it unobserved—and found no money, but books money could not buy. Browsing through them he found the Gospel of John, translated from Greek to Hebrew, as I said, and the Acts of the Apostles—as well as Matthew's Gospel, which is actually Hebrew."[3]

The Lord instructed the brother of Jared to "treasure up the things which ye have seen and heard, and show it to no man. And behold, when ye shall come unto me, ye shall write them and shall seal them up, that no one can interpret them; for ye shall write them in a language that they cannot be read" (Ether 3:21–22). Treasuring up and sealing up are parallel terms in this passage.

In *Jasher* 2:13 we read, "And in those days Cainan wrote upon tablets of stone, what was to take place in time to come, and he put them in his treasures."[4] The Falasha[5] version of the *Testament of Abraham* begins with a declaration that "the holy ᵓAtnātēwos, the patriarch of Alexandria, the servant of the only God, composed it from what he had found in the Treasury of Knowledge."[6]

The Talmud reports that Rabbi Hanan bar Tahlifa sent a message to Rabbi Yosef saying that he had encountered a man who possessed an ancient prophetic text written in the holy language (Hebrew). The man claimed to have found the text among the hidden treasures of Rome while serving in the Roman army (see TB *Sanhedrin* 97b).[7]

Some texts indicate that there is a heavenly treasury in which records of the deeds of mankind are kept. Deuteronomy 32:34 speaks of the wicked acts of men being "laid up in store with God, and sealed up among [his] treasures." In a medieval Hebrew text, Rabbi Ishmael (of the second century A.D.) reported his visit to paradise, conducted by the angel Sagansagel, who "took me and brought me into the innermost place, to the treasure-house of treasures and he took down the books and showed me the decrees of many misfortunes written therein."[8] *Merkabah Rabbah* 195–98, also attributed to Rabbi Ishmael, calls God the "Sealer of all hidden things" and speaks of the "secret (name)" that "goes forth from Your treasure-house."[9] In another medieval Hebrew text, Moses was taken through the seven heavens to the presence of God, who declared, "I . . . have shown thee my treasures and I have given thee my law."[10] In Samaritan tradition, the book of the law is equated with the heavenly treasure.[11]

Mandaean texts often speak of heaven as a treasury, usually a "treasury of light," a term also known from Gnostic Coptic documents from Egypt. One text (*Thousand and Twelve Questions* 43–44) suggests that secret things are kept in the heavenly treasury:

> For these mysteries with thee are guardians; were it not so, guardians of this treasure would come to thee and bring thee these mysteries at the command of my Father, the Great and Lofty One whose like none have beheld. Nevertheless, on the appointed days I will impart these mysteries to thee, for on those days these mysteries which thou hast (*mentioned*?) were (*created*?) . . . Then, from the presence of the Great and Lofty One, there came a decree that these mysteries should be given to *Šišlam*-Rba, and Mara-*d*-Rabutha commanded him to swear oaths that were strong and constraining. And he swore him (to secrecy) with those same oaths that his (own) Teacher had imposed upon him. In like manner *Šišlam*-Rba swore: "These mysteries I will not reveal. Nevertheless, to whom amongst us shall I reveal them?"[12]

The text then responds to the question by describing how any who would receive the heavenly secrets will be examined for worthiness.

Scrolls Kept in the Temple

Elder Orson Pratt suggested that the records of the Nephites had been hidden up and kept "under the charge of holy angels, until the day should come for them to be transferred to the sacred temple of Zion."[13] His brother, Elder Parley P. Pratt, wrote of a room inside the New Jerusalem temple that would be set aside to hold these and other sacred records.[14]

Some evidence suggests that sacred scrolls were also stored in the ancient temple in Jerusalem. In the days of King Josiah (circa 640–609 B.C.), a scroll of the Law (Torah) was discovered in the temple (see 2 Kings 22:8–20; 2 Chronicles 34:15–32). More than seven centuries later, the Jewish historian Josephus appealed to the "books laid up in the temple" as confirmation of what he had written.[15]

According to *Pseudo-Aristeas* 176, when the Jews of Alexandria wanted to translate the Bible into Greek, the high priest in Jerusalem sent them a copy of the Torah for that purpose. Evidently, the Hebrew copies of the Torah in Alexandria were considered to be corrupt (see *Pseudo-Aristeas* 30).

Rabbinic sources mention the "book of the Temple Court," apparently a standard scroll for public reading on holy days. They also mention the books of the prophets in the temple court. Corrections of the book of the temple court were maintained from the public treasury (see TY *Šeqalim* 48a). One passage speaks of correcting the temple scroll itself (see Mishnah *Moʾed Qaṭan* 3.4). The Jerusalem Talmud notes that in the temple in Jerusalem were three copies of the Torah that did not agree with one another in all particulars, and that when two of the three agreed in a given passage, the rule of majority applied.[16]

The idea of keeping books in the sanctuary actually predates Solomon's building of the temple in Jerusalem. The tables of the law of Moses were kept in the ark of the covenant inside the tabernacle and later in the temple in Jerusalem (see Deuteronomy 10:1–5; 1 Kings 8:9; 2 Chronicles 5:10). When the prophet Samuel chose Saul as Israel's first king, he "told the people the manner of the kingdom, and wrote it in a book, and laid it up before the Lord," evidently in the tabernacle of Moses, then still in use (1 Samuel 10:25).

In *Life of Adam and Eve* 50:1–2, we read that Eve, before her death, instructed her posterity to make tablets of stone and clay and to write on them the life of their parents. Accordingly, Seth made the two types of tablets and wrote on them the life of his parents and their teachings. He placed them in the house of his father and they were seen by many after the flood. Solomon prayed about them and was told by an angel to build the temple on the site where they were kept.

Egyptian Temple Libraries

The Egyptians, too, kept their sacred texts in temples. In 1931 a cache of papyri from the second century was found in the basement of a house adjacent to the temple of Suchos in Tebtunis (modern Umm el-Breigat).[17] One of these, Papyrus Petese, in a very fragmentary portion of the text, speaks of "hidden books which came into existence in the temple," where "the treasuries of [the sun-god] Re" were also located.[18]

Chapter 2, "Hidden Books," noted that chapter 137 of the Egyptian Book of the Dead speaks of "the instructions which are found in the books of Prince Herutātāf, who discovered them in a secret coffer (now they were in the handwriting of the god [Thoth] himself (*i.e.*, they were written in hieroglyphs) and had been deposited in the Temple of the goddess Unnut, the Lady of Unu) during a journey which he was making in order to inspect the temples, and the temple-estates, and the sanctuaries of the gods."[19]

Egyptian scribes copied the sacred books in the "house of life," a library attached to the nearby temple. One such library was discovered intact in the temple of Horus at Edfu. The temple itself was constructed between 237 and 57 B.C., but its library dates from 140 to 124 B.C. Inscribed on its inner walls and dedicated to Horus was a two-part catalogue of all the books kept in the room.[20] One of the inscriptions suggests that the papyrus scrolls were kept in "caskets," reminding us of the stone box in which the Book of Mormon plates were deposited.[21]

The Christian chronographer Syncellus, who lived around A.D. 800, is the sole source for the *Book of Sôthis*, or *The Sôthic Cycle*. Though the book was probably written in the fourth century A.D., Syncellus suggested that it had been written by the third-century-B.C. Egyptian priest Manetho, who presented it to King Ptolemy Philadelphus. According to this story, when the king wanted to learn the future of the universe, Manetho sent to him sacred books that had originally been written by Thoth, the first Hermes, in Egyptian hieratic script. After the flood, these books had been translated by Agathodaemôn, son of the second Hermes, or Hermes Trimegistus, and deposited in Egyptian temples.[22] The books of Thoth kept in the temples of Egypt were also noted by Plato (see *Phaedra* 274d) and Philo of Byblos (see fragment 1, 805.8–10).[23]

Other Temple Libraries

Other peoples also kept records in their temples. William J. Hamblin, citing Plutarch (see *Moralia*: "Quaestiones Convivales," 5.2, 675B) notes that "a golden book containing the poetry of Aristomache of Erythrae, was deposited in the Treasury of the Sicyonians at Delphi."[24] The second-century writer Lucian, in his *Alexander the False Prophet* 10, wrote of the discovery of a record written on bronze tablets that had been buried inside the temple of Apollo in Chalcedon.[25]

A bronze tablet (18C) found during archaeological excavations at the Hittite capital of Hatti is inscribed with a treaty that notes at the end, "This document is made in seven copies and is sealed with the seal of the Sun-goddess of Arinna and the seal of the Storm-god of Hatti. One tablet is deposited in the presence of the Sun-goddess of Arinna, one tablet in the presence of the Storm-god of Hatti, one tablet in the presence of Lelwani, one tablet in the presence of Hebat of Kizzuwatna, one tablet in the presence of the Storm-god of Lightning, and one tablet in the presence of Zithariya. And Karunta, king of the land of Tarhuntassa, has one tablet in his residence" (§28 iv 44–51).[26]

The Sikhs keep their sacred scriptures, the *Adi Granth* (First Book) in the "golden temple," the temple of God (Hari-Mandir) at Amritsar, in the Punjab province of India. To reach the shrine, which is on an island, one must wade through the "tank of the immortals," or the "pool of immortality," an artificial tank 510 feet long in the center of which stands the island.[27]

Even Latter-day Saints have used temples as repositories for records. Various relics, including written records, were placed in a record stone near the southeast corner of the Salt Lake Temple in 1857, and others were included in the capstone of the central eastern tower (where the statue of the angel

Moroni sits) in 1892. The contents of the cornerstone were removed in 1993, during the temple's centennial.[28]

Summary

Though to modern readers it seems strange to read of books being kept in a treasury, the practice is ancient and is attested in numerous documents unknown in Joseph Smith's time. Thus another unusual pronouncement in the Book of Mormon is confirmed.

Notes

1. The Mandaeans, who number a few ten thousand in Iraq and Iran, claim to be the descendants of the disciples of John the Baptist. Their religion contains many elements common to early Christianity, Judaism, and pagan religions of ancient Mesopotamia.

2. See Hugh Nibley, *An Approach to the Book of Mormon,* 3rd ed. (Salt Lake City: Deseret Book and FARMS, 1988), 174–75.

3. Frank Williams, trans., *The Panarion of Epiphanius of Salamis* (Leiden: E. J. Brill 1987), 1:124.

4. *The Book of Jasher* (Salt Lake City: J. H. Parry and Co., 1887), 4.

5. The Falasha are the "black Jews" of Ethiopia. Some of their writings, such as the *Testament of Abraham,* were borrowed from their Christian neighbors.

6. Wolf Leslau, *Falasha Anthology* (New Haven: Yale University Press, 1951), 96.

7. The Roman historian Tacitus recorded the story of a lunatic named Caselius Bassus, who came from Carthage in North Africa to visit the emperor Nero in Rome. Bassus claimed to have discovered on his estate a very deep cave containing a large amount of gold bullion hidden away by the Phoenician queen Dido when she fled to Carthage after the Trojan war. The greedy emperor dispatched warships full of men to retrieve the gold. Bassus took them from place to place, digging up the ground in a futile search for the cave. He then

admitted that it had all been a hallucination. See Tacitus, *The Annals of Imperial Rome* 16.

8. Moses Gaster, *Studies and Texts* (New York: Ktav Publishing House, 1971), 1.162.

9. Martin Samuel Cohen, *The Shiʿur Qomah: Texts and Recensions* (Tübingen: Mohr, 1985), 75.

10. Geo Widengren, *The Ascension of the Apostle and the Heavenly Book* (Uppsala, Sweden: Uppsala Universitets Årsskrift, 1946), 40, citing the text published by Moses Gaster, "Hebrew Visions of Hell and Paradise," *Journal of the Royal Asiatic Society* (1893): 571–611.

11. See A. E. Cowley, ed., *The Samaritan Liturgy* (Oxford: Clarendon, 1909), 1:49, 55, cited in Widengren, *Ascension of the Apostle,* 45.

12. E. S. Drower, *The Thousand and Twelve Questions* (Berlin: Akademie-Verlag, 1960), 124.

13. O. Pratt, "The Hill Cumorah; or the Sacred Depository of Wisdom and Understanding," *Millennial Star* 28 (1866): 417.

14. See Parley P. Pratt, *The Angel of the Prairies* (Salt Lake City: Deseret News, 1880), 20–21. I am indebted to Matthew B. Brown for bringing to my attention the information about the Pratt brothers.

15. Flavius Josephus, *Antiquities of the Jews* 5.1.17, 3.1.7; see *Jewish War* 7.5.5.

16. See *TY Taʿanit* 4.2; compare *Sipre* 2.356; *Soperim* 6.4; *ʾAbot de Rabbi Nathan* 2.46.

17. See Jürgen Osing, *Hieratische Papyru aus Tebtunis I* (Copenhagen: University of Copenhagen, 1998), 19.

18. K. Ryholt, *The Story of Petese, Son of Petetum and Seventy Other Good and Bad Stories* (Copenhagen: University of Copenhagen, 1999), 53.

19. Ernest A. Wallis Budge, *The Book of the Dead* (New Hyde Park, N.Y.: University Books, 1960), 660–61.

20. See Garth Fowden, *The Egyptian Hermes: A Historical Approach to the Late Pagan Mind* (Cambridge: Cambridge University Press, 1986), 57.

21. For a discussion of boxes as repositories for sacred texts, see chapter 3 of this volume, "Hiding Records in Boxes."

22. See W. G. Waddell, *Manetho* (Cambridge: Harvard University Press, 1971), xxvii-xxviii, 209–11.

23. See Fowden, *Egyptian Hermes,* 32 n. 115. For a discussion of the Hermetic literature, see chapter 2 of this volume, "Hidden Records."

24. William J. Hamblin, "Sacred Writings on Bronze Plates in the Ancient Mediterranean" (FARMS, 1994), 13.

25. See A. M. Harmon, trans., *Lucian* (Cambridge: Harvard University Press, 1969), 4:189.

26. Gary Beckman, *Hittite Diplomatic Texts,* 2nd ed. (Atlanta: Scholars Press, 1999), 123.

27. E. Royston Pike, "Amritsar," in *Encyclopaedia of Religion and Religions* (New York: Meridian, 1958), 16.

28. See Matthew B. Brown and Paul Thomas Smith, *Symbols in Stone: Symbolism on the Early Temples of the Restoration* (American Fork, Utah: Covenant, 1997), 127.

chapter 10

The Records Come Forth

For, behold, saith the Lamb: I will manifest myself unto thy seed, that they shall write many things which I shall minister unto them, which shall be plain and precious; and after thy seed shall be destroyed, and dwindle in unbelief, and also the seed of thy brethren, behold, these things shall be hid up, to come forth unto the Gentiles, by the gift and power of the Lamb. And in them shall be written my gospel, saith the Lamb, and my rock and my salvation. (1 Nephi 13:35–36)

A number of Book of Mormon passages speak of the coming forth of ancient records in the last days. Nephi noted a vision in which he "beheld other books, which came forth by the power of the Lamb" (1 Nephi 13:39) and noted that God had shown others "all things, and they have written them; and they are sealed up to come forth in their purity, according to the truth which is in the Lamb" (1 Nephi 14:26). Nephi was permitted to see the same vision given to the apostle John, as recorded in the book of Revelation, but allowed to write only part of what he saw. The Lord instructed him, "But the things  which thou shalt see hereafter thou shalt not write; for the

Lord God hath ordained the apostle of the Lamb of God that he should write them. And also others who have been, to them hath he shown all things, and they have written them; and they are sealed up to come forth in their purity, according to the truth which is in the Lamb, in the own due time of the Lord, unto the house of Israel" (1 Nephi 14:25–26).

Among the books to come forth was the Book of Mormon, which Nephi wrote about when likening the prophecy found in Isaiah 29 to his own people and their records. He wrote of a sealed book that would be "kept . . . until the own due time of the Lord, that they may come forth" (2 Nephi 27:10). This book, he noted, "shall come forth, and be written unto the Gentiles, and sealed up again unto the Lord" (2 Nephi 30:3). The Lord directed Nephi to write to Joseph Smith, the future translator of the work, "Touch not the things which are sealed, for I will bring them forth in mine own due time," then instructed him to "seal up the book again, and hide it up unto me, that I may preserve the words which thou hast not read, until I shall see fit in mine own wisdom to reveal all things unto the children of men" (2 Nephi 27:21–22). Referring to Isaiah 29:4, Nephi wrote that "those who shall be destroyed shall speak unto them out of the ground, and their speech shall be low out of the dust, and their voice shall be as one that hath a familiar spirit" (2 Nephi 26:16). He noted in the farewell at the end of his record, "I speak unto you as the voice of one crying from the dust" (2 Nephi 33:13).

A later Nephite prophet, Mormon, noted "that wickedness will not bring them forth unto them; and they are to be hid up unto the Lord that they may come forth in his own due time. And this is the commandment which I have received; and behold, they shall come forth according to the commandment of the Lord, when he shall see fit, in his wisdom" (Mormon

5:12–13). The Lord made a similar comment regarding the Jaredite record, instructing the brother of Jared to "show them in mine own due time unto the children of men" (Ether 3:27; see 3:24).

On the title page of the Book of Mormon, Moroni described his father's abridgment as a record "*to come forth* by the gift and power of God unto the interpretation thereof—Sealed by the hand of Moroni, and hid up unto the Lord, *to come forth* in due time by way of the Gentile."

Speaking of the future prophet Joseph Smith, who would translate the Nephite record, Moroni wrote, "And blessed be he that shall bring this thing to light; for it shall be brought out of darkness unto light, according to the word of God; yea, it shall be brought out of the earth, and it shall shine forth out of darkness, and come unto the knowledge of the people; and it shall be done by the power of God" (Mormon 8:16; see 3 Nephi 21:3–6). He further noted, "And no one need say they shall not come, for they surely shall, for the Lord hath spoken it; for out of the earth shall they come, by the hand of the Lord; and none can stay it; . . . and it shall come even as if one should speak from the dead" (Mormon 8:26).[1]

Discovery of Ancient Texts

When Joseph Smith translated the Book of Mormon, the concept of ancient records hidden away for future generations was foreign to Christians, who believed that the Bible was the most ancient of books and the most authoritative record from antiquity. All that was to change over the next century and a half, as new discoveries were made.

Because ancient records had been revealed to the prophet Joseph Smith (the Book of Mormon and the records of Enoch, Moses, and Abraham, plus portions of the Doctrine and

Covenants), early Latter-day Saints became very interested in extrabiblical books. Lost books such as *Jasher* and *Enoch* were subjects of speculation in the earliest days of the restored church.[2] The discovery and translation of the Ethiopic *Book of Enoch* and the English publication of the thirteenth-century midrashic book of *Jasher* (from the Hebrew meaning "book of the righeous [one]") was also noted in early LDS periodicals, with some extracts from the latter.[3] Indeed, one of the first English translations of *Jasher* was published by J. H. Parry and Company of Salt Lake City in 1887 and is still available in reprints. The first English version of the pseudepigraphic *Apocalypse of Abraham* was published in the *Improvement Era* in 1898.[4]

Early Latter-day Saint interest in such books is also evidenced by the English version of the *Testaments of the Twelve Patriarchs.* The book was published by Samuel Downes, an elder of the church, in Manchester, England, in 1843 and dedicated to an LDS patriarch, John Albitson (read "Albertson"). A copy of the book is found in the Harold B. Lee Library at Brigham Young University, and a notice of the publication was included in the *Millennial Star.*[5]

Documents from the Near East

Large numbers of ancient Near Eastern documents have been discovered since the publication of the Book of Mormon. The largest collections are the clay tablets known from dozens of sites in Iraq, Iran, Turkey, and Syria, some of which date to the third millennium B.C. The number of known tablets is in the tens of thousands, while untold numbers lie beneath the earth waiting to be discovered.

Biblical and other documents have been discovered among the Dead Sea Scrolls and at nearby sites such as Masada, Naḥal

Ḥever, Naḥal Ṣe'ēlîm, Wadi Murabbaʿat, Khirbet Mird, and Wadi Daliyah.

Other interesting collections of documents have been found in Egypt, including the Bodmer and Anastasi papyri, the *Pistis Sophia* and *1* and *2 Jeu*, and, of course, the Nag Hammadi collection. As late as February 1998, Canadian archaeologists unearthed a collection of about two thousand papyrus rolls at Esment el-Kharab, near the Dakhla oasis in western Egypt.

Unfortunately, some documents were lost after their original discovery. Some went down in ships at sea, while others fell victim to the ravages of war. Codex Berolensis 8502, a Coptic collection on papyrus dating to the fifth century, was acquired in Cairo in 1896 by Dr. Rheinhardt and taken to Germany, where it disappeared during the fall of Berlin in 1945. It contains the Gospel of Mary, the Secret Book of John, the Sophia of Jesus Christ, and the Acts of Peter. Though its whereabouts are unknown, it is possible that it may someday reappear on the black market.

The *Copper Scroll*, one of the most famous of the Dead Sea Scrolls, indicates that there are still buried treasures and records to be found. It lists various buried artifacts and written documents, including a copy of the *Copper Scroll* itself. To date, none of these have been unearthed.

Other Ancient Records

In 1899 a Chinese Taoist monk named Wang Yuan-lu was renovating a large chapel in the Caves of the Thousand Buddhas at Ch'ien Fo Tung oasis in the province of Kansu in Chinese Turkestan when he discovered that a frescoed wall was hollow. Breaking down the wall, he discovered a small room packed with some fifteen to twenty thousand manuscripts, paintings, and other sacred artifacts. Dating between the sixth and seventh centuries A.D., the manuscripts—most of them scrolls—had been walled up about A.D. 1035, probably in anticipation of an invasion by the barbarous Tangguts of Tibet. The documents, comprising many Buddhist scriptures and commentaries, along with some historical texts, were written in Chinese, Tibetan, Sanskrit, and other languages, including some hitherto little-known central Asian tongues. Many of them had been brought to the site from India and Tibet centuries earlier by a monk named Hsüan Tsang. Among them was the oldest known block-printed book, from A.D. 868.

In 1907 Sir Aurel Stein was exploring central Asia and visited the Caves of the Thousand Buddhas. Having heard rumors about the manuscripts, he contacted Wang and managed to acquire twenty-nine cases of materials in return for a large donation of silver to continue the restoration work. The following year, French professor Paul Pelliot headed an expedition to the region and purchased many of the remaining manuscripts and paintings. In 1911 the Chinese government ordered that the rest of the manuscripts be sent to the capital, but en route many of them were stolen by handlers and officials. Wang managed to hold back some of the manuscripts and later sold them to Stein.[6]

A ruined Chinese Buddhist tower in Gilgit also contained a great number of manuscripts, some dating to perhaps the fourth century. As late as 1996, a collection of thirteen birchbark scrolls from the ancient Buddhist kingdom of Gandhara on the Pakistani-Afghan border were found in pottery jars. Written in the Gandhari language, the first-century-A.D. scrolls are thought to be the oldest known Buddhist writings.

Summary

Nephi wrote of his vision of the future, "I beheld other books, which came forth by the power of the Lamb, from the Gentiles unto them, unto the convincing of the Gentiles and the remnant of the seed of my brethren, and also the Jews who were scattered upon all the face of the earth, that the records of the prophets and of the twelve apostles of the Lamb are true" (1 Nephi 13:39). Since the publication of the Book of Mormon in 1830, many more documents have been discovered, some of them discussed in this chapter and some in earlier chapters of this work. While the documents that were discovered are not all scriptural, they nevertheless lend support to the concept that records were hidden up to come forth in the last days. It is as the Psalmist declared: "Truth shall spring out of the earth; and righteousness shall look down from heaven" (Psalm 85:11).

Notes

1. Moroni drew the idea of speaking from the dead from the Isaiah 29:4 passage cited by Nephi in reference to the latter-day coming forth of the Nephite record. The term rendered "one that hath a familiar spirit" in the King James Version of the Bible derives from the Hebrew term for "ghost."

2. See Joseph Smith, *History of the Church of Jesus Christ of Latter-day Saints* (Salt Lake City: Deseret Book, 1980), 1:363; William W. Phelps, "Letter No. 8," *Messenger and Advocate* 1/9 (June 1835): 130; "History of Joseph Smith," *Times and Seasons* 6/3 (February 1845): 800.

3. See "The Book of Jasher," *Times and Seasons* 1/8 (June 1840): 127; "Fulfillment of a Prophecy," *Times and Seasons* 6/9 (May 1845): 902; "Ancient Ruins," *Times and Seasons* 6/1 (December 1844): 745–46; "The Apocryphal Book of Enoch," *Millennial Star* 1/3 (July

1840): 61. A poem commemorating the finds was published in Samuel Brown, "Inspired Writings," *Times and Seasons* 2/14 (May 1841): 421.

The book of Jasher has been found,
And many more hid in the ground;
All these, with Enoch's book, unfold
And spread true light from pole to pole.

4. See G. Nathanael Bonwetsch, "The Book of the Revelation of Abraham," trans. Edward H. Anderson and R. T. Haag, *Improvement Era*, August 1898, 705–14, 793–806. Hugh Nibley reprinted part of the text in his *Abraham in Egypt* (Salt Lake City: Deseret Book, 1981), 10–20.

5. See "Notices," *Millennial Star* 4/6 (October 1843): 96. I am indebted to Gordon C. Thomasson for bringing both the book and the notice to my attention.

6. For an account of the discovery, see Irene Vongehr Vincent, *The Sacred Oasis: Caves of the Thousand Buddhas, Tun Huang* (Chicago: University of Chicago, 1953), 12–14, 17–19, 33–35, 70. The story is also noted in André Dupont-Sommer, *The Dead Sea Scrolls: A Preliminary Survey*, trans. E. Margaret Rowley (New York: Macmillan, 1952), 17; Jean Doresse, *The Secret Books of the Egyptian Gnostics* (New York: Viking, 1960), 121 n. 7. From 10 December 1999 to 15 March 2000, some of the documents from the Caves of the Thousand Buddhas were on display at the Queens Library Gallery in Jamaica, New York.

chapter 11

Restoring Lost Scriptures

Come unto me, O ye Gentiles, and I will show unto you the greater things, the knowledge which is hid up because of unbelief. Come unto me, O ye house of Israel, and it shall be made manifest unto you how great things the Father hath laid up for you, from the foundation of the world; and it hath not come unto you, because of unbelief. Behold, when ye shall rend that veil of unbelief which doth cause you to remain in your awful state of wickedness, and hardness of heart, and blindness of mind, then shall the great and marvelous things which have been hid up from the foundation of the world from you. . . . And then shall my revelations which I have caused to be written by my servant John be unfolded in the eyes of all the people. Remember, when ye see these things, ye shall know that the time is at hand that they shall be made manifest in very deed. Therefore, when ye shall receive this record ye may know that the work of the Father has commenced upon all the face of the land. (Ether 4:13–17)

In translating the Book of Mormon, Joseph Smith restored a corpus of scripture lost to the world for fourteen centuries. But his work did not stop there. In connection with his revision of the King James Bible, the prophet restored information missing from either the Bible or ancient texts that were never part of the Bible despite their antiquity. Among the latter is the chapter he added to the beginning of the book of Genesis, known to us from the Pearl of Great Price as Moses 1, a revelation given to Moses on the mount but not included in the Bible (see Moses 1:1, 42).

Anticipating the mission of Joseph Smith, the Lord told Moses, "When the children of men shall esteem my words as naught and take many of them from the book which thou shalt write, behold, I will raise up another like unto thee; and they shall be had again among the children of men—among as many as shall believe" (Moses 1:41). According to *2 Enoch* 35:2, God made a similar promise to Enoch: "And I shall raise up for that generation someone who will reveal to them the books in your handwriting and those of your fathers."[1] Joseph Smith restored some of the writings of Moses and Enoch in the book of Moses.

The story of Enoch, found in Moses 6:26–7:69, is also unattested in the book of Genesis, though as Hugh Nibley has shown, it has many parallels with other ancient books attributed to Enoch.[2] But the Pearl of Great Price does not contain all of the writings of Enoch. The details in Doctrine and Covenants 107:41–56, which are not in the book of Moses, are said to have been "all written in the book of Enoch, and are to be testified of in due time" (D&C 107:57). Some of this information is confirmed in the medieval book of *Jasher*, which contains a number of early Jewish traditions about Old Testament personalities and stories.[3]

Information restored from antiquity (and sometimes suggested in other ancient Jewish and Christian texts)[4] by the Prophet Joseph contained additional details about

Melchizedek, including the fact that he and his people were translated (see Genesis 14:25–40 JST). Similarly, Joseph provided details about why God instituted the practice of circumcision in Abraham's family (see Genesis 17:3–12 JST).

Joseph Smith's revision of the Bible led to a number of other revelations, both of new information and of long-lost ancient texts.[5] For example, Doctrine and Covenants 45 is a variant of the material found in Matthew 24, which Joseph Smith also revised (Joseph Smith—Matthew in the Pearl of Great Price).[6] Doctrine and Covenants 7 is said to be a translation of a portion of a parchment hidden up by the apostle John that indicated that Jesus promised John he would not taste of death. While the text parallels the one found in John 21:20–23, it is more detailed and is a first-person account. The importance of Doctrine and Covenants 7 to our study is that it speaks of a hidden parchment and of a text that Joseph Smith partially restored (using the term "translated"),[7] despite the fact that there is no evidence that he ever saw the original.[8]

Not long before the Lord revealed Doctrine and Covenants 7 to the Prophet, he told Oliver Cowdery through the Prophet, "There are records which contain much of my gospel, which have been kept back because of the wickedness of the people; . . . if you have good desires . . . then shall you assist in bringing to light, with your gift, those parts of my scriptures which have been hidden because of iniquity" (D&C 6:26–27). Soon after giving Doctrine and Covenants 7, he again told Oliver, "Ask that you may know the mysteries of God, and that you may translate and receive knowledge from all those ancient records which have been hid up, that are sacred" (D&C 8:11). The word "all" suggests that the Lord was going to reveal more than just the text of the Book of Mormon. Later that same month, the Lord told Oliver that after the work on the Nephite record, "other records have I, that I will give unto you power that you may assist to translate" (D&C 9:2). He was undoubtedly referring to Joseph Smith's revision of the Bible and revelations related to it.

Ancient Precedents for Restoring Lost Records

There is biblical precedent for the restoration of lost scriptures. In Jeremiah we read that when the king had burned a scroll containing Jeremiah's prophecies, the Lord instructed him, "Take thee again another roll, and write in it all the former words that were in the first roll, which Jehoiakim the king of Judah hath burned. . . . Then took Jeremiah another roll, and gave it to Baruch the scribe, the son of Neriah; who wrote therein from the mouth of Jeremiah all the words of the book which Jehoiakim king of Judah had burned in the fire: and there were added besides unto them many like words" (Jeremiah 36:28, 32; see 28:21–32).

A similar story is found in an early Christian tradition of how our current Old Testament came to be. It is said that "the books of the Jews were burned three times" during their history, including when they "were taken captive to Babylon, at which time Simeon the priest asked of Abumirdan the store of the books and received them" (*Conflict of Adam and Eve* IV, 12.12–13; see *Book of the Rolls* f.139b).

According to the Christian Arabic *Book of the Rolls* f.137a–138a, at the time Nebuchadnezzar took Jerusalem, Simeon the high priest asked permission to take "the old writings," which he carried into captivity with him. En route, "he saw a well in his way among the borders of the West; and he laid the writings in it, and put with them a bronze vase, filled with glowing coals, and in it sweet smelling incense; he covered up this well, and went to Babylon." Later, the priest/scribe Ezra recovered the vase full of fire and incense and the writings, but he found the writings faded and had to restore them by revelation.[9]

In an Ethiopian variant on the story, "Simeon the priest, found favour and grace with the captain of the king's army, and requested him to give him the house [the Ethiopic word can also mean "repository, ark, chest"] of records; and he gave him a command accordingly. Then Simeon the priest came in and gathered together the ashes of the books, and laid them in a pot in a vault, and he took a censer of brass, and put fire therein, and threw pure incense upon it, and hung it in the vault over the place in which the ashes of the books lay" (*Conflict of Adam and Eve* IV, 10.16–17).[10] When the children of Israel returned from Babylon, they did not have any books. They settled in Jerusalem, and "Ezra the scribe came to the vault in which Simeon the priest had placed the ashes of the books, which Simeon the priest, had gathered together. . . . Then Ezra prayed to God, wept abundantly, and spread his hand towards the ashes of the books of the law, and of the prophets, and all of them three times. Then came the Spirit of God upon him, and the [same] Spirit spake through him that had spoken through the prophets. And he wrote the law and the prophets, new a second time" (*Conflict of Adam and Eve* IV, 11.8–13).[11]

The Syriac version of the story is told in *Cave of Treasures* 36b.1: "Now when the people had gone up [to Jerusalem] they had no Books of the Prophets. And Ezra the scribe went down into that pit [wherein Simeon had cast the Books], and he found a censer full of fire, and the perfume of the incense which rose up from it. And thrice he took some of the dust of those Books, and cast it into his mouth, and straightway God made to abide in him the spirit of prophecy, and he renewed all the Books of the Prophets."[12]

In the book of *4 Ezra*, which was included in some early Christian Bibles, Ezra told the Lord, "Your Law has been burned, and so no one knows the things which have been done or will be done by you. If then I have found favor before you, send the Holy Spirit to me, and I will write everything that has happened in the world from the beginning, the things which were written in your Law." The Lord then told Ezra to "prepare for yourself many writing tablets" and to take five men scribes with him, "and I will light in your heart the lamp of understanding, which shall not be put out until what you are about to write is finished. And when you have finished, some things you shall make public, and some you shall deliver in secret to the wise" (*4 Ezra* 14:21–26).[13]

Samaritan tradition reflects the same story, though it claims that Ezra "altered many things in the text of the Holy Torah out of hatred for the community of the children of Israel," meaning the Samaritans. "Moreover many errors were made by him in the book of the Torah; which neither he nor his people [the Jews] perceived or understood. In addition to this he gathered many sayings and writings composed by former authors and prophets, such as suited his aims and desires, and he and his colleague Nehemiah commanded his community to keep them all."[14]

Summary

When answering a question prompted by Joseph Smith's study of the Book of Mormon, the Lord told the prophet, "I gave unto thee, my servant Joseph, an appointment, and restore all things. Ask what ye will, and it shall be given unto you according to my word" (D&C 132:40). This gift enabled Joseph to restore long-forgotten scriptures and the truths found therein. It was part of his role as translator (see D&C 21:1), which in nineteenth-century parlance referred not just to one who rendered a text from one language into another, but to one who preserved and transmitted records that already existed before his time. As we have seen in this book, the practice was very ancient and involved a long chain of prophets and scribes who wrote and preserved sacred texts, often by hiding them to be uncovered by future generations. We are fortunate indeed to live in the day when the Lord is restoring these long-lost texts.

Notes

1. James H. Charlesworth, *The Old Testament Pseudepigrapha* (Garden City, N.Y.: Doubleday, 1983), 1:158.
2. See Hugh Nibley, *Enoch the Prophet* (Salt Lake City: Deseret Book and FARMS, 1986).
3. For example, Cainan's call from God (see D&C 107:45) is also mentioned in *Jasher* 2:11. Enoch's blessing at age sixty-five (see D&C 107:48) parallels his anointing as king in *Jasher* 3:12, 17. For Enoch's translation, see Genesis 5:22–24; D&C 107:49; Moses 7:69; 8:1; *Jasher* 3:27–38.
4. Several forthcoming FARMS publications will detail information given to us by the Prophet Joseph Smith that is confirmed in ancient Jewish and Christian sources.
5. See Robert J. Matthew, "The 'New Translation' of the Bible, 1830–1833: Doctrinal Development During the Kirtland Era," *BYU Studies* 11/4 (1971): 400–422.
6. I have done a rather extensive comparison of the accounts in Matthew 24; Joseph Smith—Matthew; D&C 45; Mark 13; and Luke 12–13, 17, 21, which I hope to publish elsewhere.

7. See Joseph Smith, *History of the Church of Jesus Christ of Latter-day Saints* (Salt Lake City: Deseret Book, 1980), 1:36.

8. Only in the cases of the Book of Mormon and the Book of Abraham did Joseph actually possess ancient documents. In the case of the Abraham material, some LDS scholars believe that it, too, came by direct revelation rather than by normal translation methods.

9. Margaret Dunlop Wilson, "Kitâb al Magâll, or The Book of the Rolls," in *Apocrypha Arabica* (London: C. J. Clay, 1901), 53–54.

10. S. C. Malan, *The Book of Adam and Eve, also called The Conflict of Adam and Eve with Satan* (London: Williams and Norgate, 1882), 196.

11. Ibid., 198. The restoration of text that was lost when documents were burned has its modern parallel in a project begun by the FARMS Center for the Preservation of Ancient Religious Texts in 1998. At the request of the Jordanian government, Gene Ware and Steven Booras went to Jordan to make multispectral computer scans of early Christian documents that were destroyed by fire at Petra. The process has enabled them to read formerly illegible text on the charred remains.

12. Ernest A. Wallis Budge, *The Book of the Cave of Treasures* (London: Religious Tract Society, 1927), 192.

13. Charlesworth, *Old Testament Pseudepigrapha,* 1:554.

14. John Bowman, *Samaritan Documents Relating to Their History, Religion and Life* (Pittsburgh: Pickwick Press, 1977), 102.

appendix 1

The Book of Mormon and the Apocalypse of Paul

by Steven W. Booras

When Joseph Smith proclaimed that he had seen God and Jesus Christ in the Sacred Grove in answer to his prayers, he was immediately subjected to ridicule and persecution from neighbors, strangers, and even ministers (see JS—H 1:21). Later an angel revealed to him the hiding place of an ancient scripture written on gold plates that were buried in a stone box. This was so bizarre to current beliefs of the day that the persecution increased,[1] since such a declaration was considered blasphemous.[2] However, an ancient Christian account of the discovery of the *Apocalypse of Paul* is similar to that of the coming forth of the Book of Mormon, both involving the appearance of an angel to reveal the hiding-place of an ancient scripture buried in a stone box. The two accounts of the appearance of an angel are as follows.

This appendix is based on a brown-bag lecture sponsored by the Foundation for Ancient Research and Mormon Studies (FARMS), where the author is employed at the Center for the Preservation of Ancient Religious Texts (CPART).

Joseph Smith's Account (in Joseph Smith—History)

After retiring for the evening on 21 September 1823, young Joseph began to pray for forgiveness and to know of his standing before God. He noticed that the whole room began to increase in light until it was "lighter than at noonday" (JS—H 1:30). Then a heavenly messenger appeared at his bedside, introducing himself as Moroni, an ancient prophet who lived on the American continent some fourteen centuries earlier. "He said there was a book deposited, written upon gold plates, giving an account of the former inhabitants of this continent, and the source from whence they sprang. He also said that the fulness of the everlasting Gospel was contained in it, as delivered by the Savior to the ancient inhabitants" (JS—H 1:34).

Moroni informed Joseph of the location of a buried stone box containing an ancient record with accompanying relics. He gave Joseph specific instructions on what he was to do with the record and told him of the urim and thummim, that "God had prepared them for the purpose of translating the book," and that they consisted of two stones in silver bows, fastened to a breastplate. They had been deposited with the plates "and the possession and use of these stones were what constituted 'seers' in ancient or former times" (JS—H 1:35). Moroni appeared three times that evening.[3]

Later, Moroni instructed young Joseph to go to the spot where Moroni had deposited the record centuries earlier (see JS—H 1:51).[4] So intense was the persecution that followed that Joseph had to be constantly on guard as enemies attempted to harm him and steal the plates (see JS—H 1:60).

Paul's Vision

The *Apocalypse of Paul*[5] claims to be Paul's more detailed account of the vision mentioned in his second letter to the

Corinthians. Paul was taken away in vision up to the "third heaven," but was told not to reveal the experience to others.

> It is not expedient for me doubtless to glory. I will come to visions and revelations of the Lord. I knew a man in Christ above fourteen years ago, (whether in the body, I cannot tell; or whether out of the body, I cannot tell: God knoweth;) such an one caught up to the third heaven. And I knew such a man, (whether in the body, or out of the body, I cannot tell: God knoweth;) How that he was caught up into paradise, and heard unspeakable words, which it is not lawful for a man to utter. (2 Corinthians 12:1–4)

According to an ancient Christian tradition Paul did record this vision and then hid it for a later generation.[6] Apparently a young man living in Tarsus discovered the account years after Paul recorded his vision. This account, the so-called Tarsus account preface or Tarsus Introduction now comprises the first two verses in the translation of the *Apocalypse of Paul* by Hugo Duensing and Aurelio de Santos Otero:

> In the consulate of Theodosius Augustus the Younger and of Cynegius[7] a certain respected man[8] was living in Tarsus in the house which had once belonged to St. Paul; an angel,[9] appearing to him by night, gave him a revelation telling him to break up the foundations of the house and to make public what he found. But he thought this was a delusion. However, the angel came the third time[10] and scourged[11] him and compelled him to break up the foundations. And when he had dug he discovered a marble box[12] which was inscribed on the sides; in it was the revelation of St. Paul and the shoes[13] in which he used to walk when he was teaching the word of God. But he was afraid to open the box and brought it to a judge;[14] the judge accepted it and sent it as it was, sealed with lead, to the emperor

> Theodosius; for he was afraid it might be something else.[15] And when the emperor received it he opened it and found the revelation of Saint Paul. After a copy had been made he sent the original manuscript to Jerusalem."[16]

The Tarsus preface has been dated by Tischendorf to A.D. 380.[17] Though others have dated it as early as A.D. 240–250,[18] it is not later than A.D. 380.[19] Constantin von Tischendorf is attributed with the modern rediscovery of Paul's vision in 1843. He published the Greek text along with a partial English translation in 1866.[20] The *Apocalypse of Paul* became very popular and "the importance of (the Apocalypse of) Paul . . . increased from the eighth century, so that it became one of the chief formative elements in the development of the later legends of Heaven."[21] It was circulated from Armenia in the East to England in the West and translated into the major European languages. "There are versions approximating to the original in Greek, Latin, Syriac, Coptic, Arabic, Armenian, and Slavic, in manuscripts ranging between the eighth and the seventeenth century."[22]

The similarity between the Joseph Smith narrative and the Tarsus account has now been recognized by at least one non–Latter-day Saint scholar, Willis Barnstone: "The details of the discovered scriptures [the *Apocalypse of Paul*] calls to mind the detailed evidence associated with the discovery of Mormon scriptures in New York state."[23] Several details in the Tarsus account parallel the record of Moroni's visits:

- Both heavenly messengers visited three times in a single evening.
- The purpose of both heavenly visitations was to reveal the location of buried records.
- Both records were buried in sealed stone boxes.
- Both records were accompanied by other relics.

- Both Joseph and the young nobleman were told to make the records public.

There are also some obvious differences between the two accounts:

- We do not know if the young nobleman was a prophet.
- We are unaware why Paul's record came forth at that time in history or if this angelic visitation was under any direct authority from God.[24]
- Although relics were found in both boxes, they were considerably different.
- It is not clear on what medium the *Apocalypse of Paul* was written.

There is one clue to the medium on which Paul's record was written. In a footnote to Tischendorf's translated edition we read that when King Theodosius I opened the stone box and read Paul's account, "he saw thus *inscribed* . . ."[25] According to Webster, the word *inscribed* was used to describe the record and not the box, although the box was also "inscribed." *Inscribe* means to write, engrave, "or print as a lasting record," "engraving on, for perpetuity or duration; as to inscribe a line or verse on a monument, on a column or pillar." This statement and the fact that the record was buried in a stone box sealed with lead, which was also inscribed on the sides, provide possible clues for a record written on something other than papyrus. Based on research by William J. Hamblin and H. Curtis Wright,[26] it would seem that there is a distinct possibility that the description of this buried record in a stone box could provide evidence that Paul's vision was inscribed on metal plates. Also, as noted in Tischendorf's translation, it was thought that the box contained "something of gold." Why, we do not know. The weight of the box or the fact that the box was stone and sealed may have indicated that it contained something of value. In any event, none of the accounts delineate on what medium Paul's revelation was written.

In addition to the story of Paul's apocalypse, there is another account of an ancient apostle's record that was hidden up and buried for later generations, the *Apocalypse of Stephen.*[27] The apostle Peter had a similar vision of the heavens and hell, as found in the Ethiopic text of the *Apocalypse of Peter*. Peter was also instructed to hide it up once he had recorded it.[28]

Whether the legend of the Tarsus account is factual or merely fabricated is not the issue.[29] What is important is that this ancient story provides many parallels to the Moroni account. Joseph Smith's story of the visit of an angel who disclosed the location of an ancient buried record is neither unique nor strange. Joseph's accounts of heavenly visitations, ancient records, gold plates, and accompanying relics correspond with accounts in certain ancient records. Many texts' apocryphal apocalypses deal with the same form of secrecy to protect both the sacred record and the uninitiated reader, and contain one or more elements that allow the record to come forth by divine control.

Tischendorf did not discover the record of Paul until 1843 in Germany and did not publish it until 1866, some twenty-two years after Joseph Smith's death. Perhaps the reason that Paul recorded his vision and the unique process by which it was later discovered and distributed was for the purpose of testifying to the modern enlightened world in some small way that God works the same way in all ages in establishing dispensations, including bringing forth the Book of Mormon. The Prophet Moroni testified:

> Behold, I make an end of speaking concerning this people. I am the son of Mormon, and my father was a descendant of Nephi. And I am the same who hideth up this

> record unto the Lord; the plates thereof are of no worth, because of the commandment of the Lord. For he truly saith that no one shall have them to get gain; but the record thereof is of great worth; and whoso shall bring it to light, him will the Lord bless. For none can have power to bring it to light save it be given him of God; for God wills that it shall be done with an eye single to his glory, or the welfare of the ancient and long dispersed covenant people of the Lord. (Mormon 8:13–15)

The original title page of the Book of Mormon, taken from the gold plates, further asserts:

> Wherefore, it is an abridgment of the record of the people of Nephi, and also of the Lamanites—Written to the Lamanites, who are a remnant of the house of Israel; and also to Jew and Gentile—Written by way of commandment, and also by the spirit of prophecy and of revelation—Written and sealed up, and hid up unto the Lord, that they might not be destroyed—To come forth by the gift and power of God unto the interpretation thereof—Sealed by the hand of Moroni, and hid up unto the Lord, to come forth in due time by way of the Gentile—The interpretation thereof by the gift of God.

In 1823 Moroni appeared to Joseph Smith and, under God's direction, instructed him to take the plates, translate them, and make the record available to the world. The Book of Mormon is another testament of Jesus Christ. It is indeed a sacred record for our time for our enlightenment. As the ancient record of the Book of Mormon is a witness to the fact that God deals with his children consistently, so also perhaps is the process in which God brought forth this ancient record. This Book of Mormon has come to us through preparation and planning under divine direction and is of great importance to us.

Notes

I would like to thank John A. Tvedtnes for his helpful suggestions and Wendy H. Christian and Alison Coutts for their assistance in preparing this paper for publication.

1. See Richard L. Anderson, "Book of Mormon Witnesses," *Encyclopedia of Mormonism*, ed. Daniel H. Ludlow (New York: Macmillan, 1992), 1:214–15; Dean C. Jessee, "The Original Book of Mormon Manuscript," *BYU Studies* 10/3 (1970): 259.

2. See "Great Discussion on Mormonism between Dr. West and Elder Adams, at the Marlboro' Chapel," *Times and Seasons* 3/19 (1 August 1842): 863–64. See also Hugh Nibley, *Since Cumorah* (Salt Lake City: Deseret Book and FARMS, 1988), 270–71.

3. The next day the angel Moroni came a fourth time (see JS—H 1:49) and visited Joseph many more times over the years.

4. See also JS—H 1:52–53. For a detailed description of the stone box containing the ancient Nephite record see Oliver Cowdery's Letter number 8 in *Messenger and Advocate* 2/1 (1835): 196.

5. The term *apocalypse* derives from the Greek *apokalypsis*, meaning revelation. An apocalypse is a specific type of revelation that pertains to a genre of literature having specific references to eschatological theology. Another term that might need clarification is *apocrypha* or *apocryphal*. These terms have come to mean"spurious or untrue." But this is not the meaning intended by those who anciently first applied the term. "An apocryphal book was—originally—one too sacred and *secret* to be in every one's hands: it must be reserved for the initiate, the inner circle of believers." Montague Rhodes James, *The Apocryphal New Testament* (Oxford: Clarendon, 1924), xiii–xiv, emphasis in original.

6. Richard L. Anderson wrote, "Apparently Paul's detailed knowledge of the three heavens went to the grave with him." See Richard L. Anderson, *Understanding Paul* (Salt Lake City: Deseret Book, 1983), 145. Note the conclusion of the record of the *Apocalypse of Paul:* "And I, Paul, returned unto myself, and I knew all that I had seen; and in life I had not rest that I might reveal this mystery; but I

wrote it, and deposited it under the ground and the foundation of the house of a certain faithful man, with whom I used to be in Tarsus, a city of Cillicia." Constantin von Tischendorf, trans., *Augusto de Grimm: de Educandis Domus Caesareae Russicae Principibus Meritissimo* (Germany, 1866), 68.

7. Gratianus (or Gratian) in Alexander Roberts and James Donaldson, eds., *Ante-Nicene Fathers* (1886; reprint, Peabody, Mass.: Hendrickson, 1994), 8:575. Gratianus was Co-Augustus with Theodosius I. Theodosius the Great was Emperor of the East (A.D. 379–395) and Gratianus was Emperor of the West (A.D. 375–383). See John Julius Norwich, *Byzantium: The Early Centuries* (New York: Knopf, 1997), 388.

8. Rendered "a certain nobleman" in Roberts and Donaldson, *Ante-Nicene Fathers*, 8:575 and "a certain honorable man" in James, *Apocryphal New Testament*, 526.

9. Rendered "angel of the Lord" in Roberts and Donaldson, *Ante-Nicene Fathers*, 8:575. According to Pheme Perkins, the "instructions (were) given by an angel in a dress," by which we should perhaps understand a robe. See David Noel Freedman, ed., *Anchor Bible Dictionary* (New York: Doubleday, 1992), 5:204. The Greek *himation* was the most common outer garment for both men and women. It was draped around the body. Also, the Greek *stole* was used as a "general term for the outer garment or long robe." See Freedman, *Anchor Bible Dictionary*, 2:236.

10. Rendered "but a third time the angel came" in James, *Apocryphal New Testament*, 526, and "the angel having persisted even to a third vision" in Roberts and Donaldson, *Ante-Nicene Fathers*, 8:575.

11. Tischendorf notes that the Greek means "urged him." Tischendorf, *Augusto de Grimm*, 69.

12. Tischendorf notes a translation describing the box as "a box of white glass." Ibid., 34. According to Roberts and Donaldson, *Ante-Nicene Fathers* 8:575 n. 3, a Syriac version calls it "a box of white glass." Casey referred to it as "a sealed marble box." Robert P. Casey,

"The Apocalypse of Paul," *Journal of Theological Studies* 34 (1933): 6 n. 24.

13. In the *Apocalypses Pauli,* Tischendorf reads that the box contained "his (Paul's) stockings placed by the side of this Revelation—these stockings he used to wear on his feet at the time of prayer—and his cloak folded up." Tischendorf, *Augusto de Grimm,* 34 n. 2.

14. Also, "and having taken it, he showed it to the ruler of the city." Roberts and Donaldson, *Ante-Nicene Fathers,* 8:575. Casey, "Apocalypse of Paul," 6.

15. The Syriac version states that they thought the box contained gold. See Roberts and Donaldson, *Ante-Nicene Fathers,* 8:575 n. 4. See also Tischendorf, *Augusto de Grimm,* xv, where he notes that they were "thinking that there was something of gold within it." However, it is rendered merely "something strange" in Carl H. Kraeling, "The Apocalypse of Paul and the 'Iranische Erlösungsmysterium,'" *Harvard Theological Review* 24 (1931): 241.

16. The Latin version states that Theodosius sent the copy and kept the original. Casey, "Apocalypse of Paul," 6. Wilhelm Schneemelcher, *New Testament Apocrypha* (Louisville, Ky.: Westminster/John Knox, 1991), 2:716–17. See also James, *Apocryphal New Testament,* 526. James states that the Syriac version puts the discovery story at the end of the book.

17. Tischendorf, "Theological Studies," u. Krit. XXIV, 442.

18. See Casey, "Apocalypse of Paul," 1–32; Roberts and Donaldson, *Ante-Nicene Fathers,* 8:359.

19. See Roberts and Donaldson, *Ante-Nicene Fathers,* 8:358; and Theodore Silverstein, *Visio Sancti Pauli* (London: Christophers, 1935), 91. Silverstein states that the apocalypse was originally written in Greek and probably by an Egyptian and "as early as the third century, and was reissued some time after the year 388 with a preface that sought to support the authority of the book by relating the story of its miraculous discovery in Tarsus." Silverstein, *Visio Sancti Pauli,* 3. Casey also dates the Tarsus account to A.D. 388. Casey, "Apocalypse of Paul," 6. This date does not accord with that of the Tarsus account,

which refers to the joint consulate of Theodosius and Gratianus. Gratianus was assassinated in 383 and replaced by Valentinian II. See John Julius Norwich, *Byzantium: The Early Centuries*, 109–10, 388. However, Casey points out that "M. R. James has rightly restored *Cynegius* and fixed the intended date at A.D. 388," Casey, "Apocalypse of Paul," 6.

20. Tischendorf discovered a Long Greek version in Milan in 1843. Before he published the text in 1866, a second Greek manuscript was found in Munich. See Silverstein, *Visio Sancti Pauli* (London: Christophers, 1935), 15 n.; 98–99.

21. Ibid., 3.

22. Ibid., 4–5. See also Antonette DiPaolo Healey, ed., *The Old English Vision of St. Paul* (Cambridge, Mass.: Mediaeval Academy of America, 1978), 19. Kraeling states that "evidence of another sort indicates that in the later centuries, particularly from the thirteenth to the fifteenth, the document continued to be in vogue." Kraeling, "Apocalypse of Paul," 211.

23. Willis Barnstone, ed., *The Other Bible* (San Francisco: Harper and Row, 1984), 537.

24. LDS theology recognizes any heavenly angelic visitation would seem to be under the direction of God. See Daniel H. Ludlow, ed., *Encyclopedia of Mormonism* (New York: Macmillan, 1992), 1:40. However, there is still the matter of authenticity of the account itself.

25. Tischendorf, *Augusto de Grimm*, III Apocalypses Pauli, 35. See also Casey, "Apocalypse of Paul," 6. Here Casey describes the Syriac (S1) text by stating that "it adds a long and edifying inscription found inside the box."

26. See William J. Hamblin, "Sacred Writings on Bronze Plates in the Ancient Mediterranean" (Provo, Utah: FARMS, 1994); and H. Curtis Wright, "Ancient Burials of Metal Documents in Stone Boxes," in *By Study and Also by Faith: Essays in Honor of Hugh W. Nibley*, ed. John M. Lundquist and Stephen D. Ricks (Salt Lake City: Deseret Book and FARMS, 1990), 2:273.

27. Along with Stephen's record were his relics. The text is dated around A.D. 415. See Schneemelcher, *The New Testament Apocrypha*,

2:694; James, *Apocryphal New Testament*, 564–68; and Casey, "Apocalypse of Paul," 6 n. 2.

28. According to Casey, in the Ethiopic text of the *Apocalypse of Peter*, "Jesus orders Peter to conceal his revelation in a box that men may not read it." Casey notes that "It is unlikely that the detail of the box (in Paul's account) was taken from Peter." Casey, "Apocalypse of Paul," 6. See also J. K. Elliott, ed., *The Apocryphal New Testament* (Oxford: Clarendon, 1993), 612.

29. For a brief statement concerning the background of the early controversy relating to the origins for both the discovery account and the recorded vision of Paul, see James, *Apocryphal New Testament*, 525. Kraeling refers to the Tarsus account as an "aetiological legend" from the fact that it provides time, place, purpose, and description, Kraeling, "Apocalypse of Paul," 240–42.

appendix 2

Glowing Stones in Ancient and Medieval Lore

by John A. Tvedtnes

Of all the miracles reported in the Book of Mormon, perhaps none has met with as much skepticism as the story of the glowing stones that provided light inside the Jaredite barges. After following the Lord's instructions to construct submarine-like barges, the brother of Jared, worried that he and his people would travel across the great ocean in darkness, "did molten out of a rock sixteen small stones; and they were white and clear, even as transparent glass" (Ether 3:1). He brought these before the Lord and pleaded, "Touch these stones, O Lord, with thy finger, and prepare them that they may shine forth in darkness; and they shall shine forth unto us in the vessels which we have prepared, that we may have light while we shall cross the sea" (Ether 3:4).

This appendix is an expanded version of an article of the same name that appeared in *Journal of Book of Mormon Studies* 6/2 (1997). It is included here because it discusses the urim and thummim, which Joseph Smith found buried with the plates, as glowing stones.

This appendix reviews ancient and medieval literature containing reports of glowing stones. It demonstrates that knowledge of the marvelous nature of such stones was widespread in earlier times and that traditions about glowing stones are known from Jewish and other Near Eastern sources.

Hugh Nibley calls attention to accounts from Jewish tradition of similar arrangements that were made for the ark of Noah,[1] to which the Jaredite vessels are compared in Ether 6:7. Several early Jewish sources indicate that God told Noah to suspend precious stones or pearls inside the ark to light it; in some traditions, it is a jewel-encrusted heavenly book.[2] The gem would glow during the night and grow dim during the day so that Noah, shut up in the ark, could tell the time of day and how many days had passed.[3] This was the explanation given by the rabbis for the ṣôhar that the Lord told Noah to construct in the ark. The word is rendered "window" in the King James Version of Genesis 6:16 but "light" in some other translations.[4]

A similar tradition is found among the Arabs, who may have borrowed it from the Jews. Al-Kisaʾi reported that when Noah made the ark, he put the name of one of the prophets (including those yet to be born) on each of the pegs, "and they shone like the stars, except for the one with the name of Muhammad, which shone as brightly as the sun and the moon together."[5]

Rabbi Eliezer told a similar story about the "great fish" the Lord had prepared "to swallow Jonah" (Jonah 1:17). He noted that Rabbi Tarphon said that Jonah entered the mouth of the fish in the same fashion that a man enters the great synagogue and that he stood inside it. The fish's two eyes were like windows of glass that gave light to Jonah. Eliezer further noted that Rabbi Meir spoke of a pearl being suspended inside the fish to give light like the noonday sun, and by this light Jonah was able to see all that was in the sea (see *Pirqe Rabbi Eliezer* 10). *Zohar* Exodus 48a tells a similar story, noting that the eyes of the fish shone like the noonday sun and that its interior was illuminated by a precious stone.

The idea of pearls providing light is also found in Mandaean lore. Noted folklorists Robert Graves and Raphael Patai cite a Mandaean text that asks, "Who has carried away the pearl which illumined our perishable house?"[6] The *Mandaean Canonical Prayerbook* 252 speaks of a "pure Crystal" containing arcana and guarded by an *uthra* (angel) and of a "Pearl that will enlighten darkened hearts."[7] Another Mandaean document, the *Diwan Malkuta,* also speaks of "the Pearl which came and gave them light."[8]

A medieval Jewish text, *Zohar* Exodus 188a, claims that the Arabs called the sun "the god of the shining pearl" and made oaths by "Allah of the shining pearl."[9] Jewish tradition also holds that Abraham constructed a city for the six sons born to him by Hagar and Keturah, with walls so high that sunlight could not enter therein. To compensate, he provided huge gems and pearls whose glow was more brilliant than the sun. These jewels would provide light on the earth when the Messiah comes to reign.[10] The medieval Jewish text *Bahir* speaks of "the power of the precious stones that are called *Socheret* and *Dar*,"[11] saying of the latter, "God took a thousandth of its radiance, and from it He constructed a beautiful precious stone. In it He included all the commandments. Abraham came, and He sought a power to give him. He gave him this precious stone, but he did not want it."[12] Abraham said that though he did not want the stone, he would "keep all the commandments that are included in it."[13] The document further notes that the two stones are alluded to in Habakkuk 3:4 in connection with the "rays" (KJV "horns") coming from God's hand.[14]

The fourth-century Christian father Ephraem of Syria wrote a document called *The Pearl, Seven Hymns on the Faith*, in which he mentioned a glowing pearl that today seems to be a urim and thummim: "On a certain day a pearl did I take up, my brethren; I saw in it mysteries pertaining to the Kingdom . . . In its brightness I beheld the Bright One Who cannot be clouded, and in its pureness a great mystery." "It was greater to me than the ark . . . it was a daughter of light . . . this pearl fill[s] me in the place of books, and the reading thereof, and the explanations thereof." "Thou dost not hide thyself in thy bareness, O pearl! . . . thy clothing is thy light, thy garment is thy brightness . . . In the mysteries whose type thou art, women are clothed with Light in Eden." "The pearl itself is full, for its light is full." "They saw the ray: they made it darkness, that they might grope therein: they saw the jewel, even the faith: while they pried into it, it fell and was lost. Of the pearl they made a stone, that they might stumble upon it." "In the covenant of Moses is Thy brightness shadowed forth: in the new covenant Thou dartest it forth: from those first Thy light shineth even unto those last. Blessed be He that gave us Thy gleam as well as Thy bright rays."[15]

The Urim and Thummim

The description of the stones that provided light for the ark is reminiscent of another instrument from the Lord—the urim and thummim.[16] At the same time that the Lord touched the stones for the brother of Jared to make them shine, he gave him two stones prepared for the interpretation of the record he would write (see Ether 3:22–24; 4:5). Two similar stones (if not the same ones) were in the possession of King Mosiah and were passed on with the Nephite records (see Mosiah 8:13, 19; 28:20; Alma 37:21, 24).[17] Moroni sealed up the breastplate and the urim and thummim with the gold plates (see Ether 4:4–5) and delivered them to Joseph Smith (see JS—H 1:35, 42, 52, 59, 62; D&C 10:1). According to Doctrine and Covenants 17:1, Joseph received the same urim and thummim given to the brother of Jared on the mount. Joseph Smith is apparently the "servant Gazelem"[18] to which Alma 37:23–25 refers:

> And the Lord said: I will prepare unto my servant Gazelem, *a stone, which shall shine forth in darkness unto light*, that I may discover unto my people who serve me, that I may discover unto them the works of their brethren, yea, their secret works, their works of darkness, and their wickedness and abominations. And now, my son, these interpreters were prepared that the word of God might be fulfilled, which he spake, saying: I will bring forth *out of darkness unto light* all their secret works and their abominations; and except they repent I will destroy them from off the face of the earth; and I will *bring to light* all their secrets and abominations, unto every nation that shall hereafter possess the land.

This passage implies that the "interpreters," which some have called the urim and thummim, shone in the dark. The idea is confirmed by David Whitmer, who wrote that in order to use the seer stone, which operated like the interpreters, Joseph Smith would place it in a hat, evidently to exclude the light in the room. Then "in the darkness the spiritual light would shine."[19] A similar description is given of the urim and thummim mounted in the breastplate of the Israelite high priest, through which the priest consulted the Lord (see Exodus 28:30; 39:6–7; Leviticus 8:8; Numbers 27:21;

Deuteronomy 33:8; 1 Samuel 28:6; Ezra 2:63; Nehemiah 7:65).[20] Josephus wrote that in addition to the twelve precious stones mounted on the breastplate (see Exodus 25:7; 28:17–21; 35:9, 27; 39:10–14), there was one stone like a button on the high priest's right shoulder from which rays of light would shine. He further claimed that the twelve stones shone whenever the Israelite army was marching to victory. He noted, however, that the breastplate and the sardonyx had ceased shining two centuries before his time because of the wickedness of the people.[21] Some have seen, in the word "urim," a plural form deriving from Hebrew *ʾôr* (light).

In *Zohar* Exodus 234b we read, "The term 'Urim' (lit. light, illumination) signifies the luminous speculum, which consisted of the engravure of the Divine Name composed of forty-two letters by which the world was created; whereas the Thummim consisted of the non-luminous speculum made of the Divine Name as manifested in the twenty-two letters. The combination of the two is thus called Urim and Thummim. Observe that by the power of these sunken letters were the other letters, namely, the raised letters forming the names of the tribes, now illuminated, now darkened."[22]

In Jewish tradition, the stones representing the tribes of Israel on the high priest's breastplate alternately glowed or became dim to detect sins committed within the tribes. Thus the sin of Achan (see Joshua 7:14–26) was discovered by the fact that the stone of his tribe, Judah, became dim when Joshua looked at the twelve stones (see *Pirqe Rabbi Eliezer* 38). The Samaritan version of the Joshua passage indicates that the stones on the breastplate grew dim when Achan's name was pronounced. Similar stories are told about other Old Testament events. When Jonathan unwittingly broke the oath his father had made for the people, all the stones in the breastplate except that of Jonathan's tribe, Benjamin, remained bright (see *Pirqe Rabbi Eliezer* 38; *Midrash Shemuel* 17:96). According to *Zohar* Exodus 230a, the letters engraved in the stones glowed to spell out answers when the high priest inquired of God.[23] The urim and thummim operated in a similar fashion.[24] When David asked the high priest, Abiathar, whether Saul would pursue him (see 1 Samuel 23:6–13), Abiathar saw the letter *yod* in the divine name (YHWH) glowing, along with the letters *resh* in Reuben's name and *dalet* in Dan's name, producing the word *yered*, "he will pursue."[25]

Zohar Exodus 231b reads, "Observe that the ephod and breastplate were 'behind and before,' and so the Priest, when clothed in them, resembled the supernal pattern. As has already been said, when his face was illumined and the letters stood out brightly, then a message was thereby conveyed to him. For this reason the breastplate and the ephod were tied together; and although they had distinct functions, they had the same symbolism and were therefore united by the four rings that held them together, back and front."[26] In *Zohar* Exodus 217b, Rabbi Simeon explained the passage in Exodus 39:30 about the plate of gold on the high priest's crown:

> Why was the plate called *z.iz.* (lit. gaze, peep)? Because it was a reflector, mirroring the character of any man gazing at it. For in that plate were graven the letters of the Divine Name, and when a righteous man appeared before it the letters so engraved bulged out and rose luminous from their sockets, from which a light shone on the man's face with a faint sparkling. For a moment the priest would notice the reflection of the letters on the man's face; but when he looked more closely he would see nothing more than a faint light, like the reflection of shining gold. But the first momentary glimpse that the priest caught was a sign to him that that man was pleasing to the Holy One, blessed be He, and that

> he was destined for the world to come, inasmuch as that light was an illumination from on high and a mark of divine favour. On the other hand, if a man's face failed to show any such sacred sign when he stood before the plate, then the priest knew that that man was an evildoer, and in need of atonement and intercession.[27]

Three fourth-century Christian fathers knew the same tradition. Epiphanius noted that the high priest had two emeralds hanging from his left shoulder and possessed a light blue diamond that constituted the urim. The color of the stone changed when the high priest entered the holy of holies in the Jerusalem temple. When the people sinned, the stone became black in color; when God wanted to send them to war, it became red; and if it became bright like snow, the people were sinless and could celebrate. Epiphanius noted that the stone had become bright when Zechariah, the father of John the Baptist, ministered in the temple.[28] Saint Augustine noted that the color of the stone changed to denote adversity or prosperity when the high priest entered the holy of holies,[29] while John Chrysostom described how the brightness of the stones foretold what would happen.[30]

Orson Pratt, referring to Doctrine and Covenants 130:6–11, suggested that "if a small stone or other material in Aaron's breastplate could be made, by the power of God, to shine forth and illuminate the vision of the Seer, then, by the same power, the whole earth could be filled with the Spirit of God, and be made to shine with celestial glory, like the sun in the firmament of heaven."[31] He further described the urim and thummim as "a stone or other substance sanctified and illuminated by the Spirit of the living God, and presented to those who are blessed with the gift of seeing. All Saints cannot see by the illuminations of the Urim and Thummim."[32] The description of the stone "illuminated by the Spirit" is similar to the Jaredite stones being illuminated by the finger of the Lord.

The glowing nature of the urim and thummim is also mentioned in the Dead Sea Scrolls. Regarding the sapphires and rubies of Isaiah 54:11–12, the *Isaiah Pesher* (4Q164 I, 4–5) says, "Its interpretation concerns the twelve [chiefs of the priests who] illuminate with the judgment of the Urim and Thummim [without] any from among them missing, like the sun in all its light."[33] From a fragmentary text that García Martínez calls *4QLiturgy of the Three Tongues of Fire* (4Q376), we read of "the anointed priest" with "urim" that "will provide you with light and he will go out with him, with tongues of fire; the stone of the left side which is at its left side will shine in the eyes of all the assembly until the priest finishes speaking. And after [the cloud(?)] has been removed [. . .] and you will keep and d[o al]l [that] he tells you . . . in accordance with all this judgment."[34]

Joseph Smith described the interpreters (which later generations have termed urim and thummim) as "two transparent stones set in the rim of a [silver] bow fastened to a breast plate."[35] The term "transparent" is used only two other times in the scriptures—in the descriptions of the glowing stones used by the Jaredites (see Ether 3:1) and of the streets of gold of the New Jerusalem that John saw descending from heaven (see Revelation 21:21). In both cases, the full description is "as . . . transparent glass."[36] In this connection, it is interesting to note that the heavenly city has foundations made of twelve precious stones and also twelve gates of pearls (see Revelation 21:19–21). This reminds us of the twelve stones in the high priest's breastplate, and indeed, John noted that the names of the twelve tribes were inscribed on the twelve gates (see Revelation 21:12), just as the names of the tribes were inscribed on the two stones worn by the high priest (see Exodus 28:9–12).

John further wrote that the heavenly Jerusalem had "the glory of God: and her *light* was like unto a *stone most precious*, even like a jasper stone, clear as crystal" (Revelation 21:11, emphasis added).[37] Because the heavenly Jerusalem will be lighted by the glory of God, it will have no night and will need neither sun nor moon (see Revelation 21:23–25). The heavenly city is very much like the residence of God and the future celestialized earth, as described in Doctrine and Covenants 130:6–9: "A globe like a sea of glass and fire . . . a great Urim and Thummim . . . like unto crystal." John saw a "sea of glass" that supported the throne of God (see Revelation 4:5–6). In Revelation 15:2, he described it as "a sea of glass mingled with fire." Joseph Smith explained that this was "the earth, in its sanctified, immortal, and eternal state" (D&C 77:1). The crystal that surrounds the throne of God is mentioned by other prophets (see Exodus 24:10; Ezekiel 1:22, 26–28; 10:1; compare 28:13–16) and in various pseudepigraphic works.

After describing the celestialized earth, Doctrine and Covenants 130:10–11 notes that "the white stone mentioned in Revelation 2:17, will become a Urim and Thummim to each individual who receives one." Significantly, this stone, like the high-priestly urim and thummim and the precious stone foundations and gates of the New Jerusalem, is inscribed—not with the names of the twelve tribes, but with a "new name [that] is the key word."[38] *Zohar* Exodus 240a–b, citing Isaiah 55:11, notes that the foundations of the future Jerusalem will be of sapphire that "will possess the radiation from the supernal light and will be embedded in the abyss so that no one will be able to loosen them. These are the sapphires that will shed their light above and below."[39]

Ginzberg mentions a story found in the *Pesiqta Rabbati* and the *Pesiqta de Rab Kahana*, according to which Rabbi Joshua, son of Levi, stood with Elijah the prophet on Mount Carmel and asked him to show him the precious stones from which the temple would be built at the end of time. Elijah agreed and the following miracle happened in response: A boat sailing on the high seas was caught in a whirlwind and was in danger. Elijah appeared to a Jewish lad on board and told him to do what he asked in exchange for the boat being saved. The lad agreed and Elijah told him to go to Rabbi Joshua in the city of Lod and show him the precious stones in a cave outside town. The boy went to Lod and had the rabbi follow him to the cave, where he showed him the precious stones. The whole of Lod was then illuminated by the brightness of the stones.[40]

The heavenly temple is also said to be constructed of jewels and pearls that glow.[41] This is reminiscent of the *ʾeben shetiyah*, which in Jewish tradition marked the center of the earth and the center of the sanctuary and was the foundation stone of the ancient temple. The stone was formed in Jacob's day, when God miraculously merged twelve gems.[42] Either the name of the messiah or the ineffable name is engraven on the stone (see *Pirqe Rabbi Eliezer* 35). Precious stones also play a role in the traditions of the Garden of Eden. After listing the precious stones of Eden[43] in verse 13, Ezekiel 28:14 and 16 mention "stones of fire."

Of particular interest is "A Parable," published in *Times and Seasons*.[44] In the story, a bride is adorned with "a crown with twelve precious diamonds" and holds "in her hand a reflecting rod[45] by which the bright rays of the sun was [*sic*] brought to reflect upon the diamonds,[46] giving light both day and night, so that she walked not in the dark, but as in the light of the noon-day sun, to guide her steps." She married the king's son, who is obviously Christ, and the king promised to "cause the rod of iron which was in the bride's hand to reflect light over all the kingdoms in the province." We are reminded that in John's vision, the heavenly Jerusalem is called the "bride" of Christ (see Revelation 21:1–2, 9–10).

The glowing rod can be tied to the rod given to Adam in the Garden of Eden, which, like the stone in Noah's ark according to some of the rabbis, was a sapphire (see *Jasher* 77:39–51). *Conflict of Adam and Eve* I, 29.6–8 informs us that golden rods had been brought by an angel from India so that Adam could put them in the cave in which he and Eve lived. The rods "should shine forth with light in the night around him, and put an end to his fear of the darkness."[47] The eleventh-century Arab writer al-Kisaʾi told of how, when brought by God to address the angels, Adam wore "a bejeweled crown of gold with four points, on each of which was a great pearl so radiant that the light of the sun and the moon was extinguished. . . . He radiated a brilliant light, which shone in every corner of Paradise. Adam stood on the pulpit in all that radiance, and God taught him all names and gave him a staff of light."[48] Elsewhere, the same writer speaks of angels carrying "ruby staffs that lit the night like daylight."[49]

The glowing rod may also be tied to the urim and thummim, which, according to Joseph Smith's brother William, was held by a rod that attached to the breastplate given to Joseph Smith.[50] According to the original wording of Doctrine and Covenants 8:6–9 (in Book of Commandments 6:3), Oliver Cowdery was to have the "gift of working with the rod," which he would hold in his hands and which would reveal truths.[51] The wording was changed to "gift of Aaron" in the Doctrine and Covenants, in line with the rod of Aaron mentioned in Exodus and Numbers (see Exodus 7:9–10, 19–20; 8:5, 16–17;

Numbers 17:6–10). Significantly, Doctrine and Covenants 8 is the revelation in which the Lord authorized Oliver to attempt to translate the plates comprising the Book of Mormon.

Brigham Young declared that "the breastplate of Aaron that you read of in the Scriptures was a Urim and Thummim, fixed in bows similar to the one Joseph Smith found. Aaron wore this Urim and Thummim on his breast, and looked into it like looking on a mirror, and the information he needed was there obtained. This earth, when it becomes purified and sanctified, or celestialized, will become like a sea of glass; and a person, by looking into it, can know things past, present, and to come; though none but celestialized beings can enjoy this privilege. They will look into the earth, and the things they desire to know will be exhibited to them, the same as the face is seen by looking into a mirror."[52]

The use of the term "mirror" to describe the urim and thummim is reminiscent of a term found in Mandaean documents. According to Mandaean tradition, the priestly vesture of Šišlam Rba had twelve mirrors,[53] bringing to mind the twelve stones in the Israelite high priest's breastplate, one for each tribe. In one Mandaean story, Hibil Ziwa went into the underworld, where he stole the hidden jewel *(gimra)* and mirror and brought them out.[54] In the Mandaean document known as the *Alma Rišaia Rba* (The Great First World) 199–201, we read that "the Lord of Greatness stretched forth His right hand to his great Treasure-chest of Radiance and to the waters with light within it, and took from it this polished mirror a beam of light which fires and enlightens all minds."[55] *Zohar* Exodus 23b declares that "Moses was possessed of the 'luminous mirror,' which is above the 'non-luminous,' which alone is vouchsafed to others."[56] *Zohar* Exodus 82b notes that "Moses derived his prophetic vision from a bright mirror, whereas the other prophets derived their vision from a dull mirror"[57]—a statement repeated in *Zohar* Genesis 170b–171a; *Zohar* Exodus 238b; and *Zohar* Deuteronomy 268b.

Glowing Images

Despite the fact that most of the precious stones in the scriptures are jewels, the Book of Mormon clearly states that the brother of Jared "did molten out of a rock sixteen small stones; and they were white and clear, even as transparent glass" (Ether 3:1). In the Bible, the term "molten" is used in reference not only to metals,[58] but also to images or idols (see Exodus 32:4, 8; 34:17; Leviticus 19:4; Numbers 33:52; Deuteronomy 9:12, 16; 27:15; Judges 17:3–4; 18:14, 17–18; 1 Kings 14:9; 2 Kings 17:16; 2 Chronicles 28:2; 34:3–4; Nehemiah 9:18). It is in the context of molten images and glowing stones that we read an ancient Jewish legend about how the tribe of Asher hid seven golden idols of the Amorites beneath Mount Shechem. When they told the judge, Kenaz, that they hid the idols, Kenaz sent someone to find them. The precious crystalline stones of which the idols were made came from Havilah and shone as daylight during the night. This caused all blind Amorites to kiss the idols and touch their eyes to receive sight. Kenaz commanded the Israelites to put the men who worshipped the glowing stones, along with their possessions and whatever was found with them, in the river Fison (biblical Pison). But when it was discovered that the idols could not be destroyed by fire, dissolved in water, or broken by iron,[59] Kenaz, following God's instructions, buried them with the Amorite books on Mount Ebarim beside the new altar. An angel of God cast the glowing Amorite stones into the depths of the sea. The next day, on the same spot, Kenaz found twelve other stones brought from the same place as the first by an angel and buried. Following God's instructions, he placed them in the high priest's breastplate and stored them in the ark of the covenant along with the tablets of the law.[60] As he did so, they shone like the sun. God told Kenaz that when Israel would sin and the temple would be destroyed, he would take those stones and the Amorite stones and hide them at their source until the last days, when they would become a light to the righteous (see *Pseudo-Philo* 25:10–12; 26:1–15; *Chronicles of Jerahmeel* 57:1–23).[61]

In this story, the river Fison evidently corresponds to the Pison of Genesis 2:11, which is where, according to the rabbinic tradition, Noah found the stone that provided light inside the ark.[62] The use of precious stones and pearls (which the rabbis said Noah hung in the ark) to manufacture idols is confirmed in *3 Enoch* 5:7.[63]

Teraphim

In the Bible, the urim and thummim is associated with the ephod, and it seems that the breastplate in which the sacred stones were mounted was attached to the ephod that was worn by the high priest (see Exodus 28:28; 39:19–21). In Judges 18:14 we read of "an ephod, and teraphim, and a graven image, and a molten image," indicating that these were items of worship that were associated one with another (compare Judges 17:5). The prophet Hosea wrote, "For the children of Israel shall abide many days without a king, and without a prince, and without a sacrifice, and without an image, and without an ephod, and without teraphim" (Hosea 3:4).

An 1841 article by W. W. Phelps refers to this passage and identifies the teraphim, which are usually considered to be "images" (see, for example, Genesis 31:19, 34, 35):

> Aaron . . . took the Urim and Thummim as instrument, that was as old as Adam for all that is known in the bible to the contrary. In fact the word *Teraphim* translated into English from the Hebrew, "images," (Gen. 31:19,) might with more propriety, be rendered spectacles or spy-glass, and actually mean the *Urim and Thummim*; for neither Laban or Abraham are charged with worshipping "images," or idols. The Urim and Thummim, Seer stones, Teraphim, and Images, whatever name is given to them; are found in the United States of America. And when Israel according to the 3rd chapter of Hosea, shall seek the Lord their God in the latter days, the same instruments of the holy offices of God, will be used as formerly. We are coming back to the light ages.[64]

The concept was first introduced (also by Phelps) in the *Evening and Morning Star* in July 1832 and January 1833.[65] It is supported by the fact that in the Bible, the teraphim are said to have been used for divination (Ezekiel 21:21; Zechariah 10:2). The *Pitaron* (Explanation) to the Samaritan *Asatir* (Secrets) of Moses indicates that Balaam, the son of Beor (see Numbers 22–24), was a descendant of Laban and owned the teraphim. It implies that this is what made him a prophet.[66]

According to *Pirqe Rabbi Eliezer* 37, the teraphim spoke when questions were addressed to them, and Rachel stole her father's teraphim so that they would not tell Laban that Jacob had fled. The passage cites Zechariah 10:2, which indicates that teraphim speak. The story is also found in other Jewish sources.[67]

The Samaritan *Asatir* 3.22–23 says that Nimrod "made a likeness of the sun and the moon of crystal and he put into the sun a golden luminous cup. And he put inside the moon a precious stone (shoham).[68] The *Pitaron* adds, "And he made a sun and a moon in the midst of the four to give light. And he placed in the midst of the sun a luminous cup of gold, and he placed in the midst of the moon a precious stone Shoham. And he said unto Gifna, 'This beacon is the first which has been made in the world.'"[69]

Sanctuary Stones

Ancient sanctuaries often contained sacred stones said to have fallen from heaven (probably meteorites), but it is the stories of glowing stones that are of particular interest. Hugh Nibley has already drawn our attention to Lucian's account (in chapter 32 of his *De syria dea*) of the shrine of the goddess Astarte, whose crown contained a luminous stone called *lychnos* (lamp) that lit up the entire sanctuary at night but had only a weak glow during the daytime. He noted the tie to the Greek version of the flood story and wrote of the Indian stories of a glowing stone called Moonfriend that borrowed its light from the sun.[70] To this we can add Pliny's report of the shining "emerald" pillar in the temple of Melkart at Tyre and the gleaming emeralds set in the eyes of a marble line at the tomb of King Hermias, which were so bright they frightened away fish (see *Naturalis historia* 37.17).

From an Egyptian tale about the legendary King Koftim, we read that "when he died his body was embalmed and placed in a cave in a rock wall where the breeze was allowed free passage and fragrant oils were burning day and night to freshen the atmosphere and spread light which reflected in the thousands of precious stones on the statues of girls which had moving hands with which they gently fanned the king during his eternal sleep. Thieves entering the cave would think the statues were alive and would run away, frightened of all the blinking eyes which were only diamonds."[71]

Another glowing sanctuary stone is noted by mineralogist George Frederick Kunz in *The Curious Lore of Precious Stones*, in which he writes that "the author of the [second- or third-century-A.D.] poem 'Lithica' says that the diamond (*adamas*), like the crystal, when placed on an altar, sent forth a flame without the aid of fire."[72]

Medieval Glowing Stones

Kunz also describes a number of other medieval stories about glowing stones. He notes, for example, that pseudo-Aristotle wrote of a "sleeping stone" that was luminous and a bright ruddy hue that gave off a bright light in the darkness.[73] He further cites an account from Plutarch about a marvelous stone that could be found in the Lydian river Tmolus, which changed color four times daily.[74] Kunz also notes Claudii Æliani's account of a woman of Tarentum named Heracleis, who was rewarded by a stork she had helped a year before. Flying overhead, the stork dropped a precious stone in her lap, which she took into the house. She awoke at night and found that the stone illuminated the entire room.[75] In another medieval story, the alchemist Albertus Magnus described a stone named orphanus set in the imperial crown of the Holy Roman Empire. According to tradition, the stone formerly shone in the nighttime but by Magnus's day no longer glowed in the dark.[76]

Kunz quotes an old English ballad that speaks of a princess who gave her lover a ring with seven diamonds. When far from home, the lover realized that the diamond had paled and, taking it as an ominous sign, rushed home just in time to prevent the princess's marriage to another. Kunz also refers to a fourteenth-century manuscript of an Old English romance that says the stone in a certain ring grew pale or red as a sign of misfortune. The text cites several similar tales of rubies and coral that lost their brilliance in times of misfortune and gained it again during good times.[77]

Another story that Kunz and Jones cite was told by Alardus of Amsterdam in his commentary on Marbodus, of the "chrysolampis," a luminous stone set in a golden tablet dedicated to Saint Adelbert. The stone was donated to the Abbey of Egmund (where Adelbert's body lay) by Hildegard, wife of Theodoric, count of Holland. The stone shone bright enough that the monks could read in the chapel at night by its light. One of the monks stole it and cast it into the sea, whence it was never recovered.[78]

A number of early stories tell of the glowing qualities of the carbuncle. Kunz writes of a luminous "carbuncle" at the shrine of Saint Elizabeth at Marburg, set above the statuette of the Virgin Mary, which reputedly glowed at night.[79] William Jones cites a story from chapter 107 of the *Gesta Romanorum* in which a clerk in Rome found a hidden subterranean royal burial chamber illuminated by a shining carbuncle.[80] He also reports from Hawe's *Pastyme of Pleasure* (1517) the story of an enormous carbuncle that lighted a room and noted that Chaucer's *Roumant of the Rose* also described a carbuncle that glowed at night.[81] An Arab source reported that one of the rooms inside the pyramid of Cheops in Egypt was lit by an egg-sized carbuncle.[82] Chalkhill's poem *Thealma and Clearchus* decribes shining carbuncles and diamonds that light a small room.[83] In an Arabian tale, the *History of the Seven Champions of Christendom*, also cited by Jones, a group of knights entered a dark hall and removed their gauntlets so that the diamonds on their fingers could provide light.[84] Medieval stories of Prester John say that at night his palace was lit by two carbuncles.[85]

Kunz notes that the ring of Saint Elizabeth was supposed to have glowed at night but did not do so when he saw it. He notes several similar tales of glowing gemstones,[86] including that of a luminous ruby of the king of Ceylon mentioned by Chau Ju-Kua, a Chinese writer of the thirteenth century. Chau said the ruby shone in the night like a torch.[87] When Henry II of France arrived at the city of Boulogne, a stranger from India presented him a luminous stone. De Thou indicates that the story was told by J. Pipin, who saw the stone and later described it in a letter to Antoine Mizauld, an occult writer.[88] Kunz and Jones also note the failed plans of a parson to light a London bridge at night by means of carbuncles.[89]

Kunz further points out that in his *Conte du Grail*, Chrétien de Troyes indicated that the Holy Grail was made of gold and encrusted with jewels that shone with a brilliance that made candles in the room dim like stars when the sun appears, while in the account by Wolfram von Eschenbach *(Parzival)*, the Holy Grail is said to be a stone that was brought down from heaven by a troop of angels. The Sacro Catino, preserved in Genoa and represented in the early sixteenth century as the cup or dish used by Christ at the last supper, was thought to be carved from a single immense emerald but was subsequently shown to be green glass. Its rival was an emerald-green dish or shallow cup, said to be the Holy Grail, kept in a monastery near Lyon, France, and noted in the fifteenth century by George Agricola.[90]

Of his visit to the palace of King Manual in Constantinople in 1161, Benjamin of Tudela wrote: "The throne in this palace is of gold and ornamented with precious stones; a golden crown hangs over it, suspended on a chain of the same material, the length of which exactly admits the emperor to sit under it. This crown is ornamented with precious stones of inestimable value. Such is the lustre of these diamonds, that, even without any other light, they illumine the room in which they are kept."[91]

Conclusions

Though the idea of stones that glow in the dark may seem strange to the modern mind, such beliefs were widespread in earlier times. The stones used to provide light in the Jaredite barges fit rather well into a larger corpus of ancient and medieval literature, including stories related directly to the biblical account. This essay does not attempt to explain what made the stones glow, and while some natural explanations might be presented, I can only say that the Book of Mormon account attributes their light to divine influence. This is the same explanation given in many of the early texts this essay has surveyed. One would do well to read the story in Ether with the eye of faith that earlier peoples demonstrated when they passed on these records.

Notes

1. See Hugh Nibley, "There Were Jaredites: The Shining Stones," *Improvement Era,* September 1956, 630–32, 672–75; *Lehi in the Desert; The World of the Jaredites; There Were Jaredites* (Salt Lake City: Deseret Book and FARMS, 1988), 366–79; *An Approach to the Book of Mormon,* 3rd ed. (Salt Lake City: Deseret Book and FARMS, 1988), 337–58; *Since Cumorah,* 2nd ed. (Salt Lake City: Deseret Book and FARMS, 1988), 209–10; *The Prophetic Book of Mormon* (Salt Lake City: Deseret Book and FARMS, 1989), 243–44. The first person to bring the Jewish tradition to the attention of Latter-day Saints was Janne M. Sjodahl, in his *An Introduction to the Study of the Book of Mormon* (Salt Lake City: Deseret News Press, 1927), 248.

2. See TB *Sanhedrin* 108b; TY *Pesaḥim* 1.1; *Targum Pseudo-Jonathan* on Genesis 6:16; *Midrash Bereshit Rabbah* 31.11; *Pirqe*

Rabbi Eliezer 23; Rashi on Genesis 6:16. For a recap of the story, see Louis Ginzberg, ed., *The Legends of the Jews* (Philadelphia: Jewish Publication Society, 1937) 1:162–63. According to the *Book of Noah*, engraved on the sapphire that glowed inside the ark was the sacred book given to Adam in the Garden of Eden. In Jewish tradition, the second set of tablets on which the law was written was made of either diamond or sapphire. See *Pirqe Rabbi Eliezer* 46; TB *Nedarim* 38a; and the references given by Ginzberg in *Legends of the Jews,* 3:141 nn. 306–7 (found in his volume 6). According to *Apocryphon of John* 73.5–12, the Ark was not a ship but a luminous cloud.

3. Rabbi Eliezer declared that the crystal surrounding the throne of God in Ezekiel 1:22 refers to precious stones and pearls that illuminate the heavens (*Pirqe Rabbi Eliezer* 4). According to *Zohar* Genesis 41a (citing Exodus 24:10), the celestial sapphire glows and provides light in the heavenly temple. *Zohar* Exodus 136b speaks of "the manner in which the heavens radiate sapphire brightness to that Glory, . . . in order that the one should complete itself in the other, and one be illuminated by the other from the luminous and sparkling radiance of the Sapphire which is reflected by the heavens back to the central glory." Harry Sperling and Maurice Simon, trans., *The Zohar* (New York: Rebecca Bennet Publications, 1958), 3:391. The Arab writer al-Kisaʾi reported that "from a green jewel, God created the Canopy [over the throne], neither the magnificence nor the light of which can be described." W. M. Thackston Jr., trans., *The Tales of the Prophets of al-Kisa'i* (Boston: Twayne, 1978), 2:6. Knappert reports a Turkish Muslim tradition in which God's throne was created out of light. See Jan Knappert, *Islamic Legends: Histories of the Heroes, Saints and Prophets of Islam* (Leiden: E. J. Brill, 1985), 1:28. The idea of glowing heavenly stones is also known from ancient Mesopotamia. Following is part of an unpublished translation of an Akkadian text (KAR 307 UAT 8917) by E. Jan Wilson, used by permission: "The upper heaven is *luludanitu* stone of Anu. He settled the 300 *Igigi* [a kind of heavenly being] inside. The middle heaven is *saggilmut* stone of the Igigi. Bel sat on a throne within on a dais of

lapis lazuli. He made glass and crystal shine inside (it). The lower heaven is jasper of the stars." The Falasha *Apocalypse of Gorgorios* describes paradise as being "like a precious pearl of various colors that shines like bright stars and like lamps that ravish the eyes. There were in it thousands of doors of sapphire brighter than the sun. The floor of this place was white as silver and as mirrors." The text says that the heavenly temple "was built of green emerald, the light of which shone in Paradise. And behold, columns and vaults, topazes, red hyacinths, and gold, and images of sky color adorned with precious pearls. . . . There was in it a white sea pearl which shone brightly, and if one opened the interior of this Íéyon it would illuminate the ends of the light. Its light was brighter than the light of the sky. It was made of a shiny pearl and of pure gold, and the crown on its top was made of a green pearl like an emerald, adorned with three white pieces of silver that shone with so brilliant a light that no eye could look at it." Wolf Leslau, *Falasha Anthology* (New Haven: Yale University Press, 1951), 84–85.

4. The idea of a "window" came from the Latin Vulgate translation and is also found in the Greek translation of Aquila. *Targum Onqelos* renders it "light."

5. Thackston, *Tales of the Prophets*, 2:98.

6. Robert Graves and Raphael Patai, *Hebrew Myths: The Book of Genesis* (New York: McGraw-Hill, 1963), 118.

7. E. S. Drower, *The Canonical Prayerbook of the Mandaeans* (Leiden: E. J. Brill, 1959), 209.

8. E. S. Drower, *The Secret Adam* (Oxford: Clarendon, 1960), 55.

9. Sperling and Simon, *The Zohar*, 4:132.

10. See Ginzberg, *Legends of the Jews*, 1:298, 5:265 n. 312. Compare the statement in *Zohar* Prologue 11a in which it is said that Rabbi Yohai possessed "a precious jewel . . . and it flashed like the radiance of the sun when he emerges from his sheath, and flooded the world with a light which radiated from heaven to earth and spread to the whole world, until the Ancient of Days was duly enthroned."

Sperling and Simon, *The Zohar*, 1:47. In *Zohar* Genesis 217a, Rabbi Judah speaks of the deceased Rabbi Simeon as a "precious jewel which used to illumine it and on which higher and lower beings were supported." Sperling and Simon, *The Zohar*, 2:304.

11. These are mentioned in the Hebrew version of Esther 1:6 and in TB *Megillah* 12a.

12. *Bahir* 190, in Aryeh Kaplan, trans., *The Bahir* (York Beach, Maine: Samuel Weiser, 1989), 75.

13. *Bahir* 192, in ibid., 77.

14. See *Bahir* 193, in ibid.

15. *The Pearl* 1.1, 2; 3.1; 4.3; 6.3, 7, in Philip Schaff and Henry Wace, eds., *Nicene and Post-Nicene Fathers*, Second Series (Peabody, Mass.: Hendrickson, 1994), 13:293, 295, 296, 298, 299.

16. Orson Pratt indicated that Noah had "a Urim and Thummim by which he was enabled to discern all things pertaining to the ark, and its pattern." Orson Pratt, in *Journal of Discourses*, 16:50. According to Abraham 3:1 and 4, it was by means of the urim and thummim that the Lord revealed to Abraham the secrets of the stars.

17. According to Mosiah 8:13–16, the use of the "interpreters" made a man a "seer," that is, "one who sees." Joseph Smith reflected this in John 1:42 JST, when Jesus gave Simon his second name, Cephas (Peter, "stone"): "Thou shalt be called Cephas, which is, by interpretation a seer, or a stone."

18. In earlier editions of the Doctrine and Covenants (before 1981), the code word *Gazelam* was used to denote Joseph Smith (see D&C 78:9; 82:11; 104:26, 43). The etymology of the word is uncertain but should be compared with *gāzrîn*, a term used in reference to diviners in Daniel 2:27; 4:4; 5:7, 11. The verbal form of the same root is used in reference to the stone "cut" without hands in Daniel 2:34, while another related noun is a heavenly "decree" in Daniel 4:17, 24 (MT 4:14, 21); compare Job 22:28. The noun form appears again in Lamentations 4:7, where we read of the "polishing" of sapphires. There is an Old Akkadian name *Gu-zu-LUM*, but since its meaning

is unknown, we cannot confirm a relationship. See I. J. Gelb, *Glossary of Old Akkadian* (Chicago: University of Chicago Press, 1973), 121. In one of the Nag Hammadi texts, VI,*1 Acts of Peter and the Twelve Apostles* 2.10–29, the apostle described how he encountered Christ in disguise, holding a book in his left hand and declaring himself to be "Lithargoel . . . the interpretation of which is, the light, gazelle-like stone." James M. Robinson, ed., *The Nag Hammadi Library,* 3rd ed. (San Francisco: HarperCollins, 1990), 290–91.

19. David Whitmer, *An Address to all Believers in Christ* (Richmond, Mo.: Whitmer, 1887), 12.

20. An Assyrian text speaks of the high priest of Bel being asked to make stones on the king's breast shine. See Charles Fossey, *La Magie Assyrienne* (Paris: Ernest Leroux, 1902), 301; George Rawlinson, *The Cuneiform Inscriptions of Western Asia* (London: Bowler, 1861–84), 4:18 n. 3, cited in George F. Kunz, *The Curious Lore of Precious Stones* (Philadelphia: Lippincott, 1913), 230.

21. See Josephus, *Antiquities of the Jews* 3.8.9.

22. Sperling and Simon, *The Zohar,* 4:300.

23. See ibid., 4:283–84. The passage also notes that the letters stood out when they glowed and that the high priest's face also glowed as a sign that he was a righteous man.

24. *Zohar* Exodus 230b explains that "Urim signifies the words illuminated, whereas Thummim points to the words in their fulfilment." Ibid., 4:285.

25. TB *Yoma* 73a–b; *Targum Yerušalmi* 7.44c, cited in Ginzberg, *Legends of the Jews,* 3:172, 6:69 n. 358.

26. Sperling and Simon, *The Zohar,* 4:289.

27. Ibid., 4:239. See also *Zohar* Exodus 218b, in ibid., 4:243.

28. See *De Duodecim Gemmis.*

29. See *Questions on Exodus* 117.

30. See *Against the Jews,* homily 6.

31. Cited by Nels B. Lundwall, *Masterful Discourses of Orson Pratt* (Salt Lake City: Bookcraft, 1962), 588. Lundwall does not give the source for this discourse and I have been unable to identify it.

Compare the story told in the Falasha *Apocalypse of Gorgorios*, in which the prophet of that name was taken to the heavenly temple by the angel Michael. The text notes that "there was in it a white sea pearl which shone brightly, and if one opened the interior of this Ṣyon it would illuminate the ends of the earth. Its light was brighter than the light of the sky. It was made of a shiny pearl and of pure gold, and the crown on its top was made of a green pearl like an emerald, adorned with three white pieces of silver that shone with so brilliant a light that no eye could look at it." Leslau, *Falasha Anthology*, 84–85.

32. Lundwall, *Masterful Discourses*, 583.

33. Florentino García Martínez, *The Dead Sea Scrolls Translated*, 2nd ed. (Leiden: E. J. Brill, 1996), 190–91.

34. Ibid., 279. An even more fragmentary version of the text (1Q29) is found on page 277.

35. Joseph Smith, *History of the Church of Jesus Christ of Latter-day Saints* (Salt Lake City: Deseret Book, 1980), 4:537.

36. In *Targum Pseudo-Jonathan* on Exodus 19:17, Mount Sinai, when the Lord's presence was upon it, is described as being "transparent like glass."

37. On two other occasions, twelve nonprecious stones were used to represent the tribes of Israel. Elijah used twelve stones to reconstruct the Lord's altar atop Mount Carmel (see 1 Kings 18:31). Joshua had men from each of the tribes retrieve a stone from the Jordan River, and the stones were set up in a circle (see Joshua 4:2–9). This story is reminiscent of the tradition that Noah found the glowing stone in a river.

38. Nibley compares the white stone and its new name with a passage from the Egyptian Book of Breathings, "Stone of Truth is thy name." Hugh Nibley, *The Message of the Joseph Smith Papyri: An Egyptian Endowment* (Salt Lake City: Deseret Book, 1975), 120. Solomon is said to have had a gold ring with a magic stone engraven with the divine name. Other divine names were cut in charm stones by early Christians in Egypt. See Ernest A. Wallis Budge, *The Bandlet*

of Righteousness: An Ethiopian Book of the Dead (London: Luzac, 1929), xi; the citation from Gollancz is from *Book of Protection* (London: H. Frowde, 1912), 1, 7, 26, 33. According to Pliny, *Naturalis historia* 38.40, the names of the sun and moon written on amethyst as an amulet protect from sorcery.

39. Sperling and Simon, *The Zohar*, 4:317.

40. See Ginzberg, *Legends of the Jews*, 4:221–22.

41. See ibid., 3:446–47. According to Josephus, *Antiquities of the Jews* 8.3.3, Solomon's temple was made of polished stones and much of the temple was covered with gold plates, making it dazzle.

42. In *Targum Pseudo-Jonathan* and *Targum Neofiti* on Genesis 28:10, it was the four stones Jacob used as a pillow that he found merged into a single stone when he awoke in the morning. The same story is told in *Zohar* Exodus 229b–230a, which identifies the twelve stones with the ones placed in the high priest's breastplate.

43. In the Ugaritic literature, precious stones are said to be part of the island where El, the chief god, has his throne.

44. See "Restoration of the Jews," *Times and Seasons* 6 (15 March 1845): 846.

45. The glowing rod is reminiscent of the scepter of fire held by God in *Pirqe Rabbi Eliezer* 4. Note also that Satan, when appearing as an angel of light, is said to have a "staff of light in his hand" in *Conflict of Adam and Eve* II, 5.4. In a Coptic text, *The Lady Euphemia and the Devil*, Michael came to rescue a woman from the devil, "bearing in his right hand a golden sceptre on which was the Sign of the Holy Cross, and the whole place was filled with light, ten thousand times brighter than that of the sun." Ernest A. Wallis Budge, *Egyptian Tales and Romances* (London: Thornton Butterworth, 1935), 245. In an Armenian document *Concerning the Creation of Adam and the Incarnation of Christ Our God* 44, the flaming sword of the angels (see Genesis 3:24) is said to be "a fiery rod." W. Lowndes Lipscomb, *The Armenian Apocryphal Adam Literature* (Philadelphia: University of Pennsylvania, 1990), 265. *Zohar* Numbers 126b speaks

of the three heavenly judges who "hold in their hands fiery rods." Sperling and Simon, *The Zohar,* 5:187.

46. This description reminds us of the Ethiopic text of the *Apocalypse of Peter*, which contains material not found in the Coptic Akhmimic version, including, "The Son . . . will make their crowns shine like crystal and like the rainbow in the time of rain, (crowns) which are perfumed with nard, and cannot be contemplated (adorned) with rubies, with the colour of emeralds shining brightly, with topazes, gems, and yellow pearls that shine like the stars of heaven, and like the rays of the sun, sparkling, which cannot be gazed upon." J. K. Elliott, *The Apocryphal New Testament* (Oxford: Clarendon, 1993), 612.

47. S. C. Malan, *The Book of Adam and Eve, also called The Conflict of Adam and Eve with Satan* (London: Williams and Norgate, 1882), 31. See also *Conflict of Adam and Eve* I, 31.12. The same text informs us that "the golden rods were from the Indian sea, where there are precious stones" (*Conflict of Adam and Eve* I, 30.6, in ibid., 32). In *Conflict of Adam and Eve* I, 40.1, Satan appeared to Adam and Eve holding "a staff of light" (ibid., 68).

48. Thackston, *Tales of the Prophets,* 2:29.

49. Ibid., 2:85.

50. See Dan Vogel, ed., *Early Mormon Documents* (Salt Lake City: Signature Books, 1996), 508. The connection between the rod and the urim and thummim and its later imitation, the crystal ball or orb, reminds us that the Jewish sages declared an image forbidden (to be employed for any useful purpose) only when, in its hand, was a rod, a bird, an orb, a dish, a sword, a coronet, or a ring. They further noted that the rod denotes rule over the world (see *Midrash Rabbah* Numbers 13:14).

51. Note that Heber C. Kimball, an early member of the Twelve Apostles, "inquired by the rod" in prayer, as indicated in his 1844–45 journal under the dates of 6 June 1844, 5 July 1844, and 25 January 1845 (in Church Historical Department); cited by D. Michael Quinn, "Latter-day Saint Prayer Circles," *BYU Studies* 19/1 (1978): 83.

52. Brigham Young, in *Journal of Discourses,* 9:86–87. *Zohar* Genesis 231b speaks of how "the righteous put on their crowns and feast themselves on the brightness of the 'pellucid mirror'—happy are they to be vouchsafed that celestial light! The light of this mirror shines on all sides, and each one of the righteous takes his appropriate portion, each according to his works in this world; and some of them are abashed because of the superior light obtained by their neighbours." Sperling and Simon, *The Zohar,* 2:341.

53. See Drower, *Canonical Prayerbook,* 221; *Coronation of the Great Šišlam* (Leiden: E. J. Brill, 1962), 15.

54. See Drower, *Secret Adam,* 57.

55. E. S. Drower, *A Pair of Naṣoraean Commentaries (Two Priestly Documents)* (Leiden: E. J. Brill, 1963), 69. The document is reminiscent of the statement in D&C 88:11: "And the light which shineth, which giveth you light, is through him who enlighteneth your eyes, which is the same light that quickeneth your understandings."

56. Sperling and Simon, *The Zohar,* 3:78.

57. Ibid., 3:248.

58. In Job 28:1–3 we read of metals being molten out of the ground and of "the stones of darkness."

59. This description reminds us that Augustine described the diamond as a stone so hard that neither iron nor fire could crack it (see *City of God* 21.4).

60. According to *2 Baruch* 6:7–9, the forty-eight precious stones kept in the holy of holies were hidden with the other temple implements before the destruction of Jerusalem, to come forth later.

61. Compare the following story: According to the *Pitaron* (Explanation) to the Samaritan *Asatir* (Secrets) of Moses, Adam was given a Book of Signs, copied on twenty-four precious stones, twelve of which were "hidden away as a secret for the last generation." The other twelve were "for the choice of the families of the children of Jacob," and the text suggests they may have been the twelve stones of the high priest's breastplate. See Moses Gaster, *The Asatir: The*

Samaritan Book of the "Secrets of Moses" (London: Royal Asiatic Society, 1927), 193, 195. In *Asatir* 2.7, Enoch "learned the Book of Signs which was given to Adam. And these are the twenty-four precious stones, twelve for the time of Divine Favour and twelve for the chosen heads of the sons of Jacob and to the descendants of the servants of the high God" (ibid., 198).

62. In addition to the story of Noah retrieving a glowing gem from the river Pison in *Targum Pseudo-Jonathan* on Genesis 6:16, the same text speaks of the precious stones and pearls of Pison in its paraphrase of Exodus 14:9 and 21, while its paraphrase of Exodus 35:27 notes that the precious stones placed in the high priest's breastplate came from the river Pison. Compare Genesis 2:11–12.

63. There is even an apocryphal story of a stone that the Lord made to resemble the prophet Jeremiah. When the people wanted to stone Jeremiah for talking about the Son of God who would come to earth, he called for a stone and said to Christ, "Light of the aeons, make this stone look just like me. . . . Then the stone, by the command of God, took on the likeness of Jeremiah." The people cast stones at the stone instead of the prophet. After delivering his message, Jeremiah was stoned and his friends set the stone on his tomb, inscribed "This is the stone (that was) the ally of Jeremiah" (*4 Baruch* 9:21–32). James H. Charlesworth, ed., *The Old Testament Pseudepigrapha* (Garden City, N.Y.: Doubleday, 1983), 2:424–25.

64. W. W. Phelps, "Despise Not Prophesyings," *Times and Seasons* 2/7 (1 February 1841): 298, emphasis added.

65. W. W. Phelps, "The Book of Mormon," *The Evening and the Morning Star* 1/2 (1832): 14; Ibid., 1/8 (1833): 58.

66. See Gaster, *The Asatir,* 263.

67. See *Midrash Tanhuma Vayeze* 12; *Yalquṭ* Genesis 130; *Yalquṭ* Zechariah 578; *Jasher* 31:41; *Targum Pseudo-Jonathan* on Genesis 31:19.

68. See Gaster, *The Asatir,* 220.

69. Ibid., 207.

70. See Nibley, *Lehi in the Desert,* 371–75; *An Approach to the*

Book of Mormon, 356–57. See also Kunz, *Curious Lore of Precious Stones*, 163.

71. Knappert, *Islamic Legends*, 1:46.

72. Kunz, *Curious Lore of Precious Stones*, 163, referring to "Lithica" line 270.

73. See ibid.

74. See ibid., citing De Mely, "Le traité des fleuves de Plutarque," *Revue des Études Grecques* 5 (1892): 331.

75. See ibid., 161–62, citing Claudii Æliani, *De animalium natura* 8:22.

76. See ibid., 147, citing Albertus Magnus, *Opera Omnia* (Paris: Borgnet, 1890), 5:42.

77. See ibid., 156–60.

78. See ibid., 164; William Jones, *History and Mystery of Precious Stones* (London: Richard Bentley and Son, 1880), 14.

79. See Kunz, *Curious Lore of Precious Stones*, 165.

80. See Jones, *History and Mystery*, 57.

81. See ibid., 61.

82. See ibid., 62–63.

83. See ibid., 63.

84. See ibid., 62.

85. See ibid., 65, 82.

86. See Kunz, *Curious Lore of Precious Stones*, 165–67.

87. See ibid., 165–66, citing the English translation of his "Chu-fan-chï" by Friedrich Hirth and W. W. Rockhill (St. Petersburg: Imperial Academy of Sciences, 1911), 72. The story is also recounted in Jones, *History and Mystery*, 60.

88. See Kunz, *Curious Lore of Precious Stones*, 166, citing Johann Beckmann, *History of Inventions* (London: Bell, 1846), 2:433.

89. See ibid., 166–68; Jones, *History and Mystery*, 63. The story was first reported in John Norton's poem, *Ordinal*, written during the reign of Edward IV.

90. See Kunz, *Curious Lore of Precious Stones*, 258–59.

91. Thomas Wright, *Early Travels in Palestine* (New York: Ktav Publishing House, 1968), 75. Originally published in 1848.

bibliography

Ancient and Medieval Works Cited

Ab Urbe Condita (From the Hidden City). A Latin text composed by the first-century Roman writer Livy. No English translation is available.

ʾAbot de Rabbi Nathan (The Fathers of/according to Rabbi Nathan). A commentary on the Mishnaic tractate *Pirqe Aboth* that is attributed to Rabbi Nathan, though its Hebrew style has suggested to some that it may date from before the Mishnah, which was written in the second century A.D., with some later additions. Different manuscripts represent different versions. For an English translation of version A, see Judah Goldin. *The Fathers according to Rabbi Nathan.* New York: Schocken, 1974. For an English translation of version B, see Anthony J. Saldarini. *The Fathers according to Rabbi Nathan: Version B.* Leiden: E. J. Brill, 1975.

Adam, Eve and the Incarnation. An Armenian Christian text of which there are three different versions. For English translations, see Michael E. Stone. *Armenian Apocrypha relating to Adam and Eve,* 8–79. Leiden: E. J. Brill, 1996.

Adi Granth (First Book). The sacred book of the Sikhs, which is preserved in their temple at Amritsar in the Punjab province of India. For an English translation, see Gopal Singh. *Adi Granth.* New York: Taplinger, 1965.

Alexander the False Prophet. A book composed by the second-century Christian writer Lucian. For an English translation, see A. M. Harmon, trans. *Lucian,* 4: 173–254. Cambridge: Harvard University Press, 1969.

Allogenes. One of the fifth-century Coptic Gnostic documents found at Nag Hammadi in Egypt in 1945 and attributed to a man named Allogenes. For an English translation, see James M. Robinson, ed. *The Nag Hammadi Library,* 490–500. 3rd ed. San Francisco: HarperCollins, 1990.

Alma Rišaia Rba (The Great First World). A Mandaean religious text. The English translation was published in E. S. Drower. *A Pair of Naṣoraean Commentaries (Two Priestly Documents),* 1–54 . Leiden: E. J. Brill, 1963.

Annals of Imperial Rome. A history of Rome during the period A.D. 14–68, written by the Roman senator Publius (or Gaius) Cornelius Tacitus (circa A.D. 56–117). For an English translation, see Michael Grant, trans. *Tacitus: The Annals of Imperial Rome.* Rev. ed. Baltimore: Penguin, 1973.

Antiquities of the Jews. A book written by the first-century Jewish historian Flavius Josephus. The most well-known English version is the oft-reprinted translation made by William Whiston in the sixteenth century.

Apocalypse of Adam. One of the fifth-century Coptic Gnostic documents found at Nag Hammadi in Egypt in 1945 and attributed to the apostle James. For an English translation, see James M. Robinson, ed. *The Nag Hammadi Library,* 277–86. 3rd ed. San Francisco: HarperCollins, 1990.

Apocalypse of Baruch (Syriac). See *2 Baruch.*

Apocalypse of Enoch (Ethiopic). See *1 Enoch.*

Apocalypse of Enoch (Slavonic). See *2 Enoch.*

Apocalypse of Paul. A document attributed to the apostle Paul, describing his vision of the heavens alluded to in 2 Corinthians 12:1–4. It was known to St. Augustine in the fourth century A.D. It was widely distributed and is known from manuscripts written in Greek (the original), Syriac, Latin, Coptic, Armenian, and Old Church Slavonic. For English translations, see Montague Rhodes James. *The Apocryphal New Testament,* 525–54. Oxford: Clarendon, 1955; Wilhelm Schneemelcher. *New Testament Apocrypha,* 2:712–47. Trans. Robert McLachlan Wilson. Rev. ed. Louisville, Ky.: Westminster/John Knox, 1991. A Coptic version of the text was found among the Nag Hammadi records, with an English translation published in James M. Robinson, ed. *The Nag Hammadi Library,* 256–59. 3rd ed. San Francisco: HarperCollins, 1990.

Apocalypse of Peter. An early Christian document attributed to the apostle Peter, known only from quotes by early church fathers and a few fragments. For a discussion and partial English translation, see Montague Rhodes James. *The Apocryphal New Testament,* 505–24. Oxford: Clarendon, 1955. A more complete translation is in Wilhelm Schneemelcher. *New Testament Apocrypha,* 2:620–38. Trans. Robert McLachlan Wilson. Rev. ed. Louisville, Ky.: Westminster/John Knox, 1991.

Apocalypse of Zephaniah. A text ascribed to the biblical prophet Zephaniah but thought to have been written in the first century B.C. or the first century A.D. For an English translation, see James H. Charlesworth, ed. *The Old Testament Pseudepigrapha,* 1:497–516. Garden City, N.Y.: Doubleday, 1983.

Apocryphon of Jacob. One of the Dead Sea Scrolls (4Q537), this fragmentary document is attributed to the Old Testament patriarch Jacob. For an English translation, see Florentino García Martínez. *The Dead Sea Scrolls Translated,* 265. 2nd ed. Leiden: E. J. Brill, 1996.

Apocryphon of James. One of the fifth-century Coptic Gnostic documents found at Nag Hammadi in Egypt in 1945 and attributed to the apostle James. For an English translation, see James M. Robinson, ed. *The Nag Hammadi Library,* 29–37. 3rd ed. San Francisco: HarperCollins, 1990.

Apocryphon of John. One of the fifth-century Coptic Gnostic documents found at Nag Hammadi in Egypt in 1945 and attributed to the apostle John. For an English translation, see James M. Robinson, ed. *The Nag Hammadi Library,* 104–23. 3rd ed. San Francisco: HarperCollins, 1990.

Asatir (Secrets). A Samaritan document also known as the *Secrets of Moses,* known from both Samaritan and Arabic versions. A midrashic text, it combines biblical and traditional stories about the history of the earth, from the time of Adam to the death of Moses, and is thought to have been compiled no later than 250–200 B.C. The Samaritans also wrote a *pitron,* or commentary, on the *Asatir* in Arabic, but the date this commentary was composed is unknown. For an English translation of the original and its commentary, see Moses Gaster. *The Asatir: The Samaritan Book of the "Secrets of Moses."* London: Royal Asiatic Society, 1927.

Assumption of Moses. See *Testament of Moses.*

2 Baruch, also known as the *Syriac Apocalypse of Baruch.* A text attributed to Baruch, scribe of the prophet Jeremiah, but thought to have been composed in the second century A.D. For English translations, see James H. Charlesworth, ed.

The Old Testament Pseudepigrapha, 1:615–52. Garden City, N.Y.: Doubleday, 1983; Robert Henry Charles. *The Apocrypha and Pseudepigrapha of the Old Testament,* 2:470–526. Oxford: Clarendon, 1913.

4 Baruch. A text attributed to Baruch, scribe of the prophet Jeremiah, but thought to have been composed in the first or second century A.D. For an English translation, see James H. Charlesworth, ed. *The Old Testament Pseudepigrapha,* 2:413–26. Garden City, N.Y.: Doubleday, 1983.

5 Baruch. A pseudepigraphic text attributed to Baruch, scribe of the biblical prophet Jeremiah, that is found in both Christian Ethiopic and Falasha versions. An English translation of the latter is found in Wolf Leslau. *Falasha Anthology,* 57–76. New Haven: Yale University Press, 1951.

Berlin Medical Papyrus. An ancient Egyptian text unavailable in English.

Bhagavata-Puranu. One of the sacred books of the Hindus of India.

Bibliotheca Graeca (Greek Library). A Latin alchemical book written in the sixteenth century by Johann Albert Fabricus. Not available in English.

Book of Apollonios, the Sage, on the Causes. A Greek Hermetic text, perhaps the same as the Arabic *Sirr ʾal-ḫaliḳah* (Secret of Creation), attributed to the Greek philosopher Apollonios (flourished 210–205 B.C.). No longer extant, the text is known only from later citations.

Book of Noah. A name given to three medieval Hebrew texts about a heavenly book delivered to Adam, Noah, and other patriarchs. The Hebrew versions of all three recensions were published in Adolph Jellinek. *Bet ha-Midrasch,* 3:155–60. Jerusalem: Wahrmann, 1967. The third recension of the *Book of Noah* forms most of the introduction of another medieval work known today by the title *Sepher ha-Razim* (q.v.).

Book of Sôthis, also known as *The Sôthic Cycle*. Though attributed to a third-century-B.C. Egyptian priest named Manetho, the book is generally thought to have been composed in the fourth century A.D. It is known to us only because the Byzantine chronographer Syncellus (circa A.D. 800) preserved it in his *Chronological History of the World*. See the English translation in W. G. Waddell. *Manetho*, 234–49. Cambridge: Harvard University Press, 1971.

Book of the Bee. A book written in the early thirteenth century A.D. in Syriac by the Armenian-born bishop Shelemon (Solomon) of Basra, using the Bible and early commentaries on the Bible. It is closely related to the *Book of the Cave of Treasures*, the *Book of the Rolls*, and the *Conflict of Adam and Eve*. An Arabic translation of the text is on a manuscript at Oxford University. For an English translation, see Ernest A. Wallis Budge. *The Book of the Bee*. Oxford: Clarendon, 1886.

Book of the Dead. A collection of ancient Egyptian magical spells designed to assist the deceased in his afterlife journey. The English translation by Ernest A. Wallis Budge has been reissued many times by different publishers. See, for example, *The Book of the Dead*. New Hyde Park, N.Y.: University Books, 1967.

Book of the Mysteries of the Heavens and the Earth. An Ethiopic Christian text written in the thirteenth century by Bakhayla Mîkâ᾽êl, also known as Zôsîmâs. For an English translation, see Ernest A. Wallis Budge. *The Book of the Mysteries of the Heavens and the Earth and Other Works of*

Bakhayla Mîkâ'êl (Zôsîmâs). London: Oxford University Press, 1935.

Book of the Resurrection of Christ by Bartholomew the Disciple. An apocryphal work attributed to the apostle Bartholomew and known only from Coptic manuscripts. See the English translation in Ernest A. Wallis Budge. *Coptic Apocrypha in the Dialect of Upper Egypt,* 1–48. New York: AMS Press, 1977 (originally published in 1913). A resume of the text is included in Montague Rhodes James. *The Apocryphal New Testament,* 181–86. Oxford: Clarendon, 1955; Wilhelm Schneemelcher. *New Testament Apocrypha,* 1:553–57. Trans. Robert McLachlan Wilson. Rev. ed. Louisville, Ky.: Westminster/John Knox, 1991.

Book of the Rolls. An Arabic version of a book attributed to the first-century-A.D. writer Clement of Rome. An English translation appears in Margaret Dunlop Wilson, ed. and trans. "*Kitab al-Magall,* or The Book of the Rolls." In *Apocrypha Arabica.* London: C. J. Clay, 1901.

Cave of Treasures. A Syriac text composed in the fourth century A.D. by Saint Ephram Syrus. It shares a common source with the *Conflict of Adam and Eve,* and the *Book of the Rolls,* and, to a lesser extent, the *Book of the Bee.* See the English text in Ernest A. Wallis Budge. *The Book of the Cave of Treasures.* London: Religious Tract Society, 1927.

Chronicle Adler. A collection of Samaritan historical traditions whose latest iteration in Samaritan was prepared in 1900. For an English translation, see John Bowman, ed. and trans. *Samaritan Documents relating to their History, Religion and Life,* 87–113. Pittsburgh: Pickwick Press, 1977.

Chronicles of Jerahmeel. A history of the Jews, written in the twelfth century by Jerahmeel ben Solomon, who gathered traditions found in a number of earlier texts, some of which have survived. For an English translation, see Moses Gaster. *The Chronicles of Jerahmeel; or, The Hebrew Bible Historiale.* New York: Ktav 1971.

Chronicon (Chronicle). A book written by the Christian historian Eusebius (circa A.D. 260–339). No English translation is available.

City of God. A book by St. Augustine, bishop of Hippo (died A.D. 430), sometimes known by its Latin name, *De civitate Dei.* For an English translation, see Philip Schaff and Henry Wace, eds. *Nicene and Post-Nicene Fathers,* 2:1–511. First Series. Peabody, Mass.: Hendrickson, 1994 (originally published in 1887).

Clementine Homilies. Attributed to Clement of Rome (died A.D. 90). For an English translation, see Alexander Roberts and James Donaldson, eds. *Ante-Nicene Fathers,* 8:215–360. Peabody, Mass.: Hendrickson, 1994.

Cologne Mani Codex. A fifth-century-A.D. manuscript attributed to Mani, founder of the Manichaeans, an early Christian group. For an English translation, see Ron Cameron and Arthur J. Dewey. *The Cologne Mani Codex.* Missoula, Mont.: Scholars Press, 1979.

Conflict of Adam and Eve. An Ethiopic Christian document bearing affinities to the *Book of the Bee*, the *Book of the Rolls*, and the *Cave of Treasures.* For an English translation, see S. C. Malan. *The Book of Adam and Eve, also called The Conflict of Adam and Eve with Satan.* London: Williams and Norgate, 1882.

Copper Scroll. One of the Dead Sea Scrolls (designation 3Q15), written on copper plates that had been welded together; it contains a list of items said to be hidden in various places. For an English translation, see Florentino García Martínez.

The Dead Sea Scrolls Translated, 461–63. 2nd ed. Leiden: Brill, 1996.

Corpus Hermiticum. A medieval Greek text with ancient Egyptian antecedents. See the recent translation in Brian P. Copenhaver. *Hermetica.* New York: Cambridge University Press, 1995.

Damascus Document. A document first discovered in the genizah of the Old Cairo Karaite synagogue in Egypt in the latter part of the nineteenth century. Half a century later, other copies were found among the Dead Sea Scrolls. The document is generally dated to about the second century B.C. For an English translation, see Florentino García Martínez. *The Dead Sea Scrolls Translated,* 33–73. 2nd ed. Leiden: E. J. Brill, 1996.

De Abrahamo (About Abraham). A philosophical treatise on the prophet Abraham, written by the first-century Alexandrian Jewish philosopher Philo Judaeus. For an English translation, see C. D. Yonge. *The Works of Philo,* 411–34. Peabody, Mass.: Hendrickson, 1993.

De civitate Dei. See *City of God.*

De Viris Illustribus Urbis Romae (Illustrious Men of Rome). A book written by St. Augustine, bishop of Hippo (died 430). No English translation exists.

Death of Moses. A Falasha text dealing with the last teachings of the prophet Moses and his death. For an English translation, see Wolf Leslau. *Falasha Anthology,* 103–11. New Haven: Yale University Press, 1951.

Description of Greece. A book written by the fourth-century-B.C. Greek historian Pausanias. For an English translation, see J. G. Frazer, ed. *Pausanias's Description of Greece.* 6 vols. New York: Biblo and Tannen, 1965.

Discourse on the Eighth and Ninth. A Coptic Gnostic text from the fifth century A.D. For an English translation, see James M. Robinson, ed. *The Nag Hammadi Library,* 321–27. 3rd ed. San Francisco: HarperCollins, 1990.

Divinarum institutionum libri VII (Divine Institutes). A book written by the fourth-century Latin church father Lucius Caelius Firmianus Lactantius. For an English translation, see Alexander Roberts and James Donaldson, eds. *Ante-Nicene Fathers,* 7:9–223. Peabody, Mass.: Hendrickson, 1994.

Ecclesiastical History. A history of the early Christian church written by Eusebius (died 339 or 340) and compiled from earlier documents, some of which are no longer extant. For an English translation, see Philip Schaff and Henry Wace, eds. *Nicene and Post-Nicene Fathers,* 1:73–403. Second Series. Peabody, Mass.: Hendrickson, 1994.

Eighth Book of Moses. A Greek Gnostic text from Egypt (*PGM* XIII. 1–734). An English translation was published in Hans Dieter Betz. *The Greek Magical Papyri in Translation: Including the Demotic Spells,* 172–89. Chicago: University of Chicago Press, 1986.

1 Enoch, also known as the *Ethiopic Apocalypse of Enoch.* An amplification of the story of the biblical patriarch Enoch, *1 Enoch* is actually a compilation of various Enoch stories, some of which are thought to have been written as early as the third century B.C. The only complete version is in the Ethiopic language known as Geʾez, but fragments are known in Greek (mostly from Egypt), Latin, and Aramaic. The Aramaic fragments were found among the Dead Sea Scrolls and date to the first century B.C. For English translations, see James H. Charlesworth, ed. *The Old Testament Pseudepigrapha,* 1:5–90. Garden City, N.Y.: Doubleday,

1983; Robert Henry Charles. *The Apocrypha and Pseudepigrapha of the Old Testament,* 2:162–281. Oxford: Clarendon, 1913.

2 Enoch, also known as the *Slavonic Apocalypse of Enoch.* An amplification of the story of the biblical patriarch Enoch, thought to have been written in the first century A.D. Two recensions are known in Old Church Slavonic, one of which (A) is shorter than the other (J). For English translations, see James H. Charlesworth, ed. *The Old Testament Pseudepigrapha,* 1:91–222. Garden City, N.Y.: Doubleday, 1983; Robert Henry Charles. *The Apocrypha and Pseudepigrapha of the Old Testament,* 2:425–69. Oxford: Clarendon, 1913.

3 Enoch. Misnomer for a book usually known as *Sepher Hekalot* (The Book of the Palaces), *Pirqe Rabbi Yishmael* (Chapters of Rabbi Ishmael), or *The Book of Rabbi Ishmael the High Priest.* Originally written in Hebrew, it is attributed to Rabbi Ishmael, a Palestinian Jewish leader who died circa A.D. 132. It recounts what he saw during his heavenly ascent, including his encounter with Enoch, who in Jewish tradition became the heavenly scribe Metatron. For an English translation, see James H. Charlesworth, ed. *The Old Testament Pseudepigrapha,* 1:223–316. Garden City, N.Y.: Doubleday, 1983.

Enuma Elish (When on High). The Babylonian account of the creation of the world, known from tablets of various dates during the first millennium B.C. For an English translation, see James B. Pritchard. *Ancient Near Eastern Texts Relating to the Old Testament,* 60–72. 3rd ed. Princeton: Princeton University Press, 1969.

4 Ezra. An apocryphal work attributed to the Old Testament priest-scribe Ezra. Though the original text was written in

Greek, it did not form part of the Apocrypha in the Greek Septuagint version of the Bible. It is known principally from its inclusion in the Apocrypha section of the Latin Vulgate Bible and in the Syriac Peshitta. It is also known from Ethiopic and Armenian documents. For English translations, see James H. Charlesworth, ed. *The Old Testament Pseudepigrapha,* 1:517–60. Garden City, N.Y.: Doubleday, 1983; Robert Henry Charles. *The Apocrypha and Pseudepigrapha of the Old Testament,* 2:542–624. Oxford: Clarendon, 1913.

Factorum et Dictorum Memorabilia (Memorable Deeds and Sayings). A book written by the Roman Valerius Maximus in the first century A.D. For a French translation, see C. A. F. Frémion. *Factorum et dictorum memorabilium.* 3 vols. Paris: C. L. F. Panckoucke, 1834–35.

Ginza Rba (The Great Treasure/Library). One of the principal religious texts of the Mandaeans of Iraq and Iran. While no complete English translation is available, portions were published in Werner Foerster. *Gnosis: A Selection of Gnostic Texts.* Trans. Robert McLachlan Wilson. Oxford: Clarendon, 1974.

Gospel of the Egyptians. One of the fifth-century Coptic Gnostic documents found at Nag Hammadi in Egypt, said to be an early gospel account. See the English translation in James M. Robinson, ed. *The Nag Hammadi Library,* 208–19. 3rd ed. San Francisco: HarperCollins, 1990.

Haran Gawaita. A hymn of the Mandaeans, a religious group in Iraq and Iran who claim to be descendants of the disciples of John the Baptist. For an English translation, see E. S. Drower. *The Haran Gawaita and the Baptism of Hibil-Ziwa,* 3–23. Vatican: Biblioteca Apostolica Vaticana, 1953.

Hidden Book of Moses. A Christian Gnostic text written in Greek and found in Egypt (*PGM* XIII. 734–1077). For an English translation, see Hans Dieter Betz. *The Greek Magical Papyri in Translation: Including the Demotic Spells*, 189–95. Chicago: University of Chicago Press, 1986.

History of the Rechabites, also known as the *Narrative of Zosimos*. A document attributed to one Zosimos and composed sometime between the first and the fourth centuries A.D. It recounts his visit to a distant country where he visited with the Rechabites, descendants of the biblical Rechab, himself a descendant of Moses' father-in-law Jethro. For an English translation, see James H. Charlesworth, ed. *The Old Testament Pseudepigrapha*, 2:443–62. Garden City, N.Y.: Doubleday, 1983.

How Dana Nuk Visited the Seventh Heaven. A religious text of the Mandaeans of Iraq and Iran that recounts the ascension of one Dana Nuk. For an English translation, see E. S. Drower. *The Mandaeans of Iraq and Iran*, 300–305. Leiden: E. J. Brill, 1962.

Hymn of the Soul, also known as *Hymn of the Pearl*. A Christian poetic parable of the plan of salvation, incorporated into the *Acts of Thomas*, known from Greek and Syriac manuscripts. For an English translation, see Montague Rhodes James. *The Apocryphal New Testament*, 411–15. Oxford: Clarendon, 1955; Wilhelm Schneemelcher. *New Testament Apocrypha*, 2:380–85. Trans. Robert McLachlan Wilson. Rev. ed. Louisville, Ky.: Westminster/John Knox, 1991.

Hymn of the Pearl. See *Hymn of the Soul*.

Hymns on the Nativity. A collection of poems written in the fourth century by the Syriac Christian St. Ephraim Syrus. For an English translation, see Philip Schaff and Henry

Wace, eds. *Nicene and Post-Nicene Fathers*, 13:221–62. Second Series. Peabody, Mass.: Hendrickson, 1994 (originally published in 1898).

Jasher. Though the title of the book is the same as that of the book of Jasher mentioned in the Bible, it is not the ancient book, but a product of thirteenth-century-A.D. Spain. Nevertheless, because it collects much older Jewish traditions, it has some value. The most readily available English translation is the much reprinted *The Book of Jasher*. Salt Lake City, Utah: J. H. Parry & Co., 1887.

Jewish War. A book written by the first-century Jewish historian Flavius Josephus. The most well-known English version is the oft-reprinted translation by William Whiston, made in the seventeenth century.

Jubilees. A reworking of the account of the biblical book of Genesis, including stories of the patriarchs not found in the Bible. Though originally a Jewish work, it was preserved through the centuries mostly in its Ethiopic translation by the Christians of Abyssinia (Ethiopia), though there are also fragments in Greek, Syriac, and Latin. Fragments of the Hebrew version were found among the Dead Sea Scrolls in the mid-twentieth century. For an English translation, see James H. Charlesworth, ed. *The Old Testament Pseudepigrapha*, 2:35–142. Garden City, N.Y.: Doubleday, 1983; Robert Henry Charles. *The Apocrypha and Pseudepigrapha of the Old Testament*, 2:2–82. Oxford: Clarendon, 1913.

Kitāb ḏaḫīrat Aliskandar (The Book of the Treasures of Alexander). An Arabic Hermetic book not available in English.

Kore Kosmou (Daughter of the Cosmos). A Greek Hermetic text not available in English.

Krates-Book. A Greek Hermetic text attributed to one Krates, not available in English.

Lefafa Sedek (Bandlet of Righteousness). An Ethiopic Christian magical text that derives from earlier Egyptian magical texts via Coptic Christian intermediaries. For an English translation, see Ernest A. Wallis Budge. *The Bandlet of Righteousness: An Ethiopian Book of the Dead.* London: Luzac, 1929.

Letter of Aristeas. See *Pseudo-Aristeas.*

Life of Adam and Eve. A Latin text thought to have been originally written in Hebrew in the first century A.D. The account was first published in German in 1878. An English translation is published in parallel columns with its Greek equivalent, the *Apocalypse of Moses,* in James H. Charlesworth, ed. *The Old Testament Pseudepigrapha,* 2:249–96. Garden City, N.Y.: Doubleday, 1983; Robert Henry Charles. *The Apocrypha and Pseudepigrapha of the Old Testament,* 2:123–54. Oxford: Clarendon, 1913.

Life of Apollonius of Tyana. A biography written by the Greek historian Philostratus of Athens (second to third centuries B.C.). A number of English translations are available.

Lives of the Prophets. A text summarizing the lives of various Old Testament prophets and written by a Jewish Egyptian in the first century A.D., perhaps during the lifetime of Christ. For an English translation, see James H. Charlesworth, ed. *The Old Testament Pseudepigrapha,* 2:379–400. Garden City, N.Y.: Doubleday, 1983.

1 Maccabees. One of the books of the Apocrypha (all the books of the Apocrypha were included in the Greek Septuagint translation of the Old Testament). The book 1 Maccabees contains a historical account of the period between the Old and New Testaments. Earlier editions of the King James

Bible, like standard Catholic Bibles, included the Apocrypha, and one can still purchase the King James translation of these books under separate cover.

2 Maccabees. One of the books of the Apocrypha (all the books of the Apocrypha were included in the Greek Septuagint translation of the Old Testament). The book 2 Maccabees contains a historical account of the period between the Old and New Testaments. Earlier editions of the King James Bible, like standard Catholic Bibles, included the Apocrypha, and one can still purchase the King James translation of these books under separate cover.

Mandaean Canonical Prayerbook. A large collection of prayers used by the Mandaeans of Iraq and Iran, who claim to be descendants of the disciples of John the Baptist. For an English translation, see E. S. Drower. *The Canonical Prayerbook of the Mandaeans*. Leiden: E. J. Brill, 1959.

Martyrdom and Ascension of Isaiah. A pseudepigraphic account of the death and heavenly ascension of the Old Testament prophet Isaiah, written sometime between the second and fourth centuries A.D. For an English translation, see James H. Charlesworth, ed. *The Old Testament Pseudepigrapha*, 2:143–76. Garden City, N.Y.: Doubleday, 1983; Robert Henry Charles. *The Apocrypha and Pseudepigrapha of the Old Testament*, 2:155–62. Oxford: Clarendon, 1913.

In Matthaeum Homiliae (Commentary on Matthew). A fifth-century Christian document falsely attributed to St. Chrysostom. The passage referred to in this volume is noted by A. F. J. Klijn. *Seth in Jewish, Christian and Gnostic Literature*, 57–58. Leiden: E. J. Brill, 1977.

Memar Marqa. A commentary on the law of Moses written in the fourth century A.D. by the Samaritan theologian

Marqa. It is available in Hebrew on Moses Gaster Manuscript 825 in the John Rylands Library.

Merkabah Rabbah (The Great Chariot). A medieval Jewish text describing the vision of the heavens of Rabbi Ishmael, the high priest. For an English translation, see Martin Samuel Cohen. *The Shiʿur Qomah: Texts and Recensions,* 53–76. Tübingen: Mohr, 1985.

Midrash Rabbah. An early rabbinic commentary on the stories found in the Old Testament books of Genesis through Deuteronomy and a few others. Though much of the material is older, the composition itself dates to the end of the fourth or the beginning of the fifth century A.D. For an English translation, see H. Freedman and Maurice Simon, eds. *Midrash Rabbah.* London: Soncino Press, 1961 (originally published in 1939).

Midrash Tanhuma. A biblical commentary attributed to the early Jewish rabbi Tanhuma but thought to have been written later, in the ninth century A.D. For an English translation, see John T. Townsend, ed. *Midrash Tanhuma.* Hoboken, N.J.: Ktav, 1989.

Mishnah (Repetition, Study). A collection of early rabbinic commentaries on the Torah, or Law, of Moses, said to have been written by Rabbi Judah the Patriarch in the second century A.D. It is the basis of the Talmud, which is a much larger collection of such commentaries by later rabbis. For an English translation, see the much reprinted Herbert Danby. *The Mishnah.* London: Oxford University Press, 1933.

Mishneh Torah (Study of the Law). An exposition of Jewish law written by the twelfth-century Jewish rabbi Moses ben Maimon, also known as Maimonides or Rambam.

Moralia (Moral Deeds). A book by the Greek biographer Plutarch (circa A.D. 46–120). For an English translation, see Frank Cole Babbitt, ed. *Plutarch's Moralia.* 15 vols. New York: G. P. Putnam's Sons, 1927.

Narrative of Zosimos. See *History of the Rechabites.*

Naturalis historia (Natural History). A book written by Gaius Plinius Secundus, better known as Pliny the Elder (A.D. 23–79), a Roman scientist and naval commander who perished in the eruption of Mount Vesuvius in A.D. 79. For an English translation, see H. Rackham, ed. *Natural History: Pliny.* 10 vols. Loeb Classical Library, 1938.

Odes of Solomon. A collection of odes attributed to Solomon but obviously of later date. The text is known from Greek, Coptic, and Syriac manuscripts. For an English translation, see James H. Charlesworth, ed. *The Old Testament Pseudepigrapha,* 2:724–71. Garden City, N.Y.: Doubleday, 1983.

On the Letter Omega. An early alchemical book written by one Zosimos that is unavailable in English.

Panarion (Refutation of All [Heresies]). A book written by the Christian Father Epiphanius, bishop of Cyprus (died 403). For an English translation, see Frank Williams. *The Panarion of Epiphanius of Salamis.* 2 vols. Leiden: E. J. Brill, 1987.

Pastor of Hermas, sometimes called *Shepherd of Hermas.* The account of a revelation given to Hermas, brother of Pius, bishop of Rome, in the second century A.D. and named from the angel who appeared to him in the form of a shepherd. The book was highly prized by early Christians and was even included in some early Bibles. For an English translation, see Alexander Roberts and James Donaldson, eds. *Ante-Nicene Fathers,* 2:9–55. Peabody, Mass.: Hendrickson, 1994.

Petirat Mosheh. A medieval Jewish text published in Adolf Jellinek. *Bet ha-Midrasch,* 1:115–29. Jerusalem: Wahrmann, 1967.

Pirqe Rabbi Eliezer (The Paragraphs of Rabbi Eliezer). A work attributed to Rabbi Eliezer, son of Hyrqanos. Eliezer lived in the latter half of the first century through the first decades of the second century A.D. While the work may have originated at an early date, its present Hebrew composition is from the twelfth or thirteenth century. Some fragments also came from the Old Cairo genizah, where the earliest copy of the *Zadokite Fragment,* or *Damascus Document,* later discovered among the Dead Sea Scrolls, was found. For an English translation, see Gerald Friedlander, trans. *Pirḳê de Rabbi Eliezer.* New York: Hermon Press, 1965. Originally published in 1916.

Pistis Sophia (The Faith of Wisdom). A fifth-century Coptic Christian Gnostic text found in Egypt, recounting post-resurrection teachings of Jesus to his disciples. For English translations, see Carl Schmidt, ed. *Pistis Sophia.* Trans. Violet MacDermot. Leiden: E. J. Brill, 1978; G. R. S. Mead. *Pistis Sophia.* London: Theosophical Publishing Society, 1896.

Praeparatio evangelica (Preparation for the Gospel). A treatise written by the fourth-century church historian Eusebius, bishop of Caesarea, that often refers to earlier texts available to him. The translation of the extract from the writings of Artapanus, cited in this work, is from James H. Charlesworth, ed. *The Old Testament Pseudepigrapha,* 2:901. Garden City, N.Y.: Doubleday, 1983.

Pseudo-Aristeas, also known as *Letter of Aristeas*. A letter purportedly written by a Jewish scholar named Aristeas in the mid-third century B.C. but which most scholars tend to date to the first century B.C. For English translations, see James H. Charlesworth, ed. *The Old Testament Pseudepigrapha,* 2:5–34. Garden City, N.Y.: Doubleday, 1983; and Robert Henry Charles. *The Apocrypha and Pseudepigrapha of the Old Testament,* 2:7–34. Oxford: Clarendon, 1913.

Pseudo-Philo, also called *Liber Antiquitatum Biblicarum* (Book of Biblical Antiquities). A book about the early history of the patriarchs and Israel, falsely attributed to the first-century Alexandrian Jewish philosopher Philo Judaeus. Linguistic aspects of the Latin and Greek versions suggests that they derive from a Hebrew original that is no longer extant. For an English translation, see James H. Charlesworth, ed. *The Old Testament Pseudepigrapha,* 2:297–378. Garden City, N.Y.: Doubleday, 1983.

Qiṣaṣ ʾal-ʾAnbiyaʾ (Tales of the Prophets). The name given to historical accounts of the biblical patriarchs and prophets. Several tenth- and eleventh-century Arab historians wrote books by this name. One of these writers was Muhammad ʾibn Allah ʾal-Kisaʾî, and an English translation of his work can be found in W. M. Thackston Jr., trans. *The Tales of the Prophets of al-Kisaʾi.* Boston: Twayne, 1978.

Rashi is an abbreviation of the Hebrew title **R**abbi **Sh**lomo ben **Y**itshaq, a Jewish scholar who lived in Troyes, France, from A.D. 1040 to 1105. He wrote a commentary on the Torah, or Pentateuch, comprising the five books of Moses (Genesis through Deuteronomy). His Hebrew text, with an English translation and additional commentary, is published in M. Rosenbaum and A. M. Silbermann. *Pentateuch* *with Targum Onkelos, Haphtaroth and Rashi's Commentary.* Jerusalem: Silbermann Family, 1973.

Refutation of All Heresies. A book written by the third-century church father Hippolytus, bishop of Portus. An English translation of Hippolytus's comments on the appearance of the angel to Alcibiades is found in Wilhelm Schneemelcher. *New Testament Apocrypha,* 2:687. Trans. Robert McLachlan Wilson. Rev. ed. Louisville, Ky.: Westminster/John Knox, 1991.

Roman History. A work composed by the fourth-century-A.D. Roman historian Ammianus Marcellinus. For an English translation, see C. D. Yonge, trans. *The Roman History of Ammianus Marcellinus.* London: George Bell and Sons, 1902.

Sepher ha-Razim (Book of the Mysteries), also known as *Sepher Razi'el* (Book of the Mystery of God). The story of the book is told in *Pirqe Rabbi Eliezer* and in two medieval kabbalistic works, the Zohar and the *Book of Noah*, with variants in the different recensions of the latter. A book entitled *Sepher Razi'el,* thought to have been compiled by Rabbi Eleazar of Worms in the thirteenth century, is said to be based on a third- or fourth-century-A.D. magical document that, in Jewish tradition, is a copy of the heavenly book that formed the basis of the Pentateuch, or Torah. For an English translation, see Michael A. Morgan. *Sepher ha-Razim, The Book of the Mysteries.* Chico, Calif.: Scholars Press, 1983.

Sepher Razi'el. See *Sepher ha-Razim.*

Shepherd of Hermas. See *Pastor of Hermas.*

Sirr 'al-ḫaliḳah (Secret of Creation). An Arabic Hermetic book, perhaps the same as the the *Book of Apollonios, the Sage, on the Causes* (q.v.).

Sôthic Cycle. See *Book of Sôthis.*

Story of Shum bar Nu (Shem the Son of Noah). A text of the Mandaeans, a religious group in Iraq and Iran who claim to be descendants of the disciples of John the Baptist. For a German translation, see M. Lidzbarski. *Das Johannesbuch der Mandäer.* Giessen: Alfred Töpelmann, 1915.

Stromata. A doctrinal treatise written by Clement of Alexandria in the second century A.D. For an English translation, see Alexander Roberts and James Donaldson, eds. *Ante-Nicene Fathers,* 2:299–568. Peabody, Mass.: Hendrickson, 1994 (originally published in 1885).

Tabula Smaragdina (Emerald Tablet). An alchemical tract thought to date to the mid-thirteenth century. Latin and Arabic versions are known. For a German translation, see J. Ruska. *Tabula Smaragdina. Ein Beitrag zur Geschichte der hermetischen Literatur.* Heidelberg: C. Winter, 1926.

Tales of the Prophets. See *Qiṣaṣ ʾal-ʾAnbiyaʾ.*

Talmud. The Babylonian Talmud is a multivolume commentary on Jewish law compiled by rabbis during the fifth and sixth centuries A.D., though it is said to include materials from earlier generations of rabbis. Several English translations are available.

Targum Pseudo-Jonathan. A second-century-A.D. Aramaic translation of portions of the Old Testament, attributed to Jonathan son of Hyrqanos. For an English translation, see Michael Maher. *Targum Pseudo-Jonathan: Genesis.* Collegeville, Minn.: Liturgical Press, 1992.

Taʾrīkh (History). A book written by the fifth- to sixth-century-A.D. Arab chronographer al-Qifṭî, unavailable in English.

Testament of Abraham. A book attributed to the biblical patriarch Abraham but thought to have been written in the first or second century A.D. For an English translation, see

James H. Charlesworth, ed. *The Old Testament Pseudepigrapha,* 1:871–902. Garden City, N.Y.: Doubleday, 1983. The Falasha also have a version of the *Testament of Abraham*, an English translation of which appears in Wolf Leslau. *Falasha Anthology,* 92–102. New Haven: Yale University Press, 1951.

Testament of Adam. A document said to have been written by Seth, son of Adam. Preserved by various Christian churches, the document is known from Syriac, Greek, Arabic, Ethiopic, Armenian, Old Georgian, and Karshuni versions. The earliest manuscript dates to the ninth century A.D. For an English translation, see James H. Charlesworth, ed. *The Old Testament Pseudepigrapha,* 1:989–95. Garden City, N.Y.: Doubleday, 1983.

Testament of Moses, also known as *Assumption of Moses*. A pseudepigraphic text attributed to the prophet Moses and purporting to be his final admonitions to his successor, Joshua. It is known only from a Latin manuscript of the sixth century A.D., but the language suggests that it was translated from Greek a century earlier, though the original may have been in Aramaic or Hebrew. For English translations, see James H. Charlesworth, ed. *The Old Testament Pseudepigrapha,* 1:919–34. Garden City, N.Y.: Doubleday, 1983; Robert Henry Charles. *The Apocrypha and Pseudepigrapha of the Old Testament,* 2:407–24. Oxford: Clarendon, 1913.

The Thousand and Twelve Questions. A text of the Mandaeans of Iraq and Iran, who claim to be descendants of the disciples of John the Baptist. For an English translation, see E. S. Drower. *The Thousand and Twelve Questions.* Berlin: Akademie-Verlag, 1960.

The World Beyond. See *World of Light.*

Tolidah (History). A Samaritan history. For an English translation, see John Bowman, ed. and trans. *Samaritan Documents relating to their History, Religion and Life,* 37–60. Pittsburgh: Pickwick Press, 1977.

Tosefta (Addition). Additions made to the Talmud by European rabbis of the twelfth and thirteenth centuries. For a German translation of the tractate *Sotah*, cited in this present work, see Hans Bietenhard. *Der Tosefta Traktat Soṭah.* Bern: Peter Lang, 1986.

Untitled Treatise. An untitled Coptic text appended to the end of the Bruce Codex. For an English translation, see Carl Schmidt, ed. *The Books of Jeu and the Untitled Text in the Bruce Codex,* 213–318. Trans. Violet MacDermot. Leiden: E. J. Brill, 1978.

Uraltes Chymisches Werck (Age-Old Chemical Work). An alchemical text written in 1735 by Rabbi Abraham Eleazar. The story is retold in Raphael Patai. *The Jewish Alchemists,* 239–53. Princeton, N.J.: Princeton University Press, 1994.

World of Light, also called *The World Beyond*. A text of the Mandaeans, a religious group in Iraq and Iran who claim to be descendants of the disciples of John the Baptist. For an English translation, see Werner Foerster. *Gnosis: A Selection of Gnostic Texts,* 2:148–58. Trans. Robert McLachlan Wilson. Oxford: Clarendon, 1974.

Zohar (Illumination). A Hebrew kabbalistic text thought to have been compiled in Spain in the thirteenth century A.D. but including numerous older traditions. Most of the text has been translated into English and is available in Harry Sperling and Maurice Simon, trans. *The Zohar.* 5 vols. New York: Rebecca Bennet Publications, 1958.

Subject Index

A

B

H

N

O

P

T

The Foundation for Ancient Research and Mormon Studies

The Foundation for Ancient Research and Mormon Studies (FARMS) encourages and supports research and publication about the Book of Mormon: Another Testament of Jesus Christ and other ancient scriptures.

FARMS is a nonprofit, tax-exempt educational foundation affiliated with Brigham Young University. Its main research interests in the scriptures include ancient history, language, literature, culture, geography, politics, religion, and law. Although research on such subjects is of secondary importance when compared with the spiritual and eternal messages of the scriptures, solid scholarly research can supply certain kinds of useful information, even if only tentatively, concerning many significant and interesting questions about the ancient backgrounds, origins, composition, and meanings of scripture.

The work of the Foundation rests on the premise that the Book of Mormon and other scriptures were written by prophets of God. Belief in this premise—in the divinity of scripture—is a matter of faith. Religious truths require divine witness to establish the faith of the believer. While scholarly research cannot replace that witness, such studies may reinforce and encourage individual testimonies by fostering understanding and appreciation of the scriptures. It is hoped that this information will help people to "come unto Christ" (Jacob 1:7) and to understand and take more seriously these ancient witnesses of the atonement of Jesus Christ, the Son of God.

The Foundation works to make interim and final reports about its research available widely, promptly, and economically, both in scholarly and in popular formats. FARMS publishes information about the Book of Mormon and other ancient scripture in the *Insights* newsletter, books and research papers, *FARMS Review of Books, Journal of Book of Mormon Studies,* reprints of published scholarly papers, and videos and audiotapes. FARMS also supports the preparation of the Collected Works of Hugh Nibley.

To facilitate the sharing of information, FARMS sponsors lectures, seminars, symposia, firesides, and radio and television broadcasts in which research findings are communicated to working scholars and to anyone interested in faithful, reliable information about the scriptures. Through Research Press, a publishing arm of the Foundation, FARMS publishes materials addressed primarily to working scholars.

For more information about the Foundation and its activities, contact the FARMS office at 1-800-327-6715 or (801) 373-5111. You can also visit the FARMS Web site at http://farms.byu.edu.

FARMS Publications

Teachings of the Book of Mormon
The Geography of Book of Mormon Events: A Source Book
The Book of Mormon Text Reformatted according to Parallelistic Patterns
Eldin Ricks's Thorough Concordance of the LDS Standard Works
A Guide to Publications on the Book of Mormon: A Selected Annotated Bibliography
Book of Mormon Authorship Revisited: The Evidence for Ancient Origins
Ancient Scrolls from the Dead Sea: Photographs and Commentary on a Unique Collection of Scrolls
LDS Perspectives on the Dead Sea Scrolls
Isaiah in the Book of Mormon
King Benjamin's Speech: "That Ye May Learn Wisdom"
Mormons, Scripture, and the Ancient World: Studies in Honor of John L. Sorenson
Latter-day Christianity: Ten Basic Issues
Illuminating the Sermon at the Temple and Sermon on the Mount
Scripture Study: Tools and Suggestions
Finding Biblical Hebrew and Other Ancient Literary Forms in the Book of Mormon
Charting the Book of Mormon: Visual Aids for Personal Study and Teaching
Pressing Forward with the Book of Mormon: The FARMS Updates of the 1990s
King Benjamin's Speech Made Simple
The Dead Sea Scrolls: Questions and Responses for Latter-day Saints
The Temple in Time and Eternity
Mormon's Map
To All the World: The Book of Mormon Articles from the *Encyclopedia of Mormonism*
The Disciple as Scholar: Essays on Scripture and the Ancient World in Honor of Richard Lloyd Anderson
The Disciple as Witness: Essays on Latter-day Saint History and Doctrine in Honor of Richard Lloyd Anderson
The Book of Mormon and Other Hidden Books: Out of Darkness into Light
A Guide to the Joseph Smith Papyri

Ancient Texts and Mormon Studies
Romans 1: Notes and Reflections
Popol Vuh: The Mythic Sections

Periodicals
Insights: A Window on the Ancient World
FARMS Review of Books
Journal of Book of Mormon Studies

Copublished with Deseret Book Company

An Ancient American Setting for the Book of Mormon
Warfare in the Book of Mormon
By Study and Also by Faith: Essays in Honor of Hugh W. Nibley
The Sermon at the Temple and the Sermon on the Mount
Rediscovering the Book of Mormon
Reexploring the Book of Mormon
Of All Things! Classic Quotations from Hugh Nibley
The Allegory of the Olive Tree
Temples of the Ancient World
Expressions of Faith: Testimonies from LDS Scholars
Feasting on the Word: The Literary Testimony of the Book of Mormon

The Collected Works of Hugh Nibley
Old Testament and Related Studies
Enoch the Prophet
The World and the Prophets
Mormonism and Early Christianity
Lehi in the Desert; The World of the Jaredites; There Were Jaredites
An Approach to the Book of Mormon
Since Cumorah
The Prophetic Book of Mormon
Approaching Zion
The Ancient State
Tinkling Cymbals and Sounding Brass
Temple and Cosmos
Brother Brigham Challenges the Saints
Abraham in Egypt

Published through Research Press

Pre-Columbian Contact with the Americas across the Oceans: An Annotated Bibliography
A Comprehensive Annotated Book of Mormon Bibliography
New World Figurine Project, vol. 1
Images of Ancient America: Visualizing Book of Mormon Life
Chiasmus in Antiquity (reprint)
Chiasmus Bibliography

Publications of the FARMS Center for the Preservation of Ancient Religious Texts

Dead Sea Scrolls Electronic Reference Library
The Incoherence of the Philosophers
The Niche of Lights
The Philosophy of Illumination